To Rita — one of the very
sweetest a[...]
my studen[...]
affection.
                    Marie Marglins

6/28/61

TORAH-VISION

TORAH·VISION

SERMONIC ESSAYS FOR OUR TIME

BY

MORRIS B. MARGOLIES

Rabbi, Temple Beth El of Manhattan Beach, 1953-61
Newly elected Rabbi

The Beth Shalom Congregation, Kansas City, Missouri

PHILIPP FELDHEIM, INC.

NEW YORK

Published and Distributed by

PHILLIPP FELDHEIM, INC.
96 East Broadway
New York 2, New York

Printed in the United States of America by
BALSHON PRINTING AND OFFSET CO.
BROOKLYN, N. Y.

In Memory of my Mother

Malka Hasia bat Moshe Menahem Mendel

TABLE OF CONTENTS

GENESIS • בראשית

Braishith

    I — "Let there be light!"   13
    II — Adam and the atom   14
    III — Creativity   16
    IV — What kind of nakedness?   18

Noah

    I — Sinking is so permanent...   20
    II — No guarantee against man-made floods   21
    III — So many colors in the rainbow!   22

Lech Le'cha

    I — Our grandfather   24
    II — The man with the great idea   25
    III — "I have made Abram rich"   28
    IV — How to be a blessing   29
    V — Isaiah to Nasser and company   31
    VI — "Is anything too hard for the Lord?"   32

Vayera

    I — A past pickled in brine   34
    II — Not even a minyan in Sodom   35
    III — Is it any of Abraham's business?   36
    IV — Twenty-twenty vision   38

Chaye Sarah

    I — Bargain basement Judaism   39
    II — The time of your life   40
    III — Nothing to live for   41

Toledot

    I — The non-identical twins   43
    II — Is it worth all that trouble?   44
    III — Who needs a birthright anyway?   46
    IV — Esau, the nihilist   47
    V — The well-digger   48
    VI — What's your angle?   50

Vayetse

    I — Jacob's stream of consciousness   52
    II — Can we ever make it to the top?   53
    III — Time to go home   55
    IV — Time to go home, indeed!   56
    V — Jacob's crucible   58
    VI — The Hunter and the Seeker   60

Vyishlach

    I — Intermarriage   62
    II — Jacob, pacifist extraordinary   63
    III — Why, Jacob, you haven't changed at all!   65

Vayeshev

    I — The comeback   66
    II — Burn the heretic!   68
    III — Ariel and Caliban are myths   69
    IV — The demagogue   71

Mikketz

    I — Such a tragic waste!   72
   II — The dreamer of the possible   73

Vayigash

    I — Collective security...   75
   II — ...Versus "rugged individualism"   76
  III — To give *and* to receive   78
  IV — Who's afraid of the big, bad truth?   80
   V — The "Miracle worker"   81

Vayechi

    I — The gentlemen *talk* of peace   83
   II — Look n o t back in anger   85
  III — "Bury me not in Egypt!"   86
  IV — The truth doesn't hurt   88
   V — The most important thing we can give
       our children   90

EXODUS • שמות

Shemot

    I — The Burning Bush   95
   II — The bush can be man himself   96
  III — What makes a good speaker?   98
  IV — Pharaoh's propoganda   100

Vaera

    I — We need Moses worse than Pharaoh does   102
   II — Foxhole religion   103

B o

    I — "Three Beautiful Blessings"   105
    II — Pharaoh is a fossil   106
    III — Shall there be a summit meeting?   108
    IV — Exodus: young and old   109

Beshalach

    I — Moses needed Miriam   110
    II — Water, water everywhere   112
    III — The Exodus is no picnic   113

Jethro

    I — Observance in the breach   115
    II — Our God and "opium-gods"   117
    III — Where, O where is God?   119
    IV — God is in the thick darkness   121
    V — Wonderful Jethro   122

Mishpatim

    I — Sweet, sweet justice   124
    II — The spirit of the laws   125
    III — Of asses and oxen   126
    IV — The society of justice   128
    V — Suicide through hypnosis   130

Terumah

    I — The art of prayer   131
    II — Buy bonds!   132
    III — All of one piece   134
    IV — The Synagogue is a taskmaster   135

Tetsaveh

— The Eternal Light   137

Ki Seesau

I — Torah-vision   139
II — The Sabbath   140
III — A lonely, lonely tent   141
IV — Soliloquy, monologue, conversation   143

Vayakhel

I — The end does not justify the means   144
II — Israel: A tabernacle in the wilderness   146

Pikudai

I — They said it couldn't be done   147
II — A Jew without a synagogue?   149
III — Chazak!   150

LEVITICUS ● ויקרא

Vayikra

I — J'accuse!   155
II — That good old guilt feeling   156

Tsav

Some mysteries should not be solved   158

Shemini

I — Alien fire   161
II — Eloquent silence   163

Tazria-Mezora

        Quarantine!   164

Acharai Mos

        The earth can vomit   165

Kedoshim

        I — The essence of Judaism   167
        II — A good Jew is God-conscious   168
        III — Cursing a deaf man   170

Emor

        Chillul Hashem   171

Behar

        "Give me liberty..."   173

Bechukosai

        I — "And give thee peace"   174
        II — My God   176
        III — Holiness and the man   178

NUMBERS ● במדבר

Bamidbar

        Numbers is a wrong translation   183

Naso

        Samson: A hero with clay feet   184

B'ha'aloscha

        I — Zecharia calling   186
        II — The voice of the bagel   187

Shelach

 A man is ten feet tall   189

Korach

 The Rabbi and his congregation   191

Chukas

 The old order changeth ...   193

Balak

 In defense of Bala'am   195

Phineas

 The still, small voice   197

Matos-Masai

 Enough of tent folding   200

DEUTERONOMY ● דברים

Va'eschanan

 I — The generation of juvenile delinquency   205
 II — Does Judaism need a code?   207

Aikev

 Poor, little Jewish girl   209

Re'ai

 What goes into the mouth *is* important   211

Shoftim

        The telephone game   212

Ki Saitsai

        Morality in the flesh   213

Ki Sauvo

        Mount Gerizim and Mount Ebal   215

Nitsavim-Vayelech

        "Therefore, choose you life!"

FESTIVALS ● ימים־טובים

Cheshbon Hanefesh   221
The day *after* **Yom Kippur . . .**   223
The universal moment   224
Rosh Hashannah

        I — "We, the defendants"   225
        II — Reveille   227

Yom Kippur

        I — The road back   228
        II — The blueprint   230

Succos

        I — Humble little hut   232
        II — Quartet   233
        III — What's happened to the Succah? 234
        IV — An embarassment of riches   236

Pesach

I —	Exodus, 20th century	239
II —	Freedom is a tyrant	241
III —	The Angel of Death is still about	243
IV —	The nature of a miracle	244
V —	Hagada vs. Kneidlach	246
VI —	Post-Pesach problem	248

Shavuot

I —	Time and time again	250
II —	An open letter to nineteen young ladies	252

Hanukah

I —	Bringing Hanukah home	254
II —	The triumph of the light-seekers	254
III —	Hanukah vs. Purim	256
IV —	Not by might	258
V —	"Broad-minded" parents	260
VI —	Zeus vs. the Menorah	261

Purim

I —	Haman's rope	262
II —	A king in his cups	264
III —	Mordecai's mistake	266
IV —	Does the Megillah have a happy ending?	267
V —	Same old Megillah	269

OCCASIONAL • לפרקים

Jewish Book Month

    I — Am hasefer or am ha'aretz   273

    II — To your books, O Israel   275

The heart of Albert Einstein   276

Jewish Education

    An open letter to 120 USY'ers   277

Mother's Day   279

בראשית

•

BRAISHITH

BRAISHITH • בראשית

I

"LET THERE BE LIGHT!"

Again we are back at the beginning. And *"In the beginning
the Lord created the heaven and the earth."* He went to a lot
of trouble to make this earth beautiful. He deluged it with
light. He suffused it with growing things. He lavished produce
upon it. He endowed it with spectacular color. He wrought it
with infinite love and — he peopled it with Adams and Eves.

It was Paradise in the beginning — idyllic, serene, blissful
and carefree. And Paradise it might well have remained save
that...

Save that man tasted of knowledge and proceeded forthwith
to misapply it. Adam learned to lie, Eve learned to beguile and
Cain learned to kill. The metamorphosis of Paradise was begun
and slowly yet steadily, the beauty was a-fading, the joy was
a-waning, the serenity was a-dying and Hell was a-borning.

And that has been the sad saga of man ever since. Knowledge,
normally a prodigious instrument for good, has been prostituted
for the service of evil. Ploughshares and pruning hooks have
given way to swords and spears. Balms and medications have
been displaced by banes and poisons. Atomic power has been
harnessed to Mammoth Monstrosities of fantastic demolition.

And now it might appear that we are at the stage not of
"In the beginning" but "at the end." The very hydrogen which
was the basic material of the Genesis may yet spell out the
post mortem of the Six Days of Creation.

Poised upon the precipice, leaning over the abyss, staring into
the bowels of chaos — we wait prayerfuly for the thundering
voice of the deity to be heard as of yore:

"Let there be light!"

13

II

ADAM AND THE ATOM

"And God divided the light from the darkness"
Genesis 1:4

It is well to distinguish between *division* and *divisiveness*. The former implies separation. The later involves discord.

Separation, in itself, is not necessarily an evil. Frequently it may be a good. The simplest form of life ,the amoeba, reproduces itself by means of division which thus constitutes the very means of its survival. Surgery, possibly the greatest life saving device known to man, is the process of separating cells which are diseased from those which are healthy, thereby militating against the spread of the malady.

The biblical account of the creation indicates that the world itself came into being as the result of several divisional operations. The Lord divided between the light and the darkness; divided the waters which were under the firmament from the waters which were above the firmament; divided between the day and the night, the summer and the winter; and finally divided between the six pedestrian days of the week and the Sabbath.

In effect, God wrought order from chaos through an orderly and systematic process of division.

But there is one important element in creation which God significantly intended to be a whole, an undivided unity. That element was the Lord's *piece de resistance* — man. Even woman, the opposite sex, was created, in the words of Adam: "bone of my bones and flesh of my flesh." "Now therefore shall a man leave his father and his mother and shall cleave unto his wife and they shall be *one flesh.*"

The unity of mankind was the supreme purpose of the Creator. The Talmud cites an interesting exchange of thoughts between two of the great scholars of the Second Century.

"Rabbi Akiba said: 'And thou shalt love thy neighbor as thyself: this is the great principle of the Torah.' Ben Azai said: 'This is the book of the generations of man': that is the great principle of the Torah."*

On the surface it is difficult to establish a connection between the statement of Rabbi Akiba and that of Ben Azai whose meaning is obscure even as an unrelated statement. A more profound examination of the words of Ben Azai, however, will serve to reveal that he was supplying the reason for Rabbi Akiba's statement. Is it not odd, muses Ben Azai, that in what is by all odds the most vital biographical account ever written, the story of the first man, that so little detail is supplied? So many questions could be asked: From what particular section of the earth was the dust taken from which man was created? What was the color of Adam's skin? What did Adam look like? How did Adam worship? Where did Adam actually live?

The silence of the Bible as to these details is the most eloquent answer to all the above questions. Adam, as the Talmud affirms, was created from dust gathered on every continent. Adam was neither black nor white nor yellow nor brown nor red. And yet he was a composite of all these colors for he was the ancestor of all men. Adam was neither semitic nor nordic nor mongolian nor teutonic nor Anglo-Saxon. And yet he was the composite of all races for he was the father of all men. Adam worshiped God. That is all. What particular *form* his religiosity assumed is not specified. Nor is it important. Adam is the spiritual father of men of all religions and of no religions.

"This is the book of the generations of man," simply man unqualified, indefinable, unlabeled and composite — man with no strings attached. That, said Ben Azai, is the great principle in the Torah for it clearly proclaims the unity and equality of

* Braishith Rabba, 24:8.

all men of all races, all colors, all creeds and all national origin. Therefore: "Love thy neighbor as thyself."

The great tragedy of man was his immediate failure to accept this principle. Man reversed God's process. He failed to divide between that which God intended to be divided and exercised division where it was contrary to God's purpose. In spite of tasting of the fruits of the tree of knowledge of good and evil man failed to divide and distinguish between them.

And Cain killed his brother Abel.

The tragedy has continued down through the ages. Man has bred divisiveness and propogated disunity in defiance of God's will. Man's attainment of knowledge would not have been tragic had he been able to divide and to distinguish between knowledge applied towards the end of good and knowledge applied towards the end of evil, between ploughshares and pruning hooks on the one hand and swords and spears on the other. But man has exhibited a much more pronounced tendency to apply the knowledge which he gained in the direction of evil. Thus it was with Cain. Thus it has been in our time with Hiroshima, Nagasaki and Atomic Energy.

The atomic bomb is itself the symbol par excellence of destructive divisiveness. It annihilates through fission. Man has learned to divide the atom. He has not yet learned to divide between its constructive and destructive uses. It would be ironic, indeed, if the end will come about as did the beginning.

In the beginning "God divided the light from the darkness."
In the end man divided the atom.

III

CREATIVITY

"In the beginning God created" — Genesis 1:1 — If we go no further in the Bible we have in these words alone the

essence of what is right and what is wrong. That is right which is creative, which improves. That is wrong which is destructive which damages.

*

"And God said: "Let there be light!" — Genesis 1:3 — That was the first edict of the Creator. To associate God with anything other than light and good is to misunderstand the essence of Judaism's conception of the deity.

*

"And God saw everything that He had made, and, behold, it was very good." — Genesis 1:31 — Indeed it was. Indeed it is. A wondrous and a beautiful world did God present to us. The misery and the corruption within it is of our own making.

*

"And God blessed the seventh day and hallowed it." — Genesis 2:3 — The Sabbath is the day which gives content and meaning to the six days of creation. It invests the world of crude matter with the Eternal Light of God's Spirit. "The Spirit of God hovering on the face of the water" when all was yet void and chaotic found its ultimate resting place within the Sabbath. To violate the Sabbath is to strike out at the very spirit of God.

*

"And the Lord called unto Adam and said unto him; 'Where art thou'?" — Genesis 3:9 — Throughout the long and oft-time tragic history of the creature called Man the Lord has been calling "Adam where art thou?" The sons of Adam who have responded to the call have vindicated their mortal existence and taken a lease as well on an iota of immortality. The sons of Adam who have not responded to the call are "the people

who walk in darkness." Their road is a maze and their destination a dead-end.

*

"By the sweat of thy brow shalt thou eat bread." — Genesis
3:19 — Is this a curse? It is not, we maintain. Indeed, it is
blessing. For if bread came easy to man he would not enjoy it.
Moreover, that creativity spoken of at the beginning can only
be the outgrowth of man's perspiration.

IV

WHAT KIND OF NAKEDNESS?

"In the beginning God created the heaven and the earth"
Genesis 1:1 — For Judaism the beginning is God. Nothing
has any meaning whatsoever apart from God, not even the
falling of an obscure leaf from an obscure tree in an obscure
forest.

*

*"Now the earth was unformed and void and darkness was
upon the face of the deep; and the spirit of God hovered over
the face of the waters."* — Genesis 1:2 — The earth shall remain
chaotic and unfulfilled and bleak darkness shall suffuse it as
long as the spirit of God is merely dangled superficially from the
tongues of men upon the bare thread of lip-service. When the
spirit of God ceases to "hover" and begins to penetrate, then —
and then only — shall there be light.

*

*"And God called the dry land Earth and the gathering to-
gether of the waters called He Seas; and God saw that it was
good."* — Genesis 1:5 — He, blessed be His name, put a perfectly
good world into our hands. Whatever is *now* wrong with the
world is man's own doing. The work of the truly religious man
is clearly set out before him: to restore the universe to its

original state of goodness. And this is the meaning of the prayer we recite thrice daily: "to perfect the world in the kingdom of the almighty."

*

"And God said: "Let there be lights in the heavens to divine the day from the night." — Genesis 1:14 — If man would only look heavenward he would readily be able to differentiate between the day and the night, the good and the evil, the right and the wrong. Morality begins with the look towards heaven.

*

"And God created Man in His own image." — Genesis 1:27 — A perfectly simple test was thus offered man. Let him periodically direct his eyes inward, into his own soul, and ascertain if he can still detect God's image therein. If yes, then he may rest at peace with his conscience. If no, then a major task of resoration lies ahead of him. And — the more man sees of *himself* as he directs his eyes inward, the less he will see of the image of God. He who is obsessed with the passion for self-glorification cannot be overly concerned with the glory of God.

*

"And they were both naked, the man and his wife (Adam and Eve) and were not ashamed." — Genesis 2:25 — The nakedness of the body — of physical accoutrements — is nothing to be ashamed of. What is shameful is the nakedness of the soul. For to cultivate and to enrich the soul is the essence of man's mission on the face of the earth. Poverty of the spirit — unlike material poverty — cannot be attributed to the injustice of others. The nourishment of the spirit is in the hands of each of us. The responsibility for his famished spirit lies at the threshhold of man himself.

NOAH • נֹחַ

I

SINKING IS SO PERMANENT...

The Ark of Noah is a beautiful bit of symbolism. Rereading the tale each year is a profoundly poetic experience for those who are neither shallow nor prosaic.

For our earth is the Ark and its inhabitants the menagerie thereof — and the flood is emblematic of the forces arrayed against us in our struggle for survival.

If we are to stay above water, we must learn to live in harmony with one another, even as the animals in Noah's Ark did. The Flood, you see, is no respecter of fine differences as between lions and eagles and bears and such. Destructively speaking, the Flood is democratic to a fault.

As an emissary of peace and serenity, the Raven is a complete failure. He looks out only for himself, little caring to overburden his bird-brain with metaphysical speculations about the greater collective good also entailing the greater individual good. The Raven will give up nothing, while his ravenous appetite will spare nothing. The Raven has little interest in bold experiments and the Pioneer Spirit simply does not abide within him.

Ah, the Dove, on the other hand, is a bird of a different feather. Her highest objective is peace and tranquility; her noblest quest, the Olive Branch. And, to reach that objective, to attain that quest, the Dove is quite willing to go a long way and to undergo great discomfort. Mind you now, the Dove need not necessarily be a so called "do-gooder," "egghead," "utopian," "visionary" or "pinko." On the contrary, she knows that everyone in the menagerie is in the same boat and that they will either swim together or sink together.

She prefers to swim. Sinking is so permanent...

II

NO GUARANTEE AGAINST MAN-MADE FLOODS

Our Torah reading states in its opening verse that *"Noah walked with God."* In these four words, I believe, is to be found the essential quality of the Religious Man. Religion to him is not something occasional or periodic. It permeates his being constantly. He lives with it and it lives with him *all the time*. Quite literally: Noah walks with God.

*

"And the earth was corrupt before God and the earth was filled with violence." — Genesis 6:11 — The inhumanity of man to man is the most severe form of rebellion against the will of God. The first of God's orders to mankind was: *"Increase and multiply."* It clearly follows that acts of violence which decrease and decimate stand in direct opposition to the will of God.

*

"And God remembered Noah and every living thing and all the cattle that were with him in the ark." — Genesis 8:1 — For sheer beauty and simplicity there is no finer statement anywhere of God's compassion fro his creatures. There is no living thing so minute as to escape the loving observation of the Creator.

*

"But the dove found no rest for the sole of her foot, and she returned unto him to the ark, for the waters were on the face of the whole earth; and he put forth his hand and took her, and brought her in unto him into the ark." — Genesis 8:9 — In this quiet and touching paragraph is the statement of the root of all mental and emotional aberration as well as the correction thereof.

The "sick" or psychotic human being can find no anchorage for the sole of his feet and is consequently terrorized by the surging waters around him. He will only be restored to mental and emotional health if some Noah can extend a powerful hand to him and draw him into an ark that will supply the necessary anchorage and impart that sense of security indispensable to the weal of all men.

A man without his ark will be lost in the flood.

"Whoso sheddeth man's blood, by man shall his blood be shed." — Genesis 9:6 — Irony of ironies! God put an end to the great flood and promised that no flood would ever be unloosed by HIM. But in this verse we find the divine warning against man-made floods, not of water, but of blood. Permit man to kill his fellow man, says the Lord, and the floodgates of endless bloodletting will have been thrown wide open. The shedding of blood leads to the shedding of blood in a vicious and never ending cycle.

III

SO MANY COLORS IN THE RAINBOW!

"Noah walked with God" — Genesis 6:9 — what a perfectly wonderful life — to walk with God! It implies several things; It means first of all that one is never alone. It means secondly that one is never afraid. It means thirdly that one can never stumble. It means finally that one is always headed in the right direction. This being so, it is truly an enigma that so few make the choice of so excellent a walking companion.

*

"And the earth was corrupt before God and the earth was filled with violence." — Genesis 6:11 — The second part of this verse explains the first. The violence we do to one another

represents the corruption of God's universe. How tragic that so much of history's bloodshed should have been committed in the name of the Almighty God who condemns it. No monstrous war has ever been fought but that it was not "justified" by the invocation of some shimmering ideal.

*

"In the six hundredth year of Noah's life, in the second month, on the seventeenth day of the month, on the same day were all the fountains of the great deep broken up, and the windows of heaven were opened." — Genesis 7:11 — The windows of heaven are always open. But such is the human animal that nothing short of tempestuous upheaval and the gaping jaws of Sheol itself will suddenly — and so oft, belatedly — magnetize his attention to the celestial windows. The foxhole, we might add, is a hell of a place to discover God. The "religion" of crisis is best described as voodoo.

*

"But the dove found no rest for the sole of her foot, and she returned unto him to the ark — and he put forth his hand, and took her, and brought her in unto him into the ark." — Genesis 8:9 — What a lesson for the would be peacemaker! The dove of peace cannot be expected to fly into his ark at no annoying inconvenience to himself. If he truly desires her he must put forth his hand and meet her halfway. To stand on ceremony while the dove of peace nervously flutters on the outside is to flirt with disaster.

*

"While the earth remaineth (said God), seedtime and harvest, and cold and heat and summer and winter, and day and night shall not cease." — Genesis 8:22 — Reliability and constancy are divine traits. In sad contrast stands God's human creature

who is always unpredictable, nearly always fickle and sometimes downright treacherous.

*

"I have set My bow (the rainbow) in the cloud and it shall be a Sign of the Covenant between Me and the earth." — Genesis 9:13 — Look at the rainbow and you will note that it seems to start from one end of the world and finish at the other. So must it be, if there is to be tranquility. It must reign everywhere or it can regin nowhere. "Gentlemen," said Maxim Litvinoff in Geneva, "peace is indivisible!" but neither Chamberlain nor Roosevelt heard him.

*

Said the builders of the Tower of Babel: *"Come let us build us a city and a tower with its top in heaven and let us make us a name..."* Genesis 11:3. An undertaking which has vanity as its motivating force cannot endure. Overweening ambition was the seed of destruction for many Tower-builders from Nebbuchadnezzar and Sennaherib to Hitler and Stalin. The motto of the Babel-builders moreover, was: "One people and one language." This motto has not changed through the ages. It is still the prescription of tyrants and absolutists who crave to stamp their image upon all people as one would stamp so many cattle. Unity, God desires. Homogeneity, He does not. Harmony, God desires. Monotone, He does not.

LECH LE'CHA • לך לך

I

OUR GRANDFATHER

We had a remarkable grandfather. He was a truly great human being. He was a living example of Jewishness and Judaism. He was a man of enormous courage. He was utterly unselfish, totally altruistic. His faith in God was profound and unlimited. His love of humanity was zealous and unswerving. His paternal instincts were tinged with poetic beauty. His filial devotion was a marvel of compliance with the Fifth Commandment.

He was a man well acquainted with suffering and disillusion. Yet from each ordeal he emerged with even greater stature. He was a man who experienced hunger and exile and loneliness and humiliation and treachery. Yet withal was his faith unseared and unscathed and unmitigated. He was a man whose origin was mean and ungodly. Yet he was to become the noblest and godliest of men. He was a man who gave all to others. Yet he demanded naught from any man. He was a Hebrew, a Jew, in the fullest possible sense of the words. Yet he recognized no barriers of any kind between him and any other member of the human race. He insisted on paying liberally for all services rendered to him. Yet he expected no payment of any kind for the multifarious services he rendered to others.

Our grandfather had pride without arrogance, militancy without bigotry, piety without superstition, integrity without obduracy. He was beyond a doubt a wonderful man. We ought to glory in the fact that he was our grandfather. We ought to study his inspirational saga with painstaking care.

For there was only one Abraham.

II

THE MAN WITH THE GREAT IDEA

Each year, as the Torah reading cycle returns to the saga of our father Abraham, I am struck anew by the altogether idyllic life and character of the first Hebrew. Abraham was the most important "first" in the saga of man. In the words of our sages: "Abraham was the first to identify his Creator."*

* Babylonian Talmud, Nedarim 32.

The name of the Chaldean-born patriot is, in itself, of immense significance. It means: "The Father of a Multitude of
Nations." Abraham discovered the great principle, indeed, the
indispensable principle, for the unification of all nations and
the brotherhood of all men: One God!

*

The principle was the most revolutionary of all time. And
like all revolutionary ideas it met with violent, uncompromising
opposition. No sooner did Abraham begin to preach it than
he became a pariah, an untouchable. It is entirely understandable, then, that the adventure of his life must perforce begin
with exile. "Now the Lord said unto Abraham: 'Get thee out
of thy country, and from thy kindred and from thy father's
house, unto the land that I will show thee.'" (Genesis 12:1)

*

Had Abraham evinced a moment's reluctance, he would have
immediately disqualified himself as the founder of a great idea.
Founders of great ideas are pioneers and wanderers on the face
of the earth. They must march on endlessly in the face of abuse,
suffering and sorrow, a living embodiment of their Great Obsession — for all to hear, to see and, yes, to humiliate. Suffering
and sorrow die with the man but the Great Idea will outlive the
mockers and the scorners.

*

The man with the Great Idea will have no use of bows and
arrows and swords. Nothing conquered by the sword ever stayed
conquered. The sword is perishable. The man with the Great
Idea is a man of peace working with a "dagger of the mind,"
a dagger which, because it has no physical substance, is not exposed to mortality or perishability. It is not the dagger that
destroys. It is the dagger that pierces — in and through and,
ultimately, through and through.

The man with the Great Idea will not consign the City of Evil to limbo. He is not a Jonah running away from a nefarious Nineveh, cursing it as he goes. He is an Abraham running towards a suffering Sodom, pitying it as he comes. Jonah is a sectarian prophet. Abraham is a universal Prophet. Jonah thinks that his people alone have a monopoly on Good. Abraham knows that there may be good even in a Sodom and that his own family has its Lots and its Ishmaels.

*

The man with the Great Idea must be free. He must be indebted to no man, that no man's bounty might serve as a leverage for the palliation or frustration of the Great Idea. "And Abram said to the king of Sodom: "I have lifted up my hand unto the Lord, God Most High, Maker of heaven and earth, that I will not take a thread nor a shoelace nor aught that is thine, lest, thou shouldest say: I have made Abram rich." — Genesis 14:22

*

The man with the Great Idea must be monomaniacal in his faith in the Idea — in the face of the most overwhelming kind of discouragement. The seed of a Great Idea, by the very nature of things, is always sown in the desert. The man with the Great Idea must truly believe that the desert will bloom. That belief, that faith, is the very irrigation of the said desert. Nothing else in the world will make the desert bloom. That is why Abraham, the childless centenarian can look toward the stars and believe that one day his children will equal them in numbers. "And he believed in the Lord; and He counted it to him for righteousness." — Genesis 15:6

"Blessed art Thou, our God and the God of our fathers — the God of Abraham..."

III

"I HAVE MADE ABRAM RICH."

...*"And in thee shall all the families of the earth be blessed..."* — Genesis 12:3 — These were among the first words God spoke to Abraham, the father of the Jewish people. If any refutation were needed of the libel that Jewry is sectarian and chauvenistic, it is readily found in these words. If any further evidence were needed to counter the nonsensical attacks upon the concept of "the chosen people," it lies in these words. Israel was chosen — as its Father Abraham was chosen — to bring blessings to *all* the families of mankind. And only the willfully ignorant can contest the fact that the Jewish people have done just that. Blind bigots of the Christian Church have often spoken of the Jews as "the cursed people," patent absurdity on the part of ecclesiasts whose own religion owes its birth and its lifeblood to Judaism.

*

...*"And Lot went with him..."* — Genesis 12:4 — At first blush this man Lot appears like an idealist, travelling the difficult pioneering route side by side with Abraham. But Lot's real intent is made clear a bit later in the story. As soon as he made his pile by dint of his Uncle Abraham's industry and good fortune, Lot up and left his benefactor. Thus has it been often in Jewish history. A Ferdinand and an Isabella would use a Don Isaac Abravanel just as long as they needed him to replenish their waning coffers. After that — the unceremonious boot and "goodbye, Don Isaac, we need you no more." Jews have consistently spent hundreds of years bringing prosperity and plenty to lands from which they were ultimately cast out like used dishwater. How does the old Yiddish proverb go? *Alleh shusters gehn borvess!"*

*

"...*I will not take a thread nor a shoe-string nor aught that is thine, lest thou shouldest say: I have made Abram rich.*" — Genesis 14:23 — Thus spoke our patriarch to the King of Sodom who was beholden to Abraham for his very life. How well Abraham must have foreseen destiny's diet for his children. Always the cry: "The Jews have become rich at our expense!" Or "the Jews are parasites upon the body economic!" Or "the Jews are the warmakers who fill their treasures of gold with the blood of our dying soldiers!" Or "the Jews control the largest part of our nation's wealth!" Always: "I have made Abram rich!" Never: "Abram has helped make me rich."

*

But then again how can a fossil (a la Toynbee) enrich anybody?

O God of Abraham, answer us!

IV

HOW TO BE A BLESSING

"*And I will bless thee and make thy name great; and be thou a blessing.*" — Genesis 12:2 — This was God's promise to Abram. How tersely does our Torah put a towering truth: one deserves to be called great only if he is a blessing to others. All the genius in the world will not elevate a man to greatness if it is not employed for the benefit of others. All the wealth in the world will not accord a man importance if it is not used to help a deservant cause.

Once upon a time, Rabbi Zvi Hirsch Cohen, patriarch of the Canadian Rabbinate in the twenties, appealed for funds to a parlor meeting of philanthropists in behalf of some notable Jewish cause. The eminent millionaire Jacob Schiff was among those present. His response was disappointing.

Rabbi Cohen turned his aristocratic visage upon the man: "Mr. Schiff," said he, "are you a respected man because of the money that *remains* in your pocket? Don't you rather think that it is the money leaving your pocket for decent purposes that has earned for you the respect you enjoy?" Mr. Schiff came through.

*

"And the Lord appeared unto Abram, and said; unto thy seed will I give this land; and he builded there an altar unto the Lord who appeared to him." — Genesis 12:7 — God's promised land did not mislead Abram into thinking that the land would be handed to his children on the proverbial silver platter. He knew full well that great sacrifices would be called for ere the promise is converted into fulfillment. Symbolically, then, he proceeded to build an altar. The mere decision to possess something does not yet guarantee its possession. Only *sacrifices* made to secure that which is so fervently desired will pave the road to triumph * * * *

To give and to sacrifice is the glory of life.

To take and to indulge is the disgrace of life.

There is the person who knows only to take; he is a self-worshipper who thinks that he has everything coming to him. Is he a happy man? Not by a long shot! He is a prisoner of a tight little stage in an empty theater with only one miserable perfomer behind the ghostly footlights; himself.

Then there is the man who knows how to give; he is a worshipper of God who knows that for every last cent he has, he ought to get down on his hands and knees and thank God who gave it to him. Is he a happy man? The happiest, I should say. He is a free man, performing a useful part in the great, broad world which God has created and which God has peopled with other human beings whom our man loves and respects and from whom in turn he receives the greatest treasure a man can have: the verdict that it is wonderful to have him around; the verdict that, like Abram, he is a blessing.

V

ISAIAH TO NASSER AND COMPANY

In the arena of global power-politics little Israel seems thoroughly isolated. The two mammoth rivals for world dominion — America and Russia — are falling all over themselves in obsequious courtship of the meanest and the pettiest Arab States. A constant torrent of venom is directed from Moscow to Jerusalem while not the slightest antidote of a kind word issues from Washington. And all around tiny Zion there is a raucous barking of two-bit Arab potentates, a veritable bevy of carping canine surrounding a lone feline and sounding off aplenty but thus far fearing to get too near.

The precarious state of peace in the Middle East is hanging by the proverbial thread and withal is being heavily taxed by the weight of Soviet arms shipments on one side and American munitions on the other. This is like filling a mischieveous boy's pockets with firecrackers on the Fourth of July and looking forward to his "safe and sane" celebration of the day. Provocation of Israel in the form of border ambushings, blackmail-tinted boycotts and flagrant violations of her right to peaceful waterway commerce continue unabated and uncensored. The UN's role in the crisis has been largely that of a free sounding-board for the most vicious sort of Arab vitriol. Topping all this off is the new insolence gained by the Kremlin and its satellites all over the world by the newest of satellites — Sputnick. Saddening is the word for all to whom Israel is sacred and precious.

Therefore it might perhaps be helpful to quote a world-famous authority on international affairs who made a statement on the world situation as it affects Israel from which its friends might take heart. Unfortunately, he is dead, having passed on two thousand five hundred years ago. But his words, I think, are very much alive — so much so, indeed that they are still read in synagogues all over the world.

Said the authority: "But thou, Israel, my servant, Jacob whom I have chosen, the seed of Abraham my friend. Thou whom I have taken hold of from the ends of the earth...Fear thou not for I am with thee, be not dismayed, for I am thy God; I strengthen thee, yea, I help thee, yea, I uphold thee with my victorious right hand. Behold all they that are incensed against thee shall be ashamed and confounded, they that strive with thee shall be as nothing, and shall perish...For I the Lord, thy God hold thy right hand, who say unto thee, fear not, I help thee. Fear not, thou worm Jacob and ye men of Israel;...Behold I make thee a new threshing sledge, having sharp teeth; thou shalt thresh the mountains and beat them small and shalt make the hills as chaff. Thou shalt fan them and the wind shall carry them away...And thou shalt rejoice in the Lord, thou shalt glory in the Holy One of Israel." — Isaiah 41:8-16, the Prophetic reading for Lech Le'cha

*

Amen.

VI

"IS ANYTHING TOO HARD FOR THE LORD?"

"Is anything too hard for the Lord?" — Genesis 18:14 — This celestial reproof was visited upon mother Sarah who was skeptical that she — an aging woman — could still bear a child. Those who speak of something as "impossible" are guilty of the deification of nature. They are saying that long experience proves such and such and therefore there is no ground for expecting anything else. They are saying, for example, "well, this is an incurable disease and therefore he will die" or "human nature will never change and therefore war is inevitable." But are nature and God identical concepts? Spinoza though so and he was excommunicated. For to the Jew *God is the creator of nature*

and nature's behavior is subject to His will. If for a billion years a natural phenomenon was everlastingly repeated it does not follow that tomorrow God yill not decide otherwise. For even a billion years are no more than a pathetic fraction of eternity, and who but God himself can see eternity whole? In His calendar, the reversal of nature's course could be an "every day" occurence.

In the truest sense, this must be the meaning of the miracle stories of the Bible: the division of the Red Sea, the Manna from heaven, the halting of the sun in Gibeon, Elishah's resuscitation of the dead, etc etc. They are the reflection of Judaism's unfaltering conviction that God rules nature, that God can alter the ways of nature, that indeed He *does* alter them when His infinite wisdom deems it fit to do so.

This, too, is the meaning of the passage in our daily prayers which reads: "in Thy goodness thou renewest the work of creation every day, constantly." Judaism refuses to accept the sun and the moon and the stars and all of nature's vast apparatus as if they were a selfwinding clockworks. God is the daily winder and God can be the unwinder as well — at any time He chooses. We must take nothing for granted, good, bad or neutral. We must perpetually direct our gaze heavenward, for it is there that all decisions are made — constantly, caringly, consciously. There in heaven is the Legislative, Executive and Judicial Arm of the Almighty forever fashioning destiny, never letting up, never looking away, never turning on a switch marked automatic.

It is precisely this Vigilance, this Watchfulness, this Providence which supplies the rationale for prayer. For what is prayer if not recourse to the Highest Court of Appeal? What indeed is all of religion if not a faith that the "inevitable" is subject to change if the Prime Mover of all that moves so wills it?

Thus can a Joshua look at the setting sun *up*setting his plan for victory and — with perfect faith — petition heaven that the day should tarry beyond its accustomed span. And what is more the petition could be granted.

Ninety year old Sarah *could* bear a child.

Cancer is *not* incurable.

War is *not* inevitable.

"Is anything too hard for the Lord?"

VAYERA ● וירא

I

A PAST PICKLED IN BRINE

Salt in small doses is quite wonderful. It makes food tasty and interesting. Salt in large doses is quite dreadful. It makes food unpalatable and repulsive. In very large quantity, salt is used as a long-time preservative.

There are people here on earth whose philosophy is a salt-philosophy. They want everything preserved, no matter what, no matter how old, no matter how out-dated. They are the champions of the *status quo,* the patrons of reaction. Their yard-stick of quality is always the past. Their pattern of behavior is always imitative, never original. They are always looking behind, never ahead.

The fact that that past which they worship may have been ugly and diseased and sanguinary does not seem to matter. Things were this way before, they "reason"; they must therefore continue in this way. Let everything be frozen in its tracks. Let everything be pickled in brine.

The wife of Lot, Abraham's nephew, thought that way. Her attraction to the past was chronic. Even when that past represented the reprehensible civilizations of Sodom and Amorah, she must needs have cast her nostalgic eyes backwards for a last, lingering, longing look at the conflagration of those two pulverized and sulphurized nests of degradation.

Therefore, she was turned into a pillar of salt — a symbol of the mania for preserving that which is rotten, and a monumental testimonial to the character of those who look behind.

If our own civilization is to survive, it must liberate itself from enslavement to its Sodomic past. It must look ahead towards new and brighter horizons, fresh and more truthful ideas, honest and more universal ideals.

The bleak and dismal past? Let's take it with a grain of salt.

II

NOT EVEN A *MINYAN* IN SODOM...

Father Abraham was a great individualist who loved individuals. He never thought of mankind in one lump unit. He never regarded such concepts as "the masses" or "the crowd" or "the mob" as morally tenable. To him a large group was basically a gathering of individuals and never did he lose sight of the solitary human being in the great multitude.

That is why he was shocked at the intelligence that Sodom was to be destroyed. To him Sodom was not an abstract unit identifiable as "a city." Sodom, in Abraham's vocabulary, was an area in which lived thousands of individual human beings — human beings who loved and wept and laughed and suffered. And in its boundless love for man, the singular, not the collective noun, Abraham's soul was agitated to the core at the prospect of the annihilation of the many individuals who lived in Sodom.

So he pleaded with God. "Wilt Thou indeed sweep away the righteous with the wicked?" Had Abraham stopped right there and said no more the implication would have been: therefore, God, save the innocent and let the guilty perish in their sin. But Abraham's infinite love for *all* people, including the wicked, is reflected in the continuation of his argument. "Peradventure there are fifty righteous within the city; wilt Thou indeed sweep away and not forgive the place for the fifty righteous that are therein?" — Genesis 18:24.

Or for the forty or for the thirty or for the twenty or for the ten? How his heart must have bled at the thought of a perishing human being! How he clutched desperately at the straws that might save Sodom from devastation! How much faith he reposited in the handful of righteous men who might redeem the large assembly of the evil!

After all, he must have mused, have not I, Abraham of Ur, the solitary Hebrew, been charged to face the whole heathen world and redeem it from the abyss of idolatry and corruption? I, Abraham of the Chaldees, versus the public opinion of all the people on earth! Yet my God believes that the one can redeem the many by emancipating them that they may redeem themselves. What, then, of Sodom, O, my God? Is it beyond redemption? O, God! is it beyond redemption?

Apparently it was. But, mark this and mark it well: *Sodom was beyond redemption only because the voice of truth and justice had died within it. It had been stifled and it had allowed itself to be stifled and it died.*

III

IS IT ANY OF ABRAHAM'S BUSINESS?

"Wilt Thou indeed sweep away the righteous with the wicked?" Thus did Abraham question God when he heard of the imminent annihilation of the wicked city of Sodom. The question is as good and as piercing now as it ever was. The evil men of the earth inevitably must pave the road to their own doom. The great tragedy, however, is the fact that they drag so many of the innocent along with them upon this same road. An Alexander, a Napoleon, a Mussolini and a Hitler will surely hang in the end. But before that end comes they manage to

hang out a long, long rope from which dangle the corpses of untold numbers of the guiltless.

*

Now the wicked are *not* the majority. They are merely more vocal and less lazy. Why it should be so is one of the most perplexing questions of the ages. But one matter is certain: Because it is so, *and only because it is so,* do Alexanders, Napoleons, Mussolinis, Hitlers — and Nassers — emerge to the forefront in the first place.

*

Noah was a passive righteous man. He really preceded Louis Quatorze with the statement: *Apres moi le deluge.* He simply didn't care to bestir himself with that propaganda of righteousness which might have averted the all-consuming flood. Abraham? Now there was an entirely different story. Abraham was the most active propagandist for righteousness the world had ever seen. Justice and truth to Abraham were not abstract albeit comforting terms. To him they were living, pulsating realities or they were nothing at all. Abraham was a wanderer who simply could not sit still. He had to spread the ideals of decency from Dan to Beersheba. He could not abide the doctrines of evil and force espoused by the Amraphel-King-of-Shinars of his generation. He could not stand by and witness the evil of a Sodom without concerning himself deeply with the possibilities of its salvation.

*

The portion of the Torah seems to fairly shout at us the warning of the appalling catastrophe which the apathy of decent men can bring upon the world.

IV

TWENTY - TWENTY VISION

Abraham is ill. The sun's rays are scorching. To catch a breath of air he sits by the door of the tent, exhausted and uncomfortable.

"And he lifted up his eyes and looked, and lo, three men stood in his line of vision, and when he saw them he ran to meet them...' — Genesis 18:2.

This is at the bottom of Abraham's character: an irresistible attraction to people — *any* people, be their description whatever it may be; be they strangers or infidels or eccentrics or men who need to have their feet washed; be they sublime angels or lowly humans.

What makes Abraham run — towards people? As Jimmie of the Mickey Mouse club used to assure my Daniel and Jonathan every evening: "Because we *like* you!" Abraham likes people, meaning: Abraham likes to do things for people. Abraham's great passion in life is to contribute to the happiness of all who were created in the image of God and that for him is a broad enough category to embrace even the citizens of Sodom and Amorah.

To have seen the three strangers at some distance in the glare of the sun and tired as he was, would seem to prove that Abraham had good vision. Indeed he had, brothers and sisters, indeed he had. And if you were to ask me how Abraham developed such vision I would give you my theory on the subject. It is briefly this: Most people's eyes narrow with suspicion at the approach of the stranger. Abraham's eyes widened with delight. Widening the eyes, opening them up all the way is, I say, wonderful excercise for the improvement of human vision.

I will say no more today.

CHAYE SARAH • חיי שרה

I

BARGAIN BASEMENT JUDAISM

"Bargains" aren't always bargains. Frequently they are extremely expensive. You go out and buy an attractive looking pair of shoes which is "marked down" to a ridiculous price. You're happy, but not for long. The shoes come apart in no time and you're back shopping again. More often than not the more expensive commodity is really the cheaper commodity in the long run. It wears longer. It gives you greater satisfaction.

Now you know all of that; you have learned it through experience. But do you know that this principle is equally true in the realm of ideas and ideals? Some ideas or ideals are pegged very low. They seem to be within the reach of everybody. To attain them, you don't have to put yourself out very much. They're a cinch. Attend God's House for Yizkor services? Let's see now, hmmmm...That's about four times a year. Now *there's* a price I can afford. That's for me! Concentrate my son's Jewish training into his Bar Mitzvah preparation? That's a snap. Five, six, seven months, a year at the most of Hebrew school and I don't have to deprive the poor, overworked kid of his stickball on Amherst Street. A short cut to Jewish learning, say, a "how to etc." in three easy lessons or "how to pack a full holiday's worth of prayer into one hour?" Fine! I'll buy that.

Bargains, bargains, bargains all. But Judaism is no "bargain" in that sense. It is a religion for the elite — exacting, demanding, highly priced. It is a way of life that has survived because of the perennial readiness of its champions to make titanic sacrifices for it without a moment's hesitation. It has lasted through several millenia because so heavy a price has been paid for it.

Abraham, our father, set the precedent at the very outset. He refused to perform the religious rite of his wife's burial at a "bargain" price. He insisted on paying heavily for her cemetery plot in the Cave of Machpelah.

II

THE TIME OF YOUR LIFE

"And the life of Sarah was a hundred years and twenty years and seven years; these were the years of the life of Sarah." — Genesis 23:1 — This opening sentence of our Torah reading is, to say the least, awkward. The information in it could easily have been condensed as follows: Sarah lived one hundred and twenty seven years. It seems to me that a major point is being made here. Every year in Sarah's life was weighty. She made her life count. The Torah, therefore, deliberately dwells upon her years; it seems, indeed, to caress each one of them as though it were a precious gem.

Time in and of itself is a vacuum, empty of content, bereft of meaning. Only the human being can, if he chooses, invest it with significance. I think that the expression "time hangs heavily on his hands" misses the mark. On the contrary, the human being who does nothing meaningful with his time is dealing with a vacuum — and a vacuum is absolutely weightless. The reason he does nothing is precisely because he takes time lightly. Only he upon whose conscience time, with its enormous potential, hangs heavily is likely to do something about making time count.

Time is often referred to as being wasted. The more profound truth, however, is that the person who does nothing with time *wastes himself.* Insofar as he permits his wonderful creative potential to lie barren he destroys that trait within him which alone can raise him above the level of the lower animals .The likeliest meaning of the expression that man was made in the image of God is that the Lord invested man with *His* bent for creativity. It would then follow that the chronic waster of time and self forfeits the image of God within him. Allowing time to flit by unfilled and unfulfilled would then constitute the most frightful crime of all.

Alas, by this standard how many are the criminals among us! The disuse and abuse of time for so many is a life-pattern of mountainous proportions. The long hours we spend in childish patter over telephone wires, the staggering bite taken out of our precious time by cinematic and videonic "entertainment" bordering on the moronic, the huge chunks of day spent dyeing and undyeing feminine hair, the endless slices of evening spent in the company of the Deuce of Spades — these and so many other destroyers of the Great Potential are responsible — *more than anything else* — for the tragic state of a world poised upon a thermonuclear precipice.

"The days of our years..." Ah, the days of our years. What do they say? What do they represent? What do they mean? O, mother Sarah, preach to us! O preach to us, mother Sarah!

III

NOTHING TO LIVE FOR

"And Abraham rose up from before his dead." — Genesis 23:3 — Abraham loved Sarah dearly. She was in the truest sense his life's companion who shared his work, his weal and his woe. In her death, he sustained a fearful loss. We may be sure that his mourning was deep and true. But *Abraham rose up from before his dead* in supreme conviction that further sorrow would be futile, that capitulation to tragedy is abdication from responsibility, that the dead must loosen their grip upon the living if life means anything at all.

I have often heard the following words: "Rabbi, she's dead now. She was everything in the world to me. Now that she's gone I don't care for anything anymore. Nothing means anything anymore. I'd just as soon be dead myself." Amazing it is how so many different people have used virtually the identical words.

With all of my deepest compassion for the bereaved people so moved, I submit that they are guilty of idolatry. When the content of life is bound up with one human being, however precious, we are witnesses to the deification of mortal man. God has created a colossal universe, has populated it with myriad forms of life, has bequeathed to man a boundless field of constructive activity, has endowed man with a marvellous thinking apparatus and enriched him with the capacity to experience a multitude of sensations, has furnished His world with infinite varieties of tastes, colors, aromas, shapes and sounds, has overwhelmed man with never-ending challenges to mind, heart, hand and will, has — in fine — invested Life with infinite content and inexhaustible fascination. What, then, is this talk of "nothing to live for anymore" if not the bankruptcy of human spirit? By God, there are a billion things to live for and if we lived a billion years we should not have exhausted the things left to live for! If a life lost was so dear to us, as we say, the more reason to dedicate ourselves to life and to the cause of the living; the more reason to bind up the wounds of our fellow flesh-and-blood; the more reason to comfort the despairing and to cheer the bereft; the more reason to feed the hungry and clothe the naked; the more reason to educate the unknowing and to inspire the unfeeling; the more reason to strengthen ramparts and to rebuild the ruins; the more reason to defy death in celebrating life.

It will be time enough for us to die. We will be rejoining the dead much, much sooner than they will be rejoining us. What is the hurry? Will our masochistic suffering benefit the departed? Will our breast beating restore them to life? Will our self-flagella-

tion beat them into consciousness? Judaism forsook the cult
of the dead and its macabre ancestor-worship when the children
of Israel left Egypt and its mummies and its tombs and its
lachrymose crocodiles behind. No shrines hath Judaism which
claim to preserve the tongues and the toenails of Hebraic
Saint Anthonys. Our "prayer of mourning" is the Kaddish in
which not a word of mourning is to be found! It thunders forth
the words: *Yisgadal, V'yiskadash Shmay Rabbaw,* "May the name
of the Lord be glorified!" He, and He alone, is the object of
our worship. *Be'olmo dee vraw chirusay* "throughout the world
which He has created," that rich, splendid bountiful, infinitely
endowed world in which there is so much for us to do, so much
for us to do.....

TOLEDOT • תולדות

I

THE NON-IDENTICAL TWINS

What is the important factor in the personality development
of a child? The question is not new and neither are the answers.
One school of thought among psychologists has held that
heredity is the important factor; that the character of the parents
(and more remote antecedents) is transmitted to the child in
much the same manner as are physical characteristics. Another
school of thought has favored the notion that *environment* is
the determinant element; that the surroundings in which the
child finds himself will, despite heredity, govern his character
development. The current consensus of the psychologists is that
personality is the creature of both factors and that the degree
of the importance of either is variable.

I was thinking about all this as I re-read the Genesis story
of Jacob and Esau in preparation for the Friday evening sermon.

Jacob and Esau as you must know were brothers. More than
that, they were twins. Both came from Rebecca's womb. Both
were fathered by Isaac. Both enjoyed an excellent home environment. And yet — there was a world of difference in their
personalities. Esau was passionate, temperamental, homicidal and
boisterous. Jacob was meditative, studious, considerate and serene (or as serene as Esau's raucous personality permitted him
to be). Esau was the man of the sword. Jacob was the man of
the book. What does this do to the theory of the heredetists?
What does it do to the theory of the environmentalists? Does
it throw them into a cocked hat?

I don't think so. Heredity and environment play their roles,
and very important roles they are. But there is a "third force"
— the most important perhaps. That force, I dare say, is in-
definite, abstract, ethereal and withal very real. It is the spark
of the divinity within each of us; "the image of God" alluded
to at the genesis of Genesis. What happens to that spark with
which everyone of us is born is what we do with it. Some of
us fan it into a flame and endow our surroundings with warmth
and spirit. Some of us are hell-bent on extinguishing it with
the result that the area in our vicinity is frost-bitten and dismally
repellant.

II

IS IT WORTH ALL THAT TROUBLE?

Our Torah Reading for this Sabbath begins as follows: "And
these are the generations of Isaac, Abraham's son." — Genesis
25:19 — It is the first time that our Torah begins to relate the
story of Man's progeny by speaking first of his father. Isaac is
the first major personage who need not have been ashamed of
his parentage.

Like his father Abraham, Isaac, too, was long afflicted with
childlessness. There can be no mistaking the Torah's intention

to emphasize and re-emphasize the enormous responsibilities of Jewish parenthood. The child is potentially both the promise and the fulfillment of Judaism.

Heredity and environment are each a vital factor in the moral development of the human being. Esau and Jacob came from the same womb, were twins in fact, were sired by the same man — but each created his own environment. "Esau was a cunning hunter" — influenced by the law of the jungle. "Jacob was a quiet man, dwelling in tents" — a man of moderation and meditation.

Esau's environment conditioned him for a *weltanschaung* in which physical prowess was pre-eminent. Jacob's environment developed within him a philosophy of life predicated upon a moral-spiritual-religious foundation.

These are polar outlooks on the meaning of human existence. They must inevitably clash. They cannot "co-exist." The Torah foreshadows this conflict in admirable fashion: "And the children struggled together within her, (Rebecca) and she said: 'If it be so, wherefore do I live?'" — Genesis 25:22

With Rebecca, all men of good will sometimes ask this question. It might be put thus: "Is the uncertain prospect of future triumph sufficient compensation for the agony of the present?"

To that question only God can supply the answer. "And she went to inquire of the Lord." — Genesis 25:22 — The Lord's answer was immediate and emphatic: Suffer on, Rebecca, suffer on! For Triumph can be born only of travail and the pangs of childbearing must perforce be the prelude to Delivery and Salvation.

Beautiful, wonderful, heroic Rebecca! You are the very incarnation of Mother. You are God's co-worker in the supreme act of creation. Your womb is the repository of the morrow and the guarantor of eternity. Your tears are as the fertilizing rains upon the parched dust of the Here-and-Now and your pains are as the rays of a sun which was born yesterday casting their life-giving magic upon the endless tiers of the generations. Beautiful, wonderful, heroic Rebecca! Thou instrument of fulfillment of the infinite bounty of God! It was He who removed the Tree of Life from the storied Garden of Eden and transplanted it into your womb. Thou bearest a sacred trust, Rebecca. Bear it with dignity and with courage and with faith and immortality will be thine.

III

WHO NEEDS A BIRTHRIGHT ANYWAY?

"And these are the generations of Isaac, Abraham's son: Abrahab begot Isaac." — Genesis 25:19 — This is not idle repetition of one fact. It is, on the contrary, emphasis of an important truth. That truth is: Isaac was no accident. He was what he was because Abraham helped make him so. The idealism which Isaac symbolized was not fashioned in a vacuum. It was bred in his father's house.

"And Jacob was a quiet man, dwelling in tents." — Genesis 25:27 — Yet later on in this Torah text Jacob is distinguished by his voice: "The voice," says Isaac, "is the voice of Jacob." This is further proof that eloquence is not a function of volume. So often in history eloquence has emanated from the Quiet Man. One of the most elquent communications of humankind with God was accomplished by Hannah of whom it was said: "Her lips move, but her voice is inaudible."

"And Esau said to Jacob: 'let me swallow, I pray thee, some of this red red pottage; for I am faint." — Genesis 25:30 — Isn't the "success" of the Red, Red Pottage of communism today the result of the faintness from hunger of so many of the people of the world? And wouldn't the best answer to Communism be the concerted attempt of all good men to wipe hunger off the map?

Yet satiety of the stomach alone will not save mankind. Herein did a possibly well-intentioned Karl Marx make his fundamental error. No, "man doth not live by bread alone." Bread without liberty, for example, is a horror — the horror of the well fed, but caged animal. Pumping food into the stomach with no corresponding provision for pumping food into the soul will (and has) reduce the human being to the level of wild beasts. And is that what God put us on earth for? To fill our bellies, to empty them and to die? Absurdity twice compounded!

Esau had his bread and his pottage of lentils and he did eat and he did drink and went his way. *"So Esau despised his birthright."* — Genesis 25:34.

And, mind you, no Horn of Plenty and no Pot of Lentils and no Point Four will save us as long as we despise our birthright.

IV

ESAU, THE NIHILIST

"And Esau said: 'Behold, I am at the point to die; and what profit shall the birthright do to me'." — Genesis 25.32.

This, of course, is nihilism at its barest. It says: What is the point of living well if tomorrow we must die? Birth is not a privilege but a burden. Life is not a call to responsibility but a license for dissipation.

I am an accident, says Esau. There was no conscious purpose for my creation and hence there can be no purpose to my life. Do not talk to me about morality. Speak to me not about doing good. There *is* no morality. There *is* no good. All is senseless, meaningless, aimless chance. We are flotsam and we are jetsam and we are the sparks from a soul-less anvil and we are the splinters of a spiritless axe.

Nobody invited me here so nobody has the right to demand that I behave myself. The mess was here when I was pushed into it. It will be here when I'm pushed out of it. It is not my duty to clean it up and I cannot be blamed if I make it even messier. *"Behold, I am at the point to die; and what profit shall the birth-right do to me?"*

Esau, nihilist extraordinary, is, as might be expected a slipshod student. He scanned the second verse of the Book of Genesis which reads: *"Now the earth was unformed and void, and darkness was on the face of the deep..."* And there is where Esau stopped reading.

But there is more to the verse, Esau, old man, there is more. It continues ...*"and the spirit of God hovered over the face of the waters."* And if you read on just a wee bit more, Esau, you will see these words: *"And God said: 'let there be light! And there was light. And God saw the light that it was good; and God divided the light from the darkness."*

There is your answer, Esau, *You are not an accident.* You are God's creature and he put you on earth to advance the cause of light and to dispel darkness. If, Esau, you will have spent your entire life without having done a thing to kindle a light-giving flame somewhere, then the day of your death will be as meaningless as the day of your birth in time and eternity.

V

THE WELL-DIGGER

Israel, the State, is wrestling once again with grim crisis. Apparently the blood and the tears of the first thirteen years of her existence sufficed only unto those thirteen years. There was no accumulation of a reserve fund to act as insurance of tranquility for some years to come. The ogre of mendacious malice still lies to all sides of her borders and particularly to the south where the perennial foe of *Mizraim* still represents the "Tiger at the Gates."

Thus was it ever with Israel, the State. The first state-builder, Johsua, in the 13th century before the common era faced the situation which was to prove prototype. Powerful King David, no less, some 300 years later was an embattled state builder throughout his career, fighting a constant war against a motley crew of nations who had one thing in common — hatred of Israel. Ahab and Ahaz and Josiah and Hosea and Joyakim and Zedekia — all kings in the land of the Patriarchs — had the Enemy to contend with. And the enemy was one or the other of the ancient nations who occupied what is now Lebanese or Iraqi or Jordanian or Syrian or Arabian or Egyptian territory.

Nor was the story different during the period of the Second Temple. Zerubabel and Ezra and Nehemiah, the first state builders of the Second Commonwealth, had to reckon with surrounding foes from the very outset. Like their forerunners of the First Temple era, these foes were consumed with a raging, uncontrollable envy over the modest successes of the indefatigable state builders. And virtually identical were the problems of Judea in the third century B. C. E. under the Ptolemies of Egypt and in the succeeding centuries under the Seleucids of Syria and the procurators of Rome.

That this sad saga of spite goes back to even earlier centuries — the centuries fully 1700 and 1800 years before the common era — is manifest in the Torah reading of this Shabbat which recounts the trials and tribulations of our Second Patriarch, Isaac. From this point on I quote Genesis 26, verses 13-23:

"And the man waxed great and grew more and more until he became very great. And he had possessions of flocks and possessions of herds and a great household and the Philistines envied him. Now all the wells which his father's servants had digged in the days of Abraham, his father, the Philistines had stopped them and filled them with earth.

"And Abimelech (read Nasser, if you will) said unto Isaac: 'Go from us, for thou art much mightier than we.' And Isaac departed thence and encamped in the valley of Gerar and dwelt there. And Isaac digged again the wells of water...and Isaac's servants digged in the valley and found there a well of living water.

"And the herdmen of Gerar strove with Isaac's herdmen, saying: 'The water is ours!' And he called the name of the well Contention because they contended with him. And they digged another well and they strove for that also. And he called the name of it Enmity. And he moved from thence and digged another well; and for that they strove not. And he called the name of it Open Spaces; and he said: 'For now the Lord has made room for us and we shall be fruitful in the land'!"

That's the answer Isaac-Israel. Don't give up! Don't put down that spade! Keep digging — and you will scoop your way to deliverance!

VI

WHAT'S YOUR ANGLE?

"Now Isaac loved Esau, because he did eat of his venison; and Rebecca loved Jacob." — Genesis 25:28

Here, in a nutshell, is the distinction between the right and the wrong kind of love. Isaac loved Esau for his venison. Rebecca loved Jacob for his own sake. In the first instance love is conditioned upon the venison. No venison, no love. In the second instance love sets no conditions at all. Obviously this kind of love is lasting where the first is transitory. Said our sages: "Whenever love depends on some material cause, with the passing away of that cause, the love too passes away; but if it be not dependent upon such a cause, it will not pass away forever."* —

Young man, examine the object of your affections (and vice versa). Why do you love her? Is it because of her father's money? Is it because she is so very pretty? Is it because she flatters you

* Babylonian Talmud, Aboth, Mishna 5.

so nicely? Is it because she comes from a "prestige" family? If it is any of these things, you don't really love her. You love yourself. But if you love her for what she is, if it's the beauty of her very being that entrances you, if the thought of her is enough to make you move mountains — in *her* behalf and not in yours — then, young man, you *are* in love.

Sir, or madame, why are you so thick with him or with her you call your very best friend? Is it because his friendship buttresses your own sense of importance? Is it because of the many things he can do or has done for you? Is it because few others will befriend you? Is it because you are bored with your own company? Is it because he plays a good game of gin and she a good game of canasta? Is it because you both hate somebody or something in common? If it is any of these things, partner, you don't have a friend. But if he whom you designate friend is one whose inner virtue and radiance attracts you, inspires you and warms you — if your friendship for him was ignited and is kept a-burning by the essence of his personality and not by the accidents of his circumstances, then, sir or madame, you *have* a friend. Hang on to him for dear life. There is nothing more precious.

And *you* worthy comrade-at-arms, what is at the source of your fervid work in behalf of the cause which — apart from your livelihood — monopolizes most of your time? Is it frustration at home or elsewhere? Is it the desire for status and recognition? Is it because it seems to be *the* thing to do in your community? Is it because time hangs heavily on your hands? If it is any of these things, comrade, the cause you serve might benefit from you, anyway, but you will not benefit from the cause at all. But if the cause is sacred to you for its nobility, illuminating qualities, for its truth, for its imperativeness, for its beauty — in a word, *for itself,* then, beloved co-member of humanity, you are, indeed working for an ideal, and — what is equally important — *the ideal is working in you.* You are a man who knows what he is doing and where he is going. You are creative in the truest meaning of the word. You are a blessing to yourself and to others. *You are a happy man!*

VAYETSE ● ויצא

I

JACOB'S STREAM OF CONSCIOUSNESS

A ladder, a ladder — my kingdom for a ladder.

O Lord, you are so exalted and I am so lowly. O Lord, I long so to sense your nearness. O Lord, I am alone, motherless, fatherless, brotherless. My Lord, my Lord, have you then forsaken me?

I would sit in my tent and ponder. I would think of infinity and immortality and timelessness and I would think of you. And my thoughts were a ladder and the ladder's topmost rung did I ever seek to conquer for there was Your Divine Presence.

But then the ladder was based in my tent and on my father's domain and near my mother's sheepcote. But now, my Lord, there is no base for my ladder. I am a fugitive and a wanderer on the face of the earth. I run not like Cain for *having* slain. I run for fear of *being* slain. And You have set no mark on my brow to protect me.

O Lord, I have left all that was mine behind. I have naught in my hand save this crooked staff. But I would happily give all that and more, o so much more, in exchange for my beloved ladder. O Lord, I move indeed, move ahead and away. I yearn to move above and beyond. How desperate is my need for the ladder!

Esau sold his birthright for lentils. I would sell my birthright, too, if the buyer's cost could be my ladder. O Lord of my Fathers Abraham and Isaac, must I henceforth and evermore be earthbound? Had my foot reached its topmost rung when it had left the womb of Rebecca? Then, say I, as did my mother, wherefore do I live?

As a harried hart panteth for water thus doth my heart desire You, O Lord. You have created me in Your image and have thereby made the comprehension of that image the content of my life and the meaning thereof. Is that content and that meaning now to be deleted by the tyranny of exile? Then is my life at an end — and I would lay me down to eternal sleep this very moment upon this very rock!

*

"And he took one of the stones of the place and put it under his head and lay down in that place to sleep. And he dreamed, and behold a ladder set up on the earth and the top of it reached to heaven. . . ." Genesis 28:11, 12

II

CAN WE EVER MAKE IT TO THE TOP?

"And he dreamed, and behold a ladder set up on the earth, and the top of it reached to heaven; and behold the angels of God ascending and descending on it." — Genesis 28:12

Jacob's immortal dream comes closer to reality than anything most people see in a state of wakefulness. It is the perfect picture of man's role in the world, of man's perennial struggle, of his triumphs and disasters.

Man is of the animal kingdom — biological, physiological, earthy and earthbound. But man has a soaring potential — the capacity to rise above his physical environment into the rarified milieu of the spirit. Thus man's estate is perfectly represented by a ladder set up on the earth but with enough rungs on it to scale the very heavens. And the whole of the history of man can be conceived as alternate ascents and descents upon this ladder. The lower the rung upon which man stands at a given historical moment, the closer he is to the rest of the animal kingdom. The higher the rung he occupies, the nearer he is to God and the angelic host, the more imminent his emancipation from the tyranny of matter.

Alas, the story of mankind cannot be told in terms of a consistent ascent towards the top of the ladder. Rather can it be seen as a feverish, oft exasperating, fluctuation between the processes of ascending and descending. Even within the limited sphere of Jewish history we can discern this alternating phenomenon. Mount Sinai was unquestionably a very high rung on the ladder — perhaps the highest yet reached. The Golden Calf fiasco, barely weeks later, was a very low point. David's reign was an ascent; Ahab's, one hundred yeads later, a descent. Josiah in 622 b.c.e. was a high; Zedekia, only forty years thereafter, a low. Mattathias, the Hasmonean, was consorting with the angels. His grandson, Jannus Alexander, seventy years later was in the company of devils. And so on up to our present day whose relative position on the ladder it will be posterity's task to decide.

And in the larger domain of universal history, it has been much the same. The beautiful Sermon on the Mount alternating with the murderous crusades; the religious democratization of Luther with the bloody Thirty Years War; the noble Declaration of the Rights of Man with the Reign of Terror; The Declaration of Independence with the unconscionable Mexican War; the Weimar Constitution with the Nurenburg Laws; the establishment of the United Nations with the advent of NATO and the Iron Curtain.

Poor, puny, struggling creature caught between the gravitational pull of earth and the stratospheric magnetism of heaven, suspended, as it were, 'twixt devil and deity, torn between the two worlds of flesh and of spirit and bewildered by the tug-o'-war within and without himself! Is there any hope of scaling the ladder and reaching the very gates of heaven, he asks in his perplexity? Or is this all too, too weak flesh of mine inescapably chained to base animalism and the attempt to snap the chain fordoomed? Is it foolhardy to think it possible, as did Meinecke, to achieve "the breakthrough and revelations of the spiritual within the causal complex of the natural?"

Jacob wakes from his dream in a cold sweat. The ladder has overwhelmed him. He perceives immediately that regardless of the enormity of the task, he must set the very top of the ladder as his destination and the ascent towards it as the very purpose of his life. The staggering effect of the challenge is soon mitigated by one decisive thought; that very thought indeed which was to make an Israel out of Jacob: "SURELY THE LORD IS IN THIS PLACE!"

III

TIME TO GO HOME

Your grandfather or your father came over "from the other side" as a splendid pauper with nothing in his possession but ambition and the will to work. He entered the sweatshop or got behind the pushcart or opened a peanut stand or collected old clothes with singleminded concentration — to make a living.

Those early days were hard and bitter and frustrating and heartbreaking. There were the terribly long hours, the cold water flat, the filth of the shop and the streets, the insufferably cramped quarters of the growing family and the difficulties of adjusting to an atmosphere as different from Galicia or Lithuania as a siddur from a Singer Sewing Machine.

But your grandfather or your father kept plugging away, without protest or complaint. He was concerned above all with providing for his children; of availing them of the many marvellous opportunities which he lacked in the Old Country, and which were so abundant in America. For the welfare of those children no sacrifice was too great, no burden too heavy.

The chances are that your grandfather or your father made some appreciable economic progress over the years — and this, despite the obstacles, the impediments, the barriers. He gave his children a good education, made some of them doctors and lawyers and teachers and "educated" people. Or, in a good many more cases, he handed them a good little business which he had built up from scratch and in which was invested his blood and his marrow.

A wonderful old man was your grandfather or father. He did everything in the world for his children — with one exception. In his zeal to conquer economic Everests for his posterity he neglected to do much about poor little Mount Sinai. He left them a plethora of flour but a dearth of Torah and Piety. For he seemed to have forgotten that even in America, nay, especially in America, the Jew without Sinai is a dead duck.

Father Jacob made his fortune, too, in the land of Laban where he began as a penniless immigrant. But when he saw that his material success was rapidly beginning to encroach upon the sprituality of his children he decided that it was time to go home.

IV

TIME TO GO HOME, INDEED!

Abraham's life was abundant in trials, but it had its periods of serenity. Isaac's youth was marked by one fearful trauma — his near sacrifice — but the rest of his career was relatively placid. Jacob's life was one long period of almost uninterrupted suffering. And Jacob is Israel — both literally and as prototype.

Jacob was the first Hebrew to be forced into exile by hatred. The primitive notion that departure from a land also means leaving the god of that land behind, very nearly possessed him as Canaan faded into the distance. But at that crucial moment he heard the voice of the *Universal* God: *"And, behold, I am with thee, and will keep thee withersoever thou goest..."* So that when Jacob heard this quite revolutionary pronouncement he had to confess: *"Surely the Lord is in this place, but I knew it not."* — Genesis 28:16.

Jaocb was the first Hebrew to experience calculated economic persecution in his exile. Though he worked for Laban with singular devotion, though he enriched Laban by remarkable industry, though he sacrificed the best years of his life upon Laban's altar, — Laban was not only not appreciative, but sullenly resentful of the modest economic gains Jacob had earned on his own behalf. Laban had the cream of the flock; Jacob, the residue. But this residue was magnified by Laban's propaganda of not-so-white lies into proportions that seemed staggering to those envious failures of society who are ever on the hunt for a scapegoat in the flock, a scapegoat upon whose shoulders their own pitiful inadequacy can be deposited.

Jacob was the first Hebrew to face the grievous peril of losing his children's souls to Laban-land. With a horrified heart he heard the voice of the diaspora: *"The daughters are my daughters and the sons are my sons."* No more shall they be called the Children of Israel. I, Mephistopheles, have paid you in sheep and goats and camels. I now claim my reward — the very souls of your children, Jacob! Pay up!

Stark terror welled-up in Father Jacob's being. *I must go home,* said he. I must go home, he said. I must go home.

I will not pay the price of my children's spirit for the "security' Laban offers me. Enough of Mesopotamia! Laban's way is not my way and it must not become Reuben's way and Judah's way and Joseph's way.

"And Jacob went on *his* way, and the angels of God met him...." Genesis 32:2

V

JACOB'S CRUCIBLE

The morning's mail brought a letter from a worthy member of the Congregation who is more than somewhat disturbed with the career and character of Father Jacob. It would seem to him that Jacob was not always ethical in his dealings with others — notably with his brother Esau and his father-in-law Laban — and that he did not devote the necessary time for the proper education of his children. Moreover Jacob seems overly dedicated to the improvement of his economic position, too pre-occupied with bread, raiment, cattle, camels and the like.

Let me begin by saying that the greatness of Father Jacob does not require my defense, nor that of anybody else. Even more than Abraham and Isaac is he the founder and the sire of the House of Israel. And this alone is the most powerful single vindication of his exalted position among "the holy and pure who shine as the brightness of the firmament". But having said this much it is necessary to shed some light on the meaning of Jacob's life by supplying the clue, perhaps, for the proper understanding of it.

Jacob was all too human and in him is reflected both the weakness and the strength of human nature. *The central point about his entire life is that in the crucible of his wanderings and sufferings his weaknesses melted away and his strength AND glory emerged triumphant.* In this, Jacob successfully realized within the compass of his tenure on earth that which alone justifies the life of man — the triumph of the spark of God within us over the naturally perverse tendencies which our Rabbis called the *yetzer hara*. Greater claim to glory than this, man hath not.

Now understand that the Torah does not justify the manner in which he obtained the Birthright, nor the way in which he won the Blessing, nor the fashion in which he achieved his economic position. It is to the eternal credit of the Torah that it speaks with complete objectivity about both its heroes and its villains. It hides nothing that might tend to discredit a Jacob, a David or even a Moses and it suppresses nothing that might shed favor upon an Esau, an Ishmael or even a Bala'am. Jacob deceived his father and for that he was punished in kind. Jacob wronged his brother and for that he paid very dearly. Both of these acts were done by Jacob not in malice but in the self-induced delusion that the pursuit of a worthy ideal justifies the employment of improper means. That he was *not* a materialist is evidenced by his passionate desire for a Birthright that would bring him no physical remuneration but only the spiritual agony of responsibility — the titanic responsibility of carrying forward the traditions of Isaac, his father and Abraham, his grandfather, and of transmitting it to the generations. Had Esau been entrusted with the Birthright, all had been lost. The progeny of Esau-Edom has a history that speaks for itself. . .

But in striving for a great and noble ideal Jacob employed the wrong tactics. And all of his subsequent life was a continuous saga of the spiritual growth and maturity of the patriarch. After twenty years with shifty, unscrupulous Laban — for whom he labored faithfully and honestly — Jacob realized that he must return to the land of the Promise and, if necessary, face the music, as it were, in facing his vegeance-bent brother. He did this and emerged with flying colors. And on the way he "struggled with God" (what a magnificent image that is!) — he came to grips with God, as it were, and with Truth. Emerging from this struggle was not *Jacob* the "heeler", the "supplanter", but Israel, which means: he who met the challenge of his God and covered himself with glory.

As for educating his children — that, dear friend, was Jacob-Israel's greatest concern in life. For that he sought the birthright. Because of that he fled to Aram and then back to Canaan. By virtue of that Joseph emerged spiritually unscathed from Pharaoh's pagan palace. Where is the seeing-eye that can withhold its tears in hearing Jacob's deathbed charge to his children and grandchildren?

"Even by the God of thy father, who shall help thee, and by the Almighty, who shall bless thee with the blessings of heaven above...

"I wait for Thy salvation, O Lord..." — Genesis 49:18.

Dying, Jacob-Israel awaits God's salvation.

Where, dear friend, have you seen greater faith?

VI

THE HUNTER AND THE SEEKER

Once upon a time there was a quiet man who loved peace and hated violence.

He hoped to live calmly in his tent and prayed that others might too.

Yet his life was not dull, nor lacking in adventure.

For his mind was ever seeking wisdom and his heart was ever throbbing with thirst for knowledge of God.

And that seeking of the mind and that throbbing of the heart was for him the most enthralling of all adventures.

To him it was the very justification of life itself.

*

But his brother was not a quiet man, nor did he love peace, nor did he hate violence.

His brother despised the calm of the tent and those who dwelt therein.

He was a man of restlessness and turbulence and a man who craved game.

At first he satisfied his craving by giving chase to the beasts of the field.

But the Hunter of animals was not content with his sway

over the creatures that are dumb and he became a Hunter of men.

He became a Hunter of his own brother who dwelt in tents. And his brother fled.

*

The Quiet Man became a nomad, running before the fury of the Hunter as chaff before the wind.

He ran for shelter but find it he did not.

For he soon learned that there were other Hunters before him as there was a Hunter behind.

And to either side there were Hunters.

At first he lost all hope and in the agony of the trapped he turned his eyes upward toward God.

It was then that he made the Great Discovery that the peace which he sought resided above him.

He was surrounded by Hunters on all sides but above there was no Hunter at all, but a Seeker.

God sought the Quiet Man just as the Quiet Man sought God.

It was then that the besieged man of peace built a ladder which he set up on earth but whose top reached to heaven.

*

The Quiet Man bequeathed the Ladder to his children.

He bade them solemnly to dedicate their lives to climbing the ladder.

For, said he, when the top rung is reached at a certain instant of eternity, that very instant will violence perish.

For at that moment will men cease to be Hunters and will instead become Seekers forevermore.

VYISHLACH • וישלח

I

INTERMARRIAGE

The first Jewish intermarriage is recorded in the Biblical reading for this week. The daughter of Jacob, Dinah, after some unfortunate developments is married to a young Canaanite prince, Schechem, by name. The union leads to very tragic consequences and the entire matter remains one of the really unsavory incidents in the chronicles of the children of Israel.

Intermarriage is a grave problem which is still with us and which represents a formidable challenge to the patience, courage and insight of Jewish parents and members of the Rabbinical profession. Hardly a month elapses without my being confronted with tearful fathers and mothers at wit's end as a result of strong entanglement between their children and a gentile of the opposite sex.

It is not my purpose to adduce at any length the unconditional opposition of Jewish law to such marriages. Obviously, the religious scruples of the young Jewish people involved could not possibly be strong in circumstances of this sort. They must however be given to understand that *practically* speaking, such marriages are fraught with the starkest danger. Statistics indicate that a disproportionate percentage of intermarriages of Jews and Gentiles end in discord. The basic social, psychic, traditional and religious cleavages, conveniently unseen, overlooked or submerged in the heat of love and passion, emerge with irresistible force as, with the passage of time, love is increasingly constrained to meet the challenge of unglamorous reality.

At best, marriage represents risk of the greatest magnitude. To be successful, it demands the complete conciliation of two *different* psychic apparatuses. The blocks, mental and physical, which obstruct the path of any marriage are of no inconsiderable proportions. A couple which has successfully negotiated the rocky

road of marital adjustments is deservant of praise unmitigated,
even under optimum conditions. To multiply the difficulties and
labyrinths inherent in marriage by mating outside of one's
religion (*especially* Judaism), is to court almost certain disaster.

II

JACOB, PACIFIST EXTRAORDINARY

Peace, it's wonderful! It would be hard indeed to find a decent
human being nowadays who would fail to give full endorsement
to this statement.

Yet, paradoxically, we are living in the most warlike and
hostile of possible worlds. Everybody pays lip service to peace —
everybody, on both sides of the iron curtain. Everybody condemns
war — *everybody* on both sides of the propaganda curtain. But
in spite of all, hardly anybody seems interested in following these
sentiments to their ultimate and logical conclusion.

*

What is the ultimate and logical conclusion? It is simply this:
war is murder. It is murder with a phony license, the license
of so called "Loyalty," "Nationalism" and "Patriotism". It was
old Samuel Johnson who, in his eighteenth century Dictionary
of the English language, defined patriotism as "The last refuge
of the scoundrel". Love of one's country can by no stretch of
the imagination serve as justification for the violation of the
Sixth Commandment, "Thou shalt not kill!" This is one of the
most unambiguous statements ever made. It means (oddly
enough) thou shalt not kill. What could be clearer than that?
What could be less complicated?

*

Through fifty centuries of recorded history, man has been
struggling pitifully towards the achievement supreme: the comprehension of this most simple of all statements. It seems strange
indeed that despite the obvious fact that such comprehension

could redound only to his benefit, obscurantism, mysticism, deceit, hypocrisy, and just plain malice have conspired to frustrate that comprehension. When the time ultimately arrives — as it must arrive — that the full meaning will seep through the mind and be absorbed by the heart of man, the world of peace and joy and serenity of which all Utopians dream will have come into being.

These thoughts come to mind again (as if they ever leave the mind at all) as one reads in the Torah of the extraordinary efforts of Father Jacob to preserve the peace. Jacob was the pacifist *par excellence.* He refused to fight. He dreaded violence. He despised bloodshed. He abhorred war. But what is most important, his entire life was a vindication of all these sentiments. One might almost say that avoiding strife and murder was a religion with him. All of the provocations of hotheaded, belligerent and violent Esau did not succeed in instigating Jacob to arms. He employed every conceivable tactic, applied every imaginable ruse, exploited every possible avenue for the preservation of peace. Considerations of "pride" never moved him to war. Quite the contrary, it was Pride in the truest sense of the word which moved him to peace at all costs.

Ethically defined, Pride is the sense of reverence for the self as a human being created in the image of God. To be consistent, that sense of reverence must perforce apply to all human beings, for all human beings were created in the image of God. True Pride is the attitude of sanctity towards that divine spark in man which presumably distinguished him from animal. The man of violence, the man of war, the assassin, the killer is the man who stands in outrageous rebellion against that divine spark and thus forfeits his right to the only possible sanction for Pride. Such a man is an unreconstructed Esau who, through the ages, has loomed as the implacable foe barring the road to Jacob's quest for peace. What shall be done with Esau? Should he be killed? Obviously not. All efforts must be made towards his spiritual rehabilitation, so that the image of God may once again be restored to his countenance.

*

This was Jacob's great mission in life. This *is* Jacob's mission in life.

III

WHY, JACOB, YOU HAVEN'T CHANGED AT ALL!

And I have oxen and asses and flocks and men-servants and maid-servants; and I have sent to tell my Lord that I may find favor in thy sight." — Genesis 32:6

The respect that some people have for others is in direct proportion to the extent of the wealth commanded by the others. Jacob knew his man Esau. He knew what would impress Esau most. Therefore he sent him a financial statement rather than a statement of principles. Dun and Bradstreet, Edom branch, were to Esau the Supreme Court with jurisdiction over Jacob's worth. And times haven't changed much since.

Yet in the final analysis Esau's respect was not for Jacob but rather for Jacob's oxen, asses, flocks, men-servants and maid-servants. How tragic if one's reputation must rest on the backs of asses and oxen!

"And he divided the people that was with him....into two camps. And he said: "If Esau come to the one camp and smite it, then the camp which is left shall escape". — Genesis 32:8, 9.

In the long, long ago warmaking was rationalized with the wishful thought that at any rate *one* of the camps will emerge unscathed, and who knows but that the fortunate camp shall be my own. No longer is this type of ratiocination possible in this thermo-nuclear age. The world is, indeed, still divided into two camps. But should war come, there shall be no escape for either camp. Esau and Jacob will both perish, so it matters

little as to which camp we choose to call by what name. It is
no longer an issue of capitalism vs. communism, America vs.
Russia, NATO vs. Iron Curtain. The issue is Life vs. Death. No
double-talk, no obscurantism, no mental acrobatics, no propagan-
distic pronunciementos can get around this issue. *It is Life vs.
Death — — regardless how you slice it.*

*"I am not worthy of all the kindnessThou hast shown unto
Thy servants; for with my staff I passed over this Jordan; and
now I am become two camps."* — Genesis 32:11

Esau might have been deluded by Jacob's riches. Not so Jacob
himself. His oxen and his asses gave him no delusions of grandeur.
He did not lose sight of the essential fact that he had crossed the
Jordan with no other accessories and baggage than his lowly
shepherd's staff. He was the same Jacob post-Laban as he had
been ante-Laban — a modest, quiet, unpretentious man. The
accidents of property did not alter his *basic* property: the soul
with which he was endowed by the good Lord. He did not
kick after having waxed prosperous. He did not repudiate his
old-time friends. He did not reject the credo of his indigent youth.
And — above all — he still prayed to the same God whose
Divine Presence hovered above his shoulders as he plunged lonely
into the River Jordan — fatherless, motherless, brotherless,
penniless, and guileless. Jacob's real triumph was not to be
measured by the change in his economic estate; it was reflected in
the glorious truth that *he* had not changed at all.

VAYESHEV • וישב

I

THE COMEBACK

Dreamers have never been popular with the masses. Jacob
was a dreamer. Esau, his twin, hated him. Joseph was a dreamer.

His brothers despised him. The prophets of Israel were all dreamers. Their people greeted their words with scorn and hostility. Many men through the tides of history were borne on the crests of dreams and visions. The Jeremiahs, the Columbuses or the Galileos of their eras, they suffered the cruel shafts of ignominy, disgrace and frustration at the hands of compatriots whose animosity and rancor were boundless.

This has been so and, in all likelihood, will forever remain so. The *avant-garde* of human thought has flourished in a climate of opposition precisely because it *was* avant-garde. The human being is by inclination conservative and atavistic. Change challenges his senses of propriety and comfort and threatens to disturb his equilibrium by confronting him with the need to reorient and rearrange his outlook upon things, to readjust his reactions to them.

Such a prospect does not appeal to most people since most people are intellectually lazy and morally lassitudinous. They seek the shelter of convention, custom and platitude and hide behind the apron-strings of the "tested and tried" — even if not necessarily found to be true.

And in a situation such as this along comes the dreamer, the visionary, the prophet, the socialist or what-have-you and makes approximately the following speech:

"Look, fellows, we must be more concerned with the future than we are with the past and so far as I can see the tools of the past are obsolescent for our future purposes. Now I should like to suggest the following", etc.

People don't like to hear that and, as a result, they try to hush such speechmakers, with varying degrees of temporary success.

And temporary it must be. For, you see, though his brothers did throw Joseph into the pit, he made a comeback — and a beautiful comeback it was, too.

II

BURN THE HERETIC!

"Behold, this dreamer cometh. Come now therefore, and let us slay him, and cast him into one of the pits."

Genesis 37:19, 20

This has been the lot of the dreamer through history. He sees visions which are beyond the realities of his time. So he is a madman. He does not conform with the standardized mores of his contemporaries. So he is an Ugly Duckling. He breaks through the sorry barrier of the what is into the stimulating atmosphere of what could be. So he is a dangerous Radical. He harangues everyone he meets with the details of his vision. So he is a Nuisance. He is an unmasker, a debunker and an exposer. So he is a Conscience.

Madman, Ugly Duckling, Radical, Nuisance and Conscience that he is — how could he possibly win a popularity contest?

Yet the naked truth remains that the dreamer of realizable dreams cannot be refuted, cannot be discounted, cannot be denied. The tools of reason are powerless against him for in the deepest sense reason is his inseparable ally. Therefore: Kill him! Down to the pit with him! A bas les juifs! To the gallows! Burn the witches! The stones for Moses! The hemlock for Socrates! The pit for Jeremiah! The flames for Jan Hus, for the Maid of Orleans, for Thomas More! A toast to the devil and the devil take the foremost!

But the burners, the hangers, the poisoners and the assassins are always guilty of one fatal error: You may burn the dreamer a thousand times over but you cannot destroy the dream. For dreams are by their very nature indestructible. They will stay. They will recur. They will haunt. They will torment. And in the end they will triumph.

III

ARIEL AND CALIBAN ARE MYTHS

The Torah reading this week begins to unfold the Joseph story, possibly the most meaningful tale ever told.

It begins with discord among brothers and it ends with the slavery of the brothers' children — and isn't that the story of mankind?

The Joseph story runs the gamut of the human potential for good and evil. The depths of human depravity are plumbed when brothers sell one of their own into bondage and the heights of human magnanimity are scaled when the wronged brother forgives.

And in between the zenith and the nadir are the multifarious shades of gray which dominate the perplexing pattern of man's behavior. There are the evils of slander and jealousy and cupidity and carnality and mendacity and hypocrity. There are the virtues of love and courage and loyalty and honesty and endurance and self-sacrifice.

The seeming paradox is that none of the colorful characters in the Joseph story have a monopoly on either the virtues or the faults. There are no clear-cut heroes; neither are there clear-cut villains — and isn't that the story of most human beings?

Joseph is guilty of slander and scornful pride but endurance and conviction and the spirit of forgiveness are among his virtues. Judah is ridden with jealousy and cupidity but courage and honesty are assets of his which rise to the fore in time of crisis.

The same Joseph who is the talebearer of evil report about his brothers is the Joseph who lovingly dedicates his life to their safety. The same Judah who instigates the dastardly treachery against Joseph is the Judah who offers himself up as a slave rather than permit the incarceration of his brother Benjamin. And the same Judah who helped perpetrate a ghastly deceit

upon his aged father is the Judah who manfully acknowledged
that a prostitute was right and he was wrong.

Shades of gray — that is the pattern of man's behavior. To
approach morality from the unrealistic vantage point of perfection pure and simple is to contribute little to the achievement
of that morality. Perfection is the domain of God, not of man.

But man's great challenge is to accentuate the white over
the black, the good above the evil, the divine within him
above the bestial within him. Shakespeare's Ariel and Caliban
are pure figments of imagination. The one is sky-spirit, the other
is an earth-demon. But Prospero is the true image of a human
being tossed about in the Tempest of human inclinations towards
both good and evil and landing safely upon a balance sheet
whose Good is predominant.

The Joseph story is perhaps the greatest of all stories because
in it is so graphically reflected the stumbling and the groping
of humanity towards more white within the shades of gray.
And, after all, *shouldn't* that be the story of mankind?

IV

THE DEMAGOGUE

The story of Joseph and his brothers is as powerful a drama
as is to be found in the literature of man. Like all truly great
narratives it is communicated on two levels of understanding:
the level of a fascinating and adventurous tale which even a
child can comprehend and that far more profound level upon
which is revealed the human soul locked in a titanic, eternal
battle with its own dross, sometimes overcoming, sometimes
overcome.

It is to be hoped that by now it is on the latter level that
we stand as the characters of this great human epic emerge
before our eyes in an array even more multicolored than the

innocent coat of many colors which was the puny prelude to a shattering tragedy.

As the leading *dramatis personnae* step forward on the biblical stage, let us, with the infallible wisdom of hindsight, supply each with a capsule sketch.

Jacob: "A man of sorrow and acquainted with grief" whose faith in God met and surpassed all challenges. A great spirit which scaled the celestial ladder the hard way — from the bottom rung up. A man who loved his children not wisely, but all too well.

Joseph: A brilliant star in the firmament whose natural light put all other stars in the shadow and thus fomented a colony of the envious and the malcontent. A little less brilliance might have produced much more light, but this was a star that was destined to learn humility by a descent into the dungeon.

Reuben: A man who hesitated to exercise his legal and moral responsibilities to the full. He hemmed and he hawed and between the hem and the haw there emerged a vacuum, and into this vacuum stepped the ever lurking, ever thirsty, ever unauthorized demagogue. After that there was a vacuum no more. There was only the pit. . .

Judah: The man with half a conscience, strong enough to ward off the extremes of evil but too weak to recognize that evil is evil in any event and that delimited amputations thereof solve no problems. "And thou shalt *eradicate* evil from thy midst!", sayeth the Law of Moses. Compromise is not the measure with which to implement morality. There is an utter contradiction in terms there. It is wrong, says Judah's half-conscience to kill our own brother. Let's just sell him into slavery, Ah, Judah, Judah, Judah, you start upon such solid ground and end upon such shifting quicksands. You are a menace Judah, because your argument is half-convincing. Sooner would I cope with a hundred Nimrods, Judah, than with one such as you. For Nimrod's stripe — the killer — is well known and well advertised. Decent men will not join his camp. But

your pussyfooting ambivalence, O Judah, has snared the soul
of many decent men. And then, of course, was their decency
evaporated!

Judah, *you* are the demagogue!

MIKKETZ • מקץ

I

SUCH A TRAGIC WASTE!

The seven lean and sickly cows swallowed the seven fat and
well-favored cows and you could not observe the difference.
The lean cows remained just as lean and sickly as ever. But
the fat and well favored cows were gone all the same.

*

Such a tragic waste! Surely we may find consolation for the
loss of the match consumed in kindling flame. It was not consumed in vain. We may seek like comfort for the loss of the
seed buried for future produce. If there is a yield, it will not
have been buried in vain. But idle consumption and barren
burial are trgaic — anr criminal.

*

Staggering is the word for the practices of waste characteristic of our civilization. Nuclear energy which finds expression in
devastating atomic explosion is, of course, the most dramatic
example of contemporary waste. The bombardment of atom
by neutron creates undreamed of power which, properly harnessed,
can be the physical salvation of *all* mankind. But thus far the
lean and sickly cows remain as lean and as sickly as ever —
much more so, indeed.

*

The quantities of good, nourishing food which find their way into American incinerators and garbage cans, can alleviate the gnawing famine of millions of Asians indefinitely. The heaps upon heaps of discarded and unwanted clothing in excellent condition can cover the bare skins of many myriads of the naked and the frost-bitten. But the lean and sickly cows remain as lean and as sickly as ever.

*

Think a moment of the mammouth mountains of energy expended by hundreds of Jewish organizations throughout this great land of ours. Jews are great belongers, dues-payers, sub-scribers, committee-makers and meeting-holders. Much of this energy is of the shadow-boxing, arm-flailing, muscle-flexing variety — aimless, senseless, meaningless, baseless. What if this energy were properly channeled into *the one really important area of Jewish activity* — Torah, Jewish education, Jewish self-enlightenment! — The Utopia of an affirmative response to this speculation if almost too lush to contemplate! But thus far the lean and sickly cows remain as lean and as sickly as ever.

*

Such a tragic waste!

II

THE DREAMER OF THE POSSIBLE

In modern society — hardboiled and cynical as it is — the dreamer is often held in biting contempt. He is regarded as a ne'er-do-well, as a neurotic, even as a hobo. Joseph, I believe, stands as a monumental refutation of these concepts of the dreamer. Joseph was a man of many dreams. Joseph was a man who took his dreams seriously. Joseph was a man who did something about his dreams.

The dreamer who is asleep is certainly of little value. His dreams are meaningless and shadowy. The rude awakening which follows his somnolent state serves only to emphasize the emptiness of the vision. But the dreamer who, dreaming, is yet awake, is the dreamer who can render great service. His dreams are not images of the impossible. They are images of the possible and, yes, the necessary. Such a dreamer was our Joseph.

*

Joseph dreamt of acres upon acres of wheat and corn and cattle; acres upon acres of the wondrous yield of the good earth intended for all mankind. In his wakeful dream he saw infinite prosperity and satiety for all children of flesh, the endless bounty of a Great Good God who provides amply for all of his children.

*

Alongside of that wakeful dream, Joseph experienced the reality that was frustrating. Joseph saw poverty, misery, disease, afflicted kine and men, interminable stretches of famine and want. And all of this he saw in the context of the opulence and magnificence and extravagence of palaces, pyramids, obelisks, and the Pharaoh who lorded it over all. He was determined, then and there, that his mission in life would be to supplant the reality with the dream.

*

"And let them gather all the food of these good years that come, and lay up corn under the hand of Pharaoh for food in the city and let them keep it. And the food shall be for a store to the land against the seven years of famine, which shall be in the land of Egypt; that the land perish not through the famine." — Genesis 41:35, 36

*

"And when all the land of Egypt was famished, the people cried to Pharaoh for bread, and Pharaoh said unto all the

Egyptians: go unto Joseph, what he saieth to you, do." —
Genesis 41:55 — The crisis forseen by the dreamer had arrived
and, for once, the dreamer was given the opportunity to apply
the remedies of his vision. Those remedies, brain children of a
visionary, saved the great masses of people from starvation.

*

I remember reading a number of years back a book by
Harvey O'Connor entitled "God's Gold", a biography of John
D. Rockefeller. I remember the zeal and the fury with which
the author attacked the Joseph of our Bible tales as the prototype of all unscrupulous capitalists and cornerers of the
market. How sadly did Mr. O'Connor miss the entire point of
the story of Joseph in Egypt! How little he saw that what The
Great Book was unfolding before us was the dream of a dreamer
who dreamt of the possible — the dream of peace, plenty, and
prosperity for all man.

VAYIGASH ● ויגש

I

COLLECTIVE SECURITY...

The expression "Collective Security" has always seemed silly
to me. What other kind of security is possible? Either security
is universal or it cannot even be local. Like peace, it is indivisible — or it is meaningless.

We say that the killer "must pay his debt to society". Nothing
can be closer to the truth. For in killing, the criminal has
wronged not merely the victim and his relatives but all men.
Murder automatically becomes the concern of the public. Acts
of murder are acts of violence against public safety or "collective
security".

Simple as these truths are, they seem to be the least observed of all the rules of logic. When Mussolini ravished Ethiopia, nobody but Haile Selassie and Maxim Litvinov seemed to care. When Hitler devoured Czechoslovakia, Chamberlain and Daladier were there to gift-wrap Masaryk's land for the Nazi ghoul. When that unspeakable butcher, Francisco Franco, bombed Barcelona, the United States adopted a "non-intervention" policy which was the greatest single contributing factor to the victory of Fascism in Spain. And today, the persistent failure of the nations to find a formula for atomic disarmament and immobilization is the most tragic of all examples of our ignorance of the meaning of Security.

That is why Judah, brother of Benjamin, refused to budge until his captive brother was released from Egyptian bondage. Either he goes free, Judah roared, or we shall all remain here as the slaves of Pharaoh. He was not threatening. He was merely stating a fact. Security can be taken only in the collective sense. Aught else is nonsense.

II

...VERSUS "RUGGED INDIVIDUALISM"

Herbert Hoover, the overpraised and overhonored mediocrity who occupied the White House from 1928 to 1932 coined the phrase "rugged individualism". Like the author thereof, the expression too has become vastly overrated. In the parlance of a good many people, "rugged individualism" is synonymous with all of the good things for which America stands.

*

In America, say these people, the key freedom is the freedom to become a "self made man" — whatever *that* phrase may mean. In America, if you've "got it", you will elbow your way to the front of the pack. You make the grade or you don't on your own merits. If you are brainy enough to "look out for yourself", resourceful enough to "outsmart the other guy" durable enough to "go fifteen rounds" — the spoils of victory will be yours.

*

If this is Americanism, God help us all! What we have here is not the law of a "more perfect union" but the law of perfect discord, the law of absolute friction, the law of total conflict — in fine, the law of the jungle.

*

That such terms as "collectivism" and "socialism" should have become onerous and distasteful and stigmatic in the vocabulary of America is symptomatic in itself of the low moral estate to which we have become heir. There is nothing after all so wonderful as the spirit of collective action for the common good. "Behold" — says the Psalmist — wild eyed subversive that he was — "how good and how pleasant it is for brothers to dwell together." Well did he realize that only in a collectivist atmosphere can peace and justice flourish.

*

"Rugged individualism" has brought us to our present cosmic impasse. Our fate hangs in the balance because men for too long have deified the chimera "every man (or every nation) for itself". The fission which has characterized society found its counterpart in the fission of the atom — poetic justice, to say the least. The road to peace is the road of fusion and union and collectivism and solidarity — not the road of fission and discord and individualism and disparity.

*

It took the brothers of Joseph a long time to discover the road to peace, to learn that brothers must stand together lest they all fall apart. It took Jacob's grief, Joseph's bondage, Canaan's famine and their own phantom of guilt to galvanize them into an indestructible unity and to bring forth from their collective throats the thunderous utterance: "Either Benjamin is freed or we shall all be slaves".

*

"Rugged individualism", indeed!

III

TO GIVE *AND* TO RECEIVE

"We have a father, an old man, and a child of his old age, a little one; and his brother is dead, and he alone is left of his mother, and his father loveth him." — Genesis 44:20

A simple, pathetic statement is this. These are the words of Judah to Joseph in our Torah narrative this week.

*

Life without companionship is as death. Life without love is as darkness. No man is poor who owns a companion. No man is miserable who is the object of love. Conversely, no man is rich who is friendless. No man is happy who is unloved.

*

The best things in life are *not* free. True enough the best things in life cannot be acquired by gold and silver. But they are not free; they must be paid for, and in kind. The best things in life are companionship and love. One cannot be the recipient of these who is not simultaneously a dispenser of these. The law of reciprocity is inexorable here. And this is exactly how it should be.

*

It is better to give than it is to receive. It is bad to give and not to receive. It is even worse to receive and not to give. But best of all is at once to give *and* to receive. Love, the most inspiring and glorious of human emotions, is the simultaneous process of giving and receiving. By the very definition of the word, companionship is the same.

*

In other words, God gave to every one of us the most precious of all assets: the capacities for bestowing love and friendship upon our fellows. Those of us who are really happy are those of us who have made use of these great assets. On the other hand, the unhappy amongst us are those who have made little or no use of the great potential within us.

*

The misery of Father Abraham was a product of Pharaoh's hostility. The troubles of Father Isaac were products of Abimelech's animosity. But most tragic of all was the suffering of Father Jacob. For in his case catastrophy was wrought from within — through the hostility of his own children towards each other.

*

Joseph went to Egypt, his brothers to exile and his father to an early grave because the sons of Jacob failed to exercise their God-given capacities for love and companionship. They all learned their lesson the hard way and the measure of that learning is reflected in the pathetic words of Genesis 44:20 — "We have a father, an old man, and a child of his old age,

a little one; and his brother is dead, and he alone is left of his
mother, and his father loveth him."

IV

WHO'S AFRAID OF THE BIG, BAD TRUTH?

*"Oh my lord, let thy servant, I pray thee, speak a word in
my lord's ears, and let not thy anger burn against thy servant."*
— Genesis 44:18 — This, from Judah to the Egyptian Prime
Minister. And how familiar it sounds! How often have you found
yourself saying (or hearing) words to the following effect: "You
don't mind if I speak to you frankly" or "Would you be
offended if I told you just what I think?"

Two things are wrong here. First: Why should anyone have
to apologize if he is going to speak the truth? Second: Why
should anyone be offended by the truth? I realize, of course,
that these are utopian questions, society being what it is, and
we being what we are. Society being what it is, we dare not
always speak the truth for fear of violating Dale Carnegie's
sublime objective. Being what we are, we cannot bear to hear
the truth about ourselves, when it does not conform to the
image we have of ourselves and that we would like others to
have of us.

I once had a friend whom I prized very highly. I admired
so many things about him. I found his intelligence illuminating
and his devotion warming. He had one blind spot. He fancied
himself a magnificent orator. Truth is, when he took to the
podium (which, alas, was very often) he was a magnificent
bore. I never talked with him about it. But one day he came
to the fore at the general meeting of the students organization
of our college and delivered himself of a half-hour humdinger
which for sheer ineptness deserved to stand all by itself. As we
walked home after the meeting he turned to me and said: "Now

what did you think of it? Remember, now, I want no flattery, I want the truth."

So I told him the truth. As I said above: "I once had a friend."

How many friends would *you* have if you were forever telling them the truth about themselves? How many people would retain your friendship if they revealed you to yourself as you appear to them? And yet, isn't the best friend a man can have the person whose conversation can be taken at face value, unpruned and undiscounted? It seems to me that a friend meeting this description is worth one hundred flatterers. Don't you see, we can never see ourselves as we appear to others, just as we can never hear our own voice as it sounds to others. How wonderful, then, if somewhere in the world there is one who cares so much for us that he is willing to lend perspective to our vision of ourselves! We should clasp such a one tightly to our bosom for his worth is immeasurable. "Once you have found him, never let him go!"

Utopian talk, you say, sheer idealism? Maybe so. Yet I am more and more persuaded that in the long run, our world will not survive unless we tear sham out of our very vitals. In an age of scandal in the studios, mendacity in the meat shops, profiteering in the pharmaceuticals, and greed in the government we must begin to establish the truth somewhere. And the easiest place to begin is right with ourselves. If it is true that charity must begin at home (and I'm not sure that it is), it is certain that truth can begin nowhere else if it is to get anywhere at all.

V

THE "MIRACLE WORKER"

"And Pharaoh said unto Joseph, 'I have dreamed a dream, and there is none that can interpret it: and I have heard say of thee, that when thou hearest a dream thou canst interpret it.'

And Joseph answered Pharaoh, saying: 'It is not in me; God will answer to the peace of Pharaoh'." — Genesis 41:15-16

So often in human relationships do we encounter the unbounded faith that a given person is the solution to severe problems. This person is the one "people swear by". He is, perhaps, the physician who will cure all maladies, the doctor with a reputation second to no one's, the "top cancer man (or eye man, or internist, or heart man) in the country." Or he may be the "finest legal mind around" who will triumphantly extricate the subject from the most abysmal civil and criminal entanglements. Or he may be the merchandising genius who will open up hitherto inaccessible markets for the company and miraculously restore it to solvency. He might even be the brilliant Rabbi who will put the congregation on the map by doubling the membership, "packing them in," raising the money, attracting the youth and "mixing" like all getout.

There is something atavistic about this type of thinking. Somehow it harks back to the days when people lived with charms, amulets and magic potions, when such slogans as "Open Sesame," "double, double, toil and trouble" and "Rumplestitskin" formed an integral part of the vernacular, and when Hellenic and Roman tyrants like Antioches Epiphanes and Gaius Caligula were identified with the gods of Olympus. This is the abdication of human reason, the descent into the Hades of obscurantism, the navigation of the river Lethe — those narcotic waters of amnesia, euphoria and idolatry.

This is the environment in which Hitlers are bred. It is an environment in which people escape the burden of thought and responsibility by cheerfully ceding it to the "Great Man", the "Hero," the "Miracle Worker", the "Expert". And who, after all, is this panacea incarnate? It is a human being who in due time will be reduced to dust and ashes. It is a human being as subject to infirmity, senility, pettiness and error as are the rest of us. To conceive of such a creature — for all his vaunted brilliance and excellence — as the ultimate solution to all that

may ail us — is to misconceive the full import of the Second
Commandment.

Not even of Moses, the best we ever had, has it been said:
"Believe in him and you shall be saved". The Jewish people
have never spelled "him" with a capital H where the pronoun
referred to a human being. Our belief in the unity of God
precludes the possibility of the promotion of man onto His
exalted, omnipotent dominion. And — by clear implication —
joins man's own God-given resources to his faith in the Creator.
The 146th psalm put it so well: "Put no trust in princes, in
mortal man who can give no help. When his breath goes, he
returns to the dust, and on that very day his designs perish.
Happy is he who has the God of Jacob as his help, whose hope
rests upon the Lord his God...."

And so, your majesty "The Big House," says Joseph, I am
not the ultimate solution to your problems. I hold no membership
card in your fraternity of sorcerers and spell-binders. I'll do all
I can, but God alone can do all.

VAYECHI • ויחי

I

THE GENTLEMEN *TALK* OF PEACE

In our tragic generation, almost everybody pays lip-service to
peace. It's the thing to do, the vogue, the mode, the style.
Kennedy wants peace and Macmillen wants peace and Mao
wants peace and Khruschev wants peace. "The Gentlemen Talk
Peace" — peace, peace but there is no peace.

The trouble seems to be that peace has become an end, a goal.
It has ceased to be (if, indeed, it ever was) a means, a method.
What I mean is that ever since Woodrow Wilson it has become
fashionable to talk in terms of fighting a war "to make the

world safe for democracy", of sanguinary campaigns for the establishment of peace.

Now isn't that somewhat of a paradox? How can you fight to outlaw fighting? How can you shed blood on a mammoth scale in order to save lives? How can you use atomic weapons to insure that atomic weapons will not be used? Downright silly, when you look at the facts squarely, isn't it?

Yet that is precisely what is happening today. Everyone seems to realize that the concepts of victors and vanquished in warfare have long since ceased to be. Victory in war henceforth belongs only to the Angel of Death and he is a genuinely democratic creature, splendidly free of bias or discrimination, equally at home both behind and in front of the iron curtain. That being the case, where is the logic in sabre-rattling and fire-eating? And why do not the "Big Powers", so called, throw their six-shooters away and sit down over a nice cup of tea, and force themselves to talk "peaceful-like and gentle"? Not as a matter of idealism and nobility, mind you, but as a matter of naked necessity, a matter of life and death, to coin a startlingly new phrase?

Ah, worthy old Father Jacob! A man of peace all the way, he was. Peace as a matter of policy, peace as a method, not merely peace as an ideal, peace as a goal. With Esau, his brother, he tried the method of peace. With the people of Schechem, he advocated the way of peace. With his Canaanite neighbors, he practiced and preached peace. And of his two hothead sons who reached for an ideal with the sword, Jacob had this to say on his deathbed.

"Simeon and Levi are brothers; weapons of violence their kinship. Let my soul not come into their council...for in their anger they slew men...Cursed be their anger for it was fierce and their wrath, for it was cruel; I will divide them in Jacob and scatter them in Israel". — Genesis 49:5-7

Bravo, Father Jacob!

II

LOOK *NOT* BACK IN ANGER

Anger and resentment directed against human objects is a double-edged sword. It stabbeth him that is on the giving end as well as him that is on the receiving end. A person who is consumed with anger is a suffering person and frequently he inflicts more punishment upon himself than upon the person with whom he is angry.

*

I once knew a men who had not spoken to his brother for twenty years though they lived on the same block and saw each other several times a day. "What a monstrous crime his brother must have committed," I mused, "to be deserving of such treatment."

*

One day, with more fortitude than discretion, I asked the man about it. Surprisingly enough, he revealed the "secret out of the dark past" Twenty years ago, he said his girl broke off their engagement and married his brother. "That sneak, that snake, that no good so and so..." was the way he concluded the account all red in the face and with the foam forming upon his lips and the veins protruding from his neck.

*

Reason enough, you might say? But tarry a moment and hear this. A) — The man of whom I speak had been happily married for nineteen years, adored his wife and had four children by her. B) — The hated brother lost his wife in an auto accident two years after their marriage, was left with an infant daughter whom he raised singlehanded, and grief-smitten from first to last, had never remarried.

*

When life is short and anger long, something is strikingly out of balance and usually, if not always, the thing out of balance is the angry, unrelenting man. He deliberately stokes the fires of a hell which he personally nurtures and cultures. And to what end and with what purpose? It is of such a one that the Gemara said: "He who is wrathful is idolatrous."*

*

"To err is human, to forgive — divine", said Alexander Pope. He was dead wrong, I think. He should have said: To err is human, *not* to forgive — inhuman. There is nothing divine about forgiveness. There is something distinctly bestial, devilish and sadistic about inordinately prolonged anger.

*

His brothers sold Joseph into slavery. Yet years later he lavished upon them the love, the affection, the concern and the care which are the antitheses of anger and resentment.

*

And Joseph was not merely being kind. He was also being wise.

III

"BURY ME NOT IN EGYPT!"

"Bury me not in Egypt"! — Genesis 47:29 — A powerful and touching request, this. They are as you know the dying words of Father Jacob to his son Joseph. And, somehow or other, one feels that in these words Jacob has supplied a challenging slogan to his posterity down to the end of time.

*

* Babylonian Talmud, Sabbath 105: (Paraphrased).

Egypt or Babylona or Assyria or Persia or Greece or Rome
or Spain or Germany or, yes, America has always threatened to
become the cemetery of Jacob-Israel. Jacob in his own land
can assimilate only with his own. Jacob in a strange land can
assimilate only with the majority in that land. And that assimilation would be the death of Jacob and his way of life. And of
that assimilation Jacob was in mortal terror. Hence: "Bury me
not in Egypt"!

*

Jacob's heart and Jacob's soul are the heart and soul of our
people. Abraham and Isaac were the two first patriarchs, it is
true, but Jacob was the prototype of the Jewish folk. It is no
accident that his given name, Israel, became the identification
tag of the Jew. In Jacob's thoughts and fears and hopes, therefore, are reflected the thoughts and the fears and the hopes of
the Jewish people.

*

Listen, then, to what he has further to say upon his deathbed:
"And now thy two sons, who were born unto thee in the land
of Egypt before I came unto thee into Egypt, are mine; Ephraim
and Manassch, even as Reuben and Simeon shall be mine." —
Genesis 48:5 — With regard to Reuben and Simeon, the sons
who were educated within Jacob's own home atmosphere, the
old man had no fear. They were safely in Israel's camp. With
regard to the grandsons, Ephraim and Manasseh, born on alien
soil and nurtured in an alien environment, the old man's doubts
were very real. Would they remain in the camp of Israel? Would
they be able to resist the blandishments of Egypt? Would they
have the spiritual insight and the moral courage not to yield to
the lure of tangible but material and temporary values at the
price of intangible but eternal and spiritual values?
O Jacob was sore afraid! He could not peacefully surrender
his life to the scythe of Time without resolving his gnawing,

devastating doubts. What can he do? What can he do but turn his eyes heavenwards and invoke the most potent weapon in his arsenal: the weapon of prayer. "And he blessed Joseph, and said: 'The God before whom my fathers Abraham and Isaac did walk, the God who had been my shepherd all my life long unto this day, the angel who hath redeemed me from all evil, may he bless the lads; and *let my name be named in them,* and the name of my fathers Abraham and Isaac; and let them grow into a multitude in the midst of the earth." — Genesis 48:15-16

*

Mind you, the Torah says "And he blessed *Joseph.*" Actually, however, the blessing is concerned exclusively with the *children* of Joseph. Here lieth a sermon that speaks for itself. Joseph's greatest blessing resides in the Jacobness, Isaacness, and Abraham-ness of his children. So long as Ephraim and Manasseh remain Ephraim and Manasseh even in Egypt, so long as they are not metamorphasized into Franklin and Manfred, (naturally we mean Franklinism and Manfredism) then the immortality of Joseph is guaranteed. Is there a greater blessing than that? Is there a greater blessing than immortality?

*

"Bury me not in Egypt!"

IV

THE TRUTH DOESN'T HURT...

Jacob said to his son Joseph: "deal kindly and truly with me." — Genesis 47:29 — Not always do kindness and truth go together. In the interests of kindness, for example, the man dying of an incurable disease and who is spiritually sustained by the hope that he can recover, should not be told the truth. In this instance, keeping the truth from the dying man will do no harm while imparting it to him will certainly do no good. However it must be said that in most situations the truth represents the truest form of kindness. There are people who will deliberately deceive themselves and others rather than face up to an unpleasant truth. They may think that this represents kindness. In reality it may constitute the harshest sort of cruelty by nurturing false illusions which when unceremoniously smashed, as is ultimately inevitable, will bring the human being crashing down with them.

I know a young man who talked himself into thinking that he had the makings of a great singing voice. In this he was initially encouraged by doting parents who may actually have persuaded themselves that their son *was* thus gifted. The truth was and is that his voice was less than mediocre. Nevertheless the encouraged self deception induced the lad to leave hearth and home, to wander for years around half the musical centers of the world to get the proper "training," to subject himself to unprincipled and expensive music teachers who kept feeding his ego with pretty-talk about his progress and potentialities.

One day he came to see me to unburden himself of his many trials and tribulations and obviously to get from me a further hypodermic of encouragement. I gave him a shot-in-the-arm all right but it wasn't the penicillin of praise. It was a full dosage of undiluted truth. I told him he never could sing, couldn't sing now and never would be able to sing; that he threw away five of the best years of his life pursuing a will-o'the wisp; that he had better go back home into his father's comfortable dry goods business before he will be fit for nothing at all.

He ranted and raved and scolded and wept. He slammed the door and went away. But the truth-serum took effect. He *did* give up his innumerable voice lessons. He *did* enter the dry goods business. And what is most important, he is very happy. Months after he had been to see me, he sent me a letter in which he jocularly thanked me for "breaking his heart." It was a bum heart," he added. "You helped replace it with a sound, if un-glamorous ticker."

Yes, indeed, *"Deal kindly and truly with me."*

V

THE MOST IMPORTANT THING WE CAN GIVE
OUR CHILDREN

*"And the time drew near that Israel (Jacob) must die and
he called his son Joseph."* — Genesis 47:29 — This was a
perfect revelation of a great truth: The child of a man is his
desperate hold on immortality. When sickness calls one sends
for his physician. When death calls one sends for his child.
We should like to feel that our children are an extension of
ourselves and, in that sense, that they represent our victory over
death.

But this feeling can only make sense if we have left our
imprint upon the child: if we bequeathed upon him not only
a legacy of things but a legacy of ideals as well; if the matters
which we held sacred during our lifetime are sacred to him too;
if, in short, the purpose of our own living becomes the purpose
of his living as well.

These are the reasons which make it so important for us to
supply our children with an understanding of the purpose of
life. But obviously we cannot supply that which we ourselves
may lack. If there is no self evaluation, no idealism, no dedication,
no holiness in our homes, it is certain that our children will
absorb none of these things there. And if they do not then the
parent has been a dismal failure in that very area where he
can do his child the most good. For it is folly to think as so
many parents do that to give a child "all the good things of
life" is to give him food, clothing, shelter, schooling or even
love in abundance. These things are of relatively minor con-
sequence, important as they are.

*The most important thing a parent can do for a child it to
help find him a purpose in life which is above and beyond
physical gratifiication and even beyond family solidarity.*

We live (and always have) in a puzzling world — a world of strife, of paradox, of anxiety, of frustration, of confusion, of chaos. With this kind of world only two categories of people can make their peace: those who are endowed with bovine insensitivity and whose life is quite full with chewing, regurgitating and the hospitality of a hay-filled barn; and those who have a definite road to travel, a particular job to do, a specific challenge to conquer — not for themselves as isolated, self-contained atoms but in behalf of the total organism of interacting, criss-crossing, colliding particles of humanity with which God chose to populate His earth.

Now we must look an important fact square in the face, much as we are inclined to ignore it: Man *was* created in the image of God and, therefore, there is a crying need within him for fulfillment of some Godly purpose. Man *cannot* live by bread alone and still retain the divine spark. A stomach deprived of food will hurt, a muscle deprived of movement will wither and a soul deprived of idealism will either atrophy or rebel. The atrophy of the human soul will ultimately mean the extinction of the human race. The rebellion of a starved human soul alone will spell mankind's salvation.

It is therefore abundantly plain that the supreme challenge of the parent is to nourish the child's soul. The parent who fails in this fails in everything. And with that kind of parent death is absolute, complete, and permanent. Jacob was not that kind of parent. When "he called his son Joseph" to his deathbed he knew full-well how much of his life was invested in Joseph. And he knew that that much as least was going to live on.

שמות

•

SHEMOT

SHEMOT • שמות

I

THE BURNING BUSH

"I met my God and He was staying
the tongue of a thirsty flame.
The fire raged with fiendish fury
a fiendish, fearful fury, frustration-fed and hell-bent.
The bush burned brightly in the dryness of the desert.
Brightly it burned, yet it cast off neither cinder nor ash.
And its light and its warmth and its power was undiminished.

I had said: I will turn aside now
and see this great sight,
Why doth not this bush die?
And then it was I met my God
and then it was I saw the light,
And it was a light far more potent than fire and flame.
It was a light of granite steadiness, unfailing and undimmed.
It was a light of healing and a light of soothing.
It was a light of Life
the light induced
by the utterance in the beginning:
Let there be Light!
And I saw that the bush could not die.
And then He saw that I had seen.
He said: The light has been kindled in your heart,
And you know that it will never be extinguished.
'Twill burn and burn and bring you pain. 'Twill give you not a
    moment of surcease.
'Twill scald you, 'Twill rend you, 'twill gnaw you, 'twill plague
    you.
Thou canst not silence it.

Then I: Alas, my God, I sense it now! How it flares and fumes!
How it stabs and stings!

Behold, I clutch at my heart, but to no avail. Alas, my God,
and what am I to do?

Then He: Get thee balm, O son of Levi. Minister to my people.
Unclose your heart that they behold the light. And having
beheld it, they shall partake of it. Then shall the burning
within Thee be eased and Thy pain assuaged. Show them thy
heart. Thou needst not speak.

And when, O my God, will pain be erased — quite, quite
erased, from my heart and from the hearts of all Thy children?
When, O my God, when?

Why, Moses, 'tis plain that when all hearts are surfeited with
My light, like this Burning Bush they shall shed brightness
but will not be consumed.

Go thou and emulate your God.

Go thou and stay the tongue of thirsty flames.

Go thou and set all men free."

II

THE BUSH CAN BE MAN HIMSELF

Enter Moses. It is quite impossible to say too much about
him: The personage is so titanic that the ordinary word, written
or spoken, must inevitably fail to render an apt description. It
is no exaggeration whatever to state that of all men who ever
walked the face of the earth he was THE GIANT.

*

Of what is greatness compounded? We dare say that it is
made up of two basic qualities: proximity to God and proximity
to man. In a sense these two qualities are but two sides of the
same coin. Of all the Lord's creation, man alone is said to have

been cast in the image of God. It follows, therefore, that a reaching for God must begin with an understanding of and a love for man.

*

Moses began his ascent towards Heaven with a descent to the Hell of human suffering. Instinctively he grasped a great truth: Jacob's ladder is not properly a stairway for the angels. It is a stairway for man. The most noble creature of the Lord's universe must be physically and spiritually unshackled before he can attain a comprehension of his Maker.

*

"And it came to pass in those days, when Moses was grown up, that he went out unto his brethren and looked on their burdens." — Exodus 2:11 — The course was clear and unmistakeable. The burden of the brethren, the burden of servitude and degradation must be lifted. But how? The problem burned into his heart, agitated his soul, destroyed his peace of mind.

*

And then he saw the Vision. A bush was in flames but it was not consumed. The bush was man. The flame was the image of God in which man was fashioned. As long as man bore that image upon his brow, he was indestructible. Life insurance for tortured, oppressed, harrassed man was the ineradicable perpetuation within him of The Great Image.

*

And when the Lord saw what Moses had seen and grasped, He issued the eternal call: Set people free that they may serve Me.

*

Now it was just a matter of time. All of the cruelty of the task-masters, all of the tyranny of the Egyptian, all of the perverseness of the Pharaoh were impotent in the face of a God-kindled humanity. Tyranny and violence and malice are perishable. The spirit of God is not.

*

Moses discovered that the divine spark alone can destroy the fibers of human bondage. The first words which God uttered at Sinai through the throat of Moses could therefore have been none other than: "I am the Lord thy God who brought thee out of the land of Egypt, out of the house of bondage!" This is the deathless legacy of Moses, the man of God, to his brothers of every age. Indeed, this is the greatest of all legacies since the dawn of time.

III

WHAT MAKES A GOOD SPEAKER?

Moses was reluctant to act as Israel's spokesman before Pharaoh because he considered himself lacking in speaking ability or oratorical talent. This intelligence comes to us from the Torah reading for the Sabbath. — Exodus 4:10

*

This raises thoughts as to the qualifications of a good speaker. Just what is it that makes one and how does one go about to become one? Is it a matter of voice or vocabulary or vigor or vehemence or veneer?

*

My point is that truly effective speaking has nothing whatever to do with any of these qualities. My point is that effective speaking is a function of truth, the truth only and — to coin a phrase — nothing but the truth.

*

We ought not to confuse show with substance or performance with instruction. There are many who can "hold" an audience with the magic of their voice and verbiage, with the artistry of their gestures and gyrations. Yet what they have to say is either untruthful or insignificant. These are not speakers. They are masters of unmusical phraseology, perhaps, but they are not speakers.

*

The speaker, properly comprehended, is a communicator of meaningful truth. He is the servant thereof. He is a means and a vehicle, not an end and a destination. He is the disembodied voice of timeless messages. And the message he carries is far more important than the vehicle which tranports it.

*

Of what effect is a magnificent jet plane which discharges smoke and hot air but discharges no cargo? Of what effect is a beautifully bound book embracing in its attractive arms voluminous blank pages? Of what effect is the orator who "packs them in" but packs nothing in them?

*

Cicero, Demosthenes, William Jennings Bryan, George Jessel — "Orators" all! How do they stand up to the rigorous, sacred requirements of the "still small voice" that pierceth the wilderness and declareth: "Prepare ye the way for the Lord!" How do they measure up to the "Voice of the Lord which whirleth the sands of the desert" which "maketh the oak trees dance and strippeth the forests bare," which "heweth out flames of fire"?

*

Moses was the greatest speaker of all time, a speaker sans facility of tongue, sans magnitude of voice, sans fluidity of expression. This, by his own testimony. But Moses was the greatest speaker of all time because he had the best speech to make. Moses died but his speech lives. The man passed on but the message remained. That message contained the Greatest Truth Ever Told. It was the message of God to mankind. It was oratory for the ages and it needed no "orator."

IV

PHARAOH'S PROPAGANDA

Exit (until next year) the Book of Genesis. Enter Exodus. At the beginning of its tragic saga of slavery and oppression we read: *"And there arose a new king over Egypt who knew not Joseph."* — Exodus 1:8 — Discrimination and bigotry are based upon ignorance, upon "knowing not" the object of the persecution. Old Ramses II (who the Exodus Pharaoh is presumed by some to have been) knew not Joseph. For all *we* know he may have thought Joseph had horns or that Joseph crucified the "divine" bull Apis or, at the least, that he poisoned the waters of the Nile and caused the Black Plague to rage furiously throughout its delta. I mean if one doesn't really know Joseph one generally will invent a thousand details about him which, while various and often even contradictory, share at least one characteristic: they all tend to distort and to render ugly the image of Joseph.

*

And what does Pharaoh get out of this distorted image? Why, a scapegoat, of course! Don't you see how perfect the scheme is? Joseph can now be blamed for all of Pharaoh's personal failings as well as for the multitude of plagues which afflict Egypt. Hunger? Put the blame on Joe! War? Joseph is the fellow who engineered it! Bad working conditions? Joseph's your culprit! Go get 'em boys! I, the great, munificent Pharaoh desire only your welfare. But what can I do if this ogre frustrates my very best intentions?

*

But then again boys (Pharaoh may well have continued) what can you expect from the descendants of non-productive parasites? They came to us to eat our precious bread when the great famine seized us. They made a mint off the sweat of our brows and the hunger in our bellies. (Here Pharaoh is publishing a revised and expurgated textbook of the History of Egypt from which some very key chapters are missing, including a very juicy one on the Interpretation of Dreams contributed by a Prof. Joseph Jacobson).

*

Furthermore (says Ramses) this Joseph character is a Trojan Horse. You can never count on his loyalty to our Fatherland. After all he's only been here two hundred and ten years. The fact that he hasn't stabbed us in the back yet doesn't mean a thing. He simply hasn't had the opportunity to do so but (and here I quote Old Ramses directly) "should it come to pass that war befell us, he will certainly join himself unto our enemies and fight against us!" — Exodus 1:10 — Here the Pharaoh displays his talents as prestidigitator, philosopher and science — fiction author rolled into one. He was so pleased with this masterful analysis that he included it over and over again in his broadcasts to the people. And, lo and behold, one day the people accept his "analysis" as an irrefutable fact of life.

*

When that happens what is left for Joseph but Exodus? And to what place can he go which will not see the repetition of the Egyptian nightmare but to a land in which *he* is master?

VAERA • וארא

I

WE NEED MOSES WORSE THAN PHARAOH DOES

God sent Moses to preach to the Jews about their inalienable right to live in their faith without being overwhelmed by an alien culture. *"And Moses spoke so unto the children of Israel; but they hearkened not unto Moses for impatience of spirit and for cruel bondage.*

"And the Lord spoke unto Moses saying: 'Go in, speak unto Pharaoh, King of Egypt, that he let the children of Israel go...'

"And Moses spoke before the Lord, saying: 'Behold, the children of Israel have not hearkened unto me; how then shall Pharaoh hear me..." — Exodus 6:9-12

A very illuminating passage, I should say, and extremely pertinent to our own status as Jews in America. We spend tens of millions of dollars annually on "Pharaoh"-directed programs — anti-defamation, "Brotherhood", social action, interfaith institutes and the like. Our presumed goal is the enlightenment of the non-Jew so that he may be more understanding of the values of Judaism and those who espouse it.

This is a commendable purpose, no doubt. But it seems to me that a far more demanding and critical piece of work has to be accomplished with *ourselves* before we can proceed to do anything with others. Teaching the non-Jew to appreciate us is fine if we have already learned self-appreciation. This we most certainly have not yet achieved in America.

As long as we remain ignorant of our language, our religion and our history, we have failed in the quest for self-appreciation. As long as we keep aloof from the observance of *mitzvoth* which are the vital links of past, present and future in Israel we have failed in the quest for self-appreciation. As long as we spend more money on gymnasia than we do on *Yeshivoth* we have failed in the quest for self-appreciation.

"And Moses spoke before the Lord, saying: 'Behold the children of Israel have not hearkened unto me; how then shall Pharaoh hear me...'"

II

FOXHOLE RELIGION

During the last war someone said: "There are no atheists in foxholes." In spite of its popular acceptance, the statement is close to being true (no typographical error here — just a bit of irony). For under stress and duress, cynicism, atheism, "scientism" and what have you generally tend to wither away.

*

Foxhole Religion is not a twentieth century development. It is old as man — as old as fear. Primitive man worshipped the elements in cowering obeisance. He was terrorized by the thunder, the rain, by the night, by the sun, by the sea — by everything which he could neither understand nor control, but which, in turn, was an ever-present menace to his survival. His "religion" was the act of placing the hand in front of the face to stave off a blow. His "religion" was founded upon sycophancy, bribery and graft. It was an attempt at the pacification of elemental fury. It was, if you will, Foxhole Religion.

*

Jonah's ship is foundering. The sea around it is a cauldron of unleashed wrath. Panic clutches the throats of its frenzied sailors. Each screams to his god — each pleads, wheedles, cringes — but the sea roars on. They pounce upon the sleeping Jonah: "What ails thee, that thou dost slumber at such a time. Get

thee up and pray to *thy* god. Perhaps *he* will still the fury of the
tempest and we shall be saved". Again — Foxhole Religion.

*

Terrible tragedy strikes. A mother is taken, or a father, or a
wife or a son or a brother. Some rebel. They shake their fists
at heaven and curse. They kick over all the traces — or so it
would appear. Others suddenly "get religion". With some of
these, the reaction is genuine, authentic, profound. They have
reacted favorably to "shock treatment" and have begun to see
things in clear perspective. With most, however, the new
religiosity is an offspring of terror, the terror of the shadow of
death, the contemplation that "I could be next". That, too is
Foxhole Religion.

*

Then there is the Jew who observes Kaddish — and nothing
else, who prays on and around Yom Kippur and at no other time.
He knows neither Festival, nor Sabbath, nor daily prayer —
neither Shaharith, nor Minha nor Ma'ariv. Three hundred and
sixty four days in the year he leads a "normal" life — and in
this normality he finds neither need nor room for the God of
Abraham, of Isaac and of Jacob. But on the 365th day, the Day
of Judgment, he comes before the Lord with a gift offering, a
genuine honest-to-goodness all-day sacrifice. This is not Judaism.
It is Foxhole Religion.

"And Pharaoh saw that the hail and the downpour had ceased,
and he resumed his sinning and he hardened his heart, he and
his servants." — Exodus 9:34 — Why not? The emergency is
over. The day of judgment is past. The foxhole is behind.

Back to Bondage, Men!

BO • בא

I

"THREE BEAUTIFUL BLESSINGS"

Say our sages: "Three beautiful blessings did the Holy One, blessed be He, give to Israel, — and the giving of them entailed suffering (on the part of the receivers): The Torah, Eretz Israel and the World to Come." (Tanhuma, Shemot).

No truer insight was ever offered into the history and mission of the Jewish people. With characteristic economy of phrase, our Rabbis succeeded in transmitting a world of meaning to those who would truly appreciate the significance of the statement quoted above.

Israel's career as a People began with Torah and can end only with the disappearance of Torah, the Lord forbid! Torah — the law and the lore, the teaching and learning, the thinking and the doing — has ever been the central pillar supporting the structure of Judaism. And Torah has ever involved suffering: suffering as the inevitable process of the acquisition of knowledge and suffering, too, in the implementation of that knowledge in a frequently hostile atmosphere.

The fierce dedication of the Jewish people to Torah has been the result of its conviction that the ideal World to Come (Olam Haba) could be achieved only through concepts and precepts of Torah. That world which "is all goodness" was blueprinted by the Creator even before the creation, and the blueprints are in the Torah. But the road to the Jewish ideal of the World to Come is necessarily arduous, difficult and painful. To reach it, false worlds built upon false foundations must first be navigated and, after all, the collective architects of these false worlds represent a die-hard vested interest...

And then, centrally located between the first and the third blessing is Eretz-Israel, the soil upon which our people's ideology was meant to be cultivated so as to serve as an inspiration and as an example: "For out of Zion shall come forth the Torah and the law of the Lord from Jerusalem." How much suffering has the acquisition of Eretz Israel entailed! Joshua and the Judges and the Kings through six hundred painful years had to fight for every inch of it only to lose it all in the end. Ezra, Nehemiah, the Hasmoneans, the Zealot leaders and finally Bar Cochba repeated the process of endless struggle for Israel's land through another six centuries and the end was again the same — defeat and exile.

But now we have returned again to Eretz Israel and are again engaged in a desperate struggle to hold it. Shall we fail again? We dare not! For it would seem that we are now upon the very crossroads of the World to Come. To justify the martyrdom and the suffering of four millennia we must make certain that the World to Come is a world which "is all goodness." In the formulation of that world Eretz Israel has a major role to play. Destiny is beckoning and we must not look the other way. The climactic decision of the age may well be at hand. We must not be found wanting.

From Jeremiah this Sabbath we read: "But fear thou not, O Jacob my servant, neither be dismayed, O Israel. For lo, I will save thee from afar, and thy seed from the land of their captivity. And Jacob shall again be quiet and at ease, and none shall make him afraid." — Jeremiah 46:27

II

PHARAOH IS A FOSSIL

"And Pharaoh's servants said unto him: 'How long shall this man (Moses) be a snare unto us? Let the men go, that they may serve their God; knowest thou not yet that Egypt is destroyed?'"

Exodus 10:7

Utterly amazing, is it not, that the King of Egypt should be in ignorance of so crucial a fact as the death of his own realm! Yet there it is in the weekly portion: Pharaoh's servants saying: "Knowest thou not yet that Egypt is destroyed?

*

At that it is not so amazing. Pharaoh's entire life was built around one sphere of reference: Egypt and everything that the word implied. Among other things Egypt meant a social and economic system whose cornerstone was slavery and a theological system whose foundations were Ptah and Apis and Isis and Osiris, to mention but a few of the more prominent denizens of the Coptic Pantheon.

*

Now spheres of references die hard, if they die at all. Especially is this so if a man's whole present and future are latched unto the particular sphere. Then he simply refuses to acknowledge such new facts as may tend to render his old orientation obsolete. Moreover to admit that one is in need of rebuilding his "world-view" (what the Germans call "weltanschaung") to tally with the newest facts is more of a blow to the human ego than most people can sustain.

*

Hence Pharaoh's solution to social revolution is simply to ignore it! "It ain't so, it ain't so, it ain't so" is the magic incantation which his tremulous lips utter over and over again in the somewhat mystic hope that the mere recitation of it will restore the *status quo* about which his planet rotates. This is somewhat in the nature of burning a hated object in effigy or sticking needles into it. Very pretty voodoo but hardly very pretty logic.

For, Pharaoh old man, you cannot push back the clock or even stop it where it is. The fact that you refuse to *recognize* the facts will not nullify them. The facts are here to stay, for a while at least. *But you are not!* Yes, even you, mighty and arrogant Pharaoh, will have to move your pomp off the arena to make room for facts which no longer include you and what you stand for. You can't stall indefinitely. Already you are an anachronism and there is no room for anachronisms in the calendar of human events.

*

Now our world today is in the greatest ferment it has likely ever experienced. Old facts are falling all over the place before the onslaught of the new. "The old order changeth" indeed. The bulwarks of feudalism, colonialism, laissezfaireism and untouchablism have been savagely assaulted even in their most traditional ramparts. Henry Wallace's "common man" is unquestionably on the move. The "Egypt" of King Arthur, Herbert Hoover, Rudyard Kipling and the Ganges River "is dead," to quote some modern Brooklynese. Trouble is that the respective Pharaohs who were so much at home in it refuse to admit it.

*

But admit or no, the Exodus will come, the Exodus will come . . .

III

SHALL THERE BE A SUMMIT MEETING?

Pharaoh suffered from a condition diagnosed as Hardening of the Heart.

Hardening of the heart is a form of masochism which consists of a refusal to look agony in the face.

It is like standing smack in the middle of the railroad tracks in the face of an onrushing locomotive.

It is a mystic incantation to the Reaper with the Hollow Sockets.

*

Say Pharaoh's advisors: Do something, else we shall all die!
Sayeth the Pharaoh: Call out the magicians.

Say Pharaoh's servants: Knowest thou not yet that Egypt is
destroyed!

Sayeth the Pharaoh: Lock all the doors.

Says Pharaoh's antagonist: Let us talk *before* the arrival of the
Angel of Death.

Sayeth the Pharaoh: Ye shall have no appointments with me;
lower the palace gates!

*

Came the Angel of Death and exit Pharaoh from the palace
into the black, black night screaming.

So what do we do now?

IV

EXODUS: YOUNG AND OLD

I said it before, I say it now, and I will say it again and
again: the spiritual progress of a synagogue is in direct proportion to the rate of increase in the number of children and
young people who frequent it. If youth can be motivated to
worship God in His House, the future of Judaism is assured.
If synagogue worship is to survive a decade or two or three
hence, it is axiomatic that those who are now youngsters will
have to be interested in that survival. To assume that that
interest will become automatic when the present generation is
gone is to indulge in the most foolhardy and suicidal sort of
reasoning.

This is why I have always felt that the youngsters must
become integrated into the regular synagogue service. It is
vital that they develop first an understanding, then a taste, and
finally a love for the services held in the synagogue proper

amid a congregation of faithful adult worshippers. It is essential
that they develop the habit of worship in the most normal
fashion as a part and parcel of the congregation. And, above
all, it is indispensable to the future survival of the synagogue
that they conceive of it not merely as a place for "old people"
but as a spiritual headquarters for all Jews of all ages.

As an inevitable corollary of the foregoing, I must stress the
inestimable value of parents attending the services together
with their children. Of all of the salutary stimuli I can think
of for the Jewish development of the child I can conceive of
none more telling than the parent's establishment of a spiritual
communion, of a sense of religious affinity with his child. And
how can that communion and that affinity be better established
than through the beautiful, the poetic, the magnificent sight of
father and son, mother and daughter worshipping together?

It was the first Rabbi of all time, Mosheh Rabainu, who, in
response to Pharaoh's suggestion that it would be sufficient if
the adults only went on to worship the Lord, thundered forth
as follows:

"We must go with our young and with our old, with our
sons and with our daughters." — Exodus 10:9

If we are to go at all, there is no other way.

BESHALACH • בשלח

I

MOSES NEEDED MIRIAM

The health of the Jewish people is in direct proportion to
the spiritual health of the Jewish woman. I insist that so far
as Jewish survival is concerned, the female is of greater import
than the male. As the Jewish woman goes, so will Judaism go.

The nature of the Jewish home is determined by the woman,
not the man of the house. The extent of the child's Jewish

education is governed by the inclination of the mother, not the father. The frequency of synagogue attendance is affected by the attitude of the lady much more than by that of the gentleman.

I hesitate to say it for obvious reasons but it is my feeling that in America particularly, the proverbial "little woman" pretty much runs the household show. Sometimes this situation obtains to a ridiculous extent, degrading from the husband's standpoint. How many times have I heard the response: "You'll have to talk to my wife about it, Rabbi", or "If you can do anything with her, Rabbi, I'm with you". And what was involved was not a social engagement or a Koffee Klotch but the Jewish education of his child or his own attendance at synagogue worship. Whether the ball and chain were actually there or whether it just served as a fictitious excuse for a pussyfooting man I couldn't always tell. But it's a fact that where Jewishness is concerned the French are right: "cherchez la femme".

I have given the charge to Bar Mitsvah boys whose fathers never showed up. I have never officiated at a Bar Mitsvah where the mother refused to attend. I have seen men who would have liked a kosher home countenance one that was strictly *trefa* because of obstinate wives. I have never seen a woman who wanted, I mean truly wanted, a kosher home, yield to a bacon-loving husband. I have seen more women make conscientious Jews of their husbands than I have seen husbands making conscientious Jewesses of their wives. I have seen more constructive and zealous work done by Hadassah over the years than by any strictly male Zionist Organization. The sisterhood of most congregations are a darn sight more active and more enthusiastic than the men.

What makes me think of these things at this time? Well, it's just the fact that our weekly Mosaic and Prophetic readings for this Sabbath feature two women who led Jews in song — Miriam and Deborah. Without Miriam, Moses would likely not have survived as a Jew. Without Deborah, the Jews would not likely have survived as anything.

II

WATER, WATER EVERYWHERE

Water, is a compound of incalculable importance. Without water, life on earth would be quite impossible. The earth would produce no food for man and beast and the dehydration that would set in everywhere would soon give way to death.

*

Yet water itself can spell death. People can drown in water and its torrential, excessive flow can encompass staggering destruction of both life and property.

*

It is interesting to note that the Children of Israel in our current Torah reading encounter both the negative and positive facets of water at the very beginning of their Great Exodus from Egypt. Fleeing from Pharaoh, they come face to face with the sea. With bondage aft and the sea fore, the waters stir up panic within their hearts and they fervently wish it were not there.

Immediately after the miracle of the crossing, the Israelites are again involved in a water problem — of a different order, to be sure. They march three days in the wilderness without finding water and when they finally locate an oasis at Marah, its waters are bitter and useless for drinking purposes. It requires still another miracle to sweeten the water. Moses casts a tree into it and it is made sweet.

*

Not so very much later, the wandering Jews arrive at Rephidim "and there was no water for the people to drink". — Exodus 17:1 — This time, no water at all. By now the seemingly ineluctable water problem has so incensed the people that they

are almost ready to stone their leader to death. Only the supreme
miracle of smiting the rock saves the day. Water flows from
the smitten rock and life is again sustained.

*

I do not believe that these several water-encounters early in
the career of the emancipated people are coincidental. I believe
that the Torah relates them all at close quarters with a purpose.
And I believe that purpose to be simply this: to teach all who
are willing to learn that — granted freedom of movement
and of choice — life is what we make of it. The mighty waters
of the sea need neither daunt nor cower the free man if he is
determined to navigate them. Bitterness to the free man is largely
a state of mind and its transformation into sweetness is largely
in his own hands. And — to make matters perfectly clear —
the Torah dramatically proclaims that no rock can be a match
to the industry of a free man.

*

Water, water everywhere — but how to use it, that is the
question. Life, life, life everywhere — but how to live it, that
is the biggest question of all.

III

THE EXODUS IS NO PICNIC

After a great deal of travail, the Exodus is finally a reality
and in the portion of the Torah for this week we read of the
departure of Israel from Egypt. "...*God led them not by the
way of the land of the Phillistines...for God said: lest peradventure the people have a change of heart when they see war,
and they return to Egypt*" — Exodus 13:17 — Yes, indeed,
many are the ambitious and worthy projects that have been

abandoned at the first sign of difficulty and challenge. Yet is any project attainable without difficulty desirable in the first place?

*

"And Moses took the bones of Joseph with him". — Exodus 13:19 — This was the fulfilment of a sacred oath imposed by Joseph upon the children of Israel before his death. One cannot avoid the melancholy observation that it was the Children of Israel who caused the exile of the living Joseph and it was left to *their* children in turn to repatriate him, if only through his mortal remains. How tragic it is that restitution for crime is so often of the *post mortem* variety! Ask Konrad Adenauer about it.

*

By day and by night the children of Israel travelled and in both cases the Lord went before them (see Exodus 13:21-22) How of the essence of Judaism is this picture! There is the daylight, bright and hopeful, and at such times the steps toward The Goal are light and springy. And there is the darkness, bleak and dismal, when the foot drags and the heart sags and hope is a-glimmering and The Goal a mirage. The people who can keep their feet in darkness and even *through the very gloom* maintain a forward march, that people's vision can detect God in the very womb of night. That people sooner or later will reach the Promised Land.

*

"For it is better for us to serve the Egyptians than that we should die in the wilderness". — Exodus 14:12 — So spoke those of frail spirit when the Exodus journey became really tough. So speak all they who would rather accept tyranny than hunger, who would willingly be mesmerized by Demagogues and Party Lines rather than be exerted in the wearying struggle for the possession of their own souls, who would rather be transfixed

by the Father — Fuehrer — Duce — Grand Llama image
than agitated by the brother image and its peace-robbing slogan:
"All men are brothers!"

*

Ah, how instinctively did even ancient Judaism fear the
disasterous products of the hegemony of a Father-Image. How
the Prophet Samuel fought (unsuccessfully) against the Israelites' desire for a King who was to be the mystic cure-all for
their troubles! How Gideon resisted the insistent call of the
masses that he accept the scepter of absolute power into his
hands that they may be relieved for all time of the burden of
all worry! How the Prophet Hosea ridiculed the infantile notion
that it wants only a "King" or a "Judge" to solve all the problems
of Israel.

*

No, Israel, no Father-image for you! There is only one Father
and He will do nothing for you which you are not prepared
to do for yourself. Nor will He absolve you from the guilt of
evil-doing. Only with His help will you cross the Red Sea,
true enough. But *you* will have to march through it and *you*
will have to get your own feet wet.

JETHRO ● יתרו

I

OBSERVANCE IN THE BREACH

It is a reflection of our modern world tragedy that the age-
old Ten Commandments have not yet gained currency in the
fabric of its civilization. On this Sabbath we shall again read
the Ten Commandments from the Torah in the midst of a
standing congregation and it may prove an instructive, if not

a cheerful, chore to question ourselves as to the degree of the implemenation of the Commandments in modern society.

Commandment One: "I am the Lord thy God who have brought thee out of...the house of bondage."

Reflection: In our time there are many so-called religionists who fail to grasp the inseverable association between God and human freedom. Catholic Spain is an example.

Commandment Two: "Thou shalt have no other gods before Me."

Reflection: Fascism, Nazism, and Communism of our time bear melancholy testimony to the violation of this commandment.

Commandment Three: "Thou shalt not take the name of the Lord, thy God, in vain."

Reflection: In our time the impassioned mouthings of idealistic principles have been matched only by the flagrant disregard of those same ideals in practice.

Commandment Four: "Remember the Sabbath Day to keep it holy."

Reflection: The function of the days of holiness and spiritual exaltation has been lost in the modern-day maze of the commercialization and secularization of the Sabbath by Christian and Jew alike.

Commandment Five: "Honor thy father and thy mother."

Reflection: Parental homage and respect for age generally would seem to have reached their lowest points in our age of arrogance and sacrilege.

Commandment Six: "Thou shalt not kill."

Reflection: Twenty five million dead in the wars of the twentieth century *thus far*. Mass-murder (genocide) developed into a polished technique in the crematoria of Satan's disciples.

Commandment Seven: "Thou shalt not commit adultery."

Reflection: The Kinsey Reports, Rita Hayworth, Ingrid Bergman et al.

Commandment Eight: "Thou shalt not steal."

Reflection: Little Czechoslovakia as one example of many: stolen first by Hitler, then by Stalin. Billions of barrels of oil stolen from the impoverished myriads of the Middle East by Anglo-American Petroleum titans.

Commandment Nine: "Thou shalt not bear false witness against thy neighbor."

Reflection: Joseph McCarthy of Wisconsin.

Commandment Ten: "Thou shalt not covet."

Reflection: World War I, World War II and World War II plus ½ — all instigated by covetousness.

Conclusion: Moses, Moses, where art Thou?

II

OUR GOD AND "OPIUM-GODS"

They begin — these Ten Commandments — with the Declaration: "I am the Lord thy God, who brought thee out of the land of Egypt, out of the house of bondage". — Exodus 20:2 — The sheer majesty of these words is unparalleled in all the annals of man. They are — these words of the First Commandment — the Declaration of the Rights of Man and the Declaration of Independence of all mankind. They say with crystal clarity that the supreme meaning of the knowledge of God is the freedom of man. The first, the topmost, the cardinal association is that of God with the emancipation and redemption of humanity. Any contrary association is not in consonance with the Mosaic concept of God. Attention (if thou canst), O Spirit of Karl Marx! For if this be opium, what then is medicinal?

*

"Thou shalt have no other gods before Me." — Exodus 20:3 — That is the Second Commandment, an inevitable corrolary of the First. More than men have observed the First have they

violated the Second. The history of humanity has been a long
succession of false gods, idols and ideals. These indeed have
been "opium gods", axes in the hands of unscrupulous grinders,
gods invented, devised and sold by men with shadowy, sordid,
selfish motives. These were — and are — enslavement of their
deluded worshippers. These were — and should continue to be
— the gods who inspire Abrahams and Jacobs and Josiahs and
Mattathiases to iconoclasm. These are gods against which all
the Godly and the free should wage unrelenting, unconditional
and unmitigated warfare. In the destruction of these gods lies
the salvation of mankind.

*

"Thou shalt not take the name of the Lord thy God in vain."
— Exodus 20:7 — Those who sanctify and sanction mundane
and unworthy pursuits in the name of God are the chief
violators of this Commandment. Anything associated with God
must perforce be noble and pure and dignified and exalted.
There is no room in the Synagogue for card playing, neither
ought there be room in our statute books for the legalization
of "Bingo".

*

"Remember the Sabbath day to keep it holy." — Exodus
20:8 — A Jew who "remembers", is a Jew who posts a fence
around his soul at least one day in the week on which is written
clearly: "all base pursuits, all materialistic considerations, all
petty nonsense — keep out. Man at work within communing
with his God."

*

"Honor thy father and thy mother". — Exodus 20:12 — A
society which does honor to its elders is a society which does itself
honor. A society which has no respect for age or seniority is
a society bound to lose its self-respect. Like charity, the quality
of deference and respect, must begin at home — or it will

begin not at all. Nor is the disrespectful and arrogant son to be fully blamed. Most of the guilt must fall upon the shoulders of pampering parents.

*

"Thou shalt not kill, Thou shalt not commit adultry. Thou shalt not steal. Thou shalt not bear false witness against thy neighbor. Thou shalt not covet." — Exodus 20:13-14 —

These are the second half of the two tablets of the Ten Commandments. Moral-minded atheists (if there are such) might be tempted to place these first. Jews cannot do so at all. Jews understand that without acceptance of the letter and the spirit of the first Five, the second Five might just as well be dashed at the foot of Sinai.

*

History has proved the Jews right.

III

WHERE, O WHERE IS GOD?

In the aftermath of the overwhelming experience at the foot of Sinai so majestically narrated in Exodus 19 and 20, there appears a quiet, unobtrusive passage of only five verses. In the wake of the thunder and smoke of the Sinaitic Revelation this short section might be in some danger of obscuration. That would be most unfortunate, for the five verses in question (Exodus 20:19-23) are of transcending importance to the nature of Judaism and, indeed, of incalculable significance to the very concept of Religion. Let us, I pray, look into these verses with some degree of concentration.

The First: *"And the Lord said unto Moses: Thus shalt thou say unto the children of Israel: Ye yourselves have seen that I have talked with you from heaven."* — Religion, which is fundamentally a belief in God as the ruler of the universe, is meaningless if it is not profoundly personal. The truly religious man must feel God at first hand, empirically. God-spoke-to-Moses-and-Moses-told-me-and-I-believe-Moses-is not good enough theology. The essence of honest faith is: I hear you calling me, O God! Indeed, *"Ye yourselves have seen that I have talked with you from heaven"*.

The Second: *"Ye shall not make with Me — gods of silver or gods of gold, ye shall not make unto you"* — Religion must not be prostituted to serve base motives and ends. One cannot justify money-making as a cult by saying, as the Puritans did, it is the will of God. Nor can one be pious about poverty saying with a shrug of the shoulders: It is God's way and who are we to challenge it? Aggressive, destructive invasion of other people's soil in the name of God in the fashion of the Christian Crusaders and the Muslim *Jehad* is not religion but idolatry. It is a remaking of God in the distorted image of man.

The Third: *"An altar of earth shalt thou make unto Me . . . In every place where I cause My name to be mentioned I will come unto thee and bless thee"*. God's abode is not to be equated with million dollar cathedrals, mosques or temples. The stairway to heaven is not diamond-studded. It is the sky-bound pathway of the humble and the quiet. Moreover, God is not the monopoly of any particular altar in any particular city. The City of God is *any* city in which there is a human being who lives by His name.

The Fourth: *"And if thou make me an altar of stone, thou shalt not build it of hewn stones; for if thou lift up thy sword upon it, thou hast profaned it"*. The Kingdom of God is not to be conquered by violence. The auto-de-fe and the brain-washing as instruments of conversion and soul-snatching are the tools of the proverbial devil, not the tools of God. Baptismal waters upon a babe abducted from a family of "unbelievers" will not *per se* "save" the infant. In the eyes of God such self-appointed dispensers of his grace will stand condemned.

The Fifth: *"Neither shalt thou go up by steps unto Mine*

altar, that thy nakedness be not uncovered thereon". God-consciousness is possible only in an environment of dignity and reverence, and human self-respect. The ancient pagans held regular orgiasmic sessions in the temples of their gods. Nakedness, lewdness and profanity reigned supreme by the legs of their altars. The man of true faith is to eschew vulgarity and indecency — in heart, in body, in soul, in speech. For the Lord, as the prophet Elijah can testify, is neither in bombast nor in pyrotechnics but in the "Still, Small, Voice".

IV

GOD IS IN THE THICK DARKNESS

"And the people stood afar off; but Moses drew near unto the thick darkness where God was." — Exodus 20:18

One does not reach God by standing afar off; one can hope to reach Him only if he reaches out after Him.

The more desirable and the more precious the object of our quest, the more likely are we to strain might and main for it. People have been known to kill themselves in frantic pursuit of wealth or power or love.

Nothing in heaven or on earth is more precious than the presence of God, for that condition having been attained — all tribulations melt away into nothingness.

Yet so many people seem to feel that this most precious of objects should fall into their relaxed laps without any expenditure of effort on their part.

And when this does not happen — as, indeed it cannot happen — they shrug their shoulders and say: "I just don't have religion. I guess I'm a non-believer."

They think that when they have walked through the doors of the synagogue they have done their share and that if "the service leaves them cold" then Judaism is not for them.

By the same reasoning they should expect to become rich merely by walking into the assembly plant of the Ford Motor Company in Dearborn.

By the same reasoning they should expect to achieve power by sitting in the gallery during a session of the United States Senate in Washington.

By the same reasoning they should expect to win love by having dinner with a closely-knit, loving and loyal family.

They want to lounge in their sportswear or loll in their smoking jackets while some Moses serves them "religion" on a silver platter in the same manner as one may have his breakfast in bed.

It can never be that way.

The quest for God is a gargantuan process reducing the fabulous chores of Hercules to the petit, the pygmy and the petty.

It demands plunging into the raging fires of Shadrach, Meshach and Abed-Nego.

It calls for wading through the turbulent waters of Nachshon ben Aminadab.

It insists on the Mosaic invasion of the region of darkness, mist and cloud which is the domain of the Unknown and which is knowable only to the rare souls whose life is an adventure of the spirit.

"And the people stood afar off; but Moses drew near unto the thick darkness where God was."

V

WONDERFUL JETHRO

The universal spirit which informs our Bible is nowhere better expressed than in the very high tribute paid to Jethro, the priest of Midian. Our Torah reading this Sabbath bears his name and, more important, the imprint of his character and his wisdom.

The clue to Jethro's character is contained in Exodus 18:9 which reads: "And Jethro rejoiced for all the goodness which the Lord had done to Israel, in that He had delivered them out of the hand of the Egyptians." A *good* character is, of course, one which is good to others, which flinches at the pain of others and exults over their joy. It is, the character guided by the transcendant moral precept: "And thou shalt love thy neighbor as thyself." Insofar as the Torah quietly tells us this about the character of Jethro just a chapter or two before the great theophany at Sinai, the Torah brilliantly foreshadows the basic foundation upon which Mosaic teaching is to rest.

Jethro was a stranger in Israel and to Israel. He was a champion of another cult and a member of another people. But Jethro "rejoiced for all the goodness which the Lord had done to Israel." How desperately is our chauvenistic world in need of this spirit!

*

The evidence of Jethro's wisdom lies in his classic evaluation of effective leadership. Seeing how mightily his son-in-law Moses labored in serving as Israel's chief — dealing with all matters, great or small personally and entrusting little to the initiative of others — Jethro was gravely disturbed. "The thing that thou doest is not good", (Exodus 18:17) said he to the inspired lawgiver. That you, brilliant and God-gifted man can execute the word of God is an axiom and no source of wonder. Neither is it a reflection of the efficacy of your leadership. Only then will your efforts have proved fruitful if others are motivated to do for themselves what you are now doing for them. A leader is one who can beget leaders, Moses. Therefore must thou "provide out of all the people able men such as fear God, men of truth...and place such over the people to be rulers of thousands, rulers of hundreds, rulers of fifties and rulers of ten." — Exodus 18:21.

The good teacher is not measured by *his* mastery of the lesson. *Cherchez l'élève,* sayeth Jethro.

MISHPATIM ● משפטים

I

SWEET, SWEET JUSTICE

"And earthly power doth then show liketh God's when mercy seasons justice" — *The Merchant of Venice.*

The Bard's idea is a wonderful epitome of the spirit of *Mishpatim* — the portion to be read from the Torah on this Sabbath.

Mishpatim — a word meaning ordinances or laws — deals primarily with mundane, everyday matters affecting social relationships. It sets forth legal procedures as to property and personal damage and liability, employment, marriage and divorce, larceny, brigandage, arson, homicide, libel, perjury and money lending.

It is the stuff that lawbooks are made of — lawbooks of every city, state, and nation of any description. And yet *Mishpatim* is much more. *Mishpatim's* distinction as a code of laws resides in the divine moment with which these laws are vested. These are not merely laws — cold, aloof, detached and unshakable. These are laws tempered with the spirit of God. This is justice seasoned with mercy, edict softened with compassion.

Heed these words of *Mishpatim*:

"Ye shall not afflict any widow or fatherless child. If you afflict them in any wise — for if they cry at all unto Me, I will surely hear their cry...

"If thou lend money unto any of My people, even to the poor with thee, thou shalt not be to him as a creditor, neither shall ye lay upon him interest. If thou at all take thy neighbor's garment as a pledge thou shalt restore it unto him before sunset. For that is his only covering, it is his garment for his skin; wherein shall he sleep? And it shall come to pass, when he crieth unto Me, that I will hear; for I am compassionate."

Exodus 22:21-26

Find words such as these in the statute books of New York State, if you will.

II

THE SPIRIT OF THE LAWS

"And these are the ordinances which thou shalt set before them", are the words which introduce the Sidrah for this Shabbos. How happily turned is the phrase "set *before* them" in the context of the whole sentence! Laws should never lag *behind* the development of people. Laws should never be permitted to vegetate or to ossify. Laws should be functions of what *is,* not of what has been. The Torah has lived so long only because its laws were vibrant, organic, and evolving. Its laws were and are good laws because they can be comprehended by looking straight ahead — not by turning back.

The famous *lex talionis* is in this very same Torah reading. At one time it was literally "an eye for an eye, a hand for a hand". Then, it was in consonance with the concepts of justice prevalent in that age. Years later our Rabbis of the Mishnah found such a law untenable. They therefore interpreted it to mean not "an eye for an eye" but the *value* of an eye for an eye. In this case — as in hundreds of others — their purpose was to keep the law in the vanguard of life and not in its rear.

*

A good system of law is a system which exalts principle above application. It is a system which allows for a wide latitude of amendment in the area of detail in order to maintain the freshness of the spirit of the laws. Dated and outmoded applications of a principle can sap the vitality of that principle. Take the issue of slavery, for instance. It is quite evident that the spirit of the Torah was an anti-slavery spirit. In their day, the

laws of the Torah modifying, regulating and restricting slavery
were very radical applications of the anti-slavery principle. In
our day, the Torah's modified-slavery program is quite insupport-
able. We can be true to the spirit of the Torah as applied to
our day only by unconditional opposition to the slightest tincture
of slavery in any shape or form. To insist today upon the
continuation in force of the measures which were anti-slavery
measures in the Torah's day would be paradoxically to sanction
slavery in the 20th century. The ancient law would survive.
The ancient principle which motivated that law in the first
place would die.

*

Said the Tanaitic scholar Ben Bag-Bag: "Study it (the Torah)
again and again, for everything is contained in it; *constantly
examine it* (my italics), grow old and gray over it, and swerve
not from it, for there is nothing more excellent than it".*
How grand an understanding did this sage possess of the true
meaning of Torah. Every generation must study it anew. Every
era must re-examine it and grow with it — not away from it
— if its immortal and immutable principles are to receive
tangible and valid expression at all times and at all seasons.

*

"And these are the ordinances which thou shalt set *before*
them".

III

OF ASSES AND OXEN

"Now these are the laws which thou shalt set before them".
                                                    Exodus 21:1

Judaism begins with the law. Love is wonderful and mercy
is lovely and compassion is noble but without law they are

* Mishna Abot.

disembodied specters floating in a vacuum of ephemeral theory.

Talk is cheap and morality even cheaper when untranslated into the ordinary business of life. Mount Sinai is a gorgeous monument but the people do not live there. Its thunder and its lightning are very impressive but life itself is not quite as spectacular. Moses first brought the people to Mount Sinai, just for the effect. But the more important part of his work was bringing Mount Sinai to the people. And that is what this portion of the Torah is all about.

At Sinai the people heard uplifting statements of principle. Love God! Love your parents! Don't lie! Don't kill! Keep the Sabbath holy! Everybody agreed that the Sinaitic sermon was just grand, that every word of it was so utterly true. Men, Women and children walked away from Sinai simply inspired. What an experience!, they all said.

But now, Moses mused, they are going back to their tents. There they will find no thunder, no lightning, no flashes of divine radiance. There they will find smelly goats and bleating sheep and stubborn mules and horn-happy oxen. How does Sinai relate to these mundane realities? It is my task to show them how it does. If I fail to do so, Sinai will have been an empty extravagenza. If I succeed in doing so, Sinai will remain with them through time and eternity.

So Moses set laws before the people: hard-tack laws, bread-and-butter laws, rat-race laws, market place laws — — — in fine life-laws. Moses translated the exalted language of Sinai into terms involving oxen and sheep, capital and labor, husbands and wives, arson, sewers, larceny (grand and petit), loans, interest, mortgages, courts, breaches of promise, food, drink, and recreation — — — and ever so much more.

Every one of these laws is permeated with the spirit of Sinai. The Mosaic law is above all else a law of life and a law for the living. It is not "Utopian", though it strives for Utopia. It is not "visionary", though it is saturated with clear vision. It is not monastic, though it aims at the realization of a "kingdom of priests". And, I believe it true to say, one of the central reasons for Jewish survival through history has been the identification of Jewish law with life itself. A society begins to disintegrate when its laws bear no relationship to the realities of its existence. Judaism has lived because of its uncanny devotion to the principle that the law was its life and its life was the law. So long as Jewish law and life remain compatible companions so long will our faith and our people abide. When law and life are out of tune with each other there is a clear mandate to amend one or the other or both so as to reintroduce that indispensible harmony of the two which already at the very beginning was the titanic work of the Great Lawgiver.

IV

THE SOCIETY OF JUSTICE

If through some terrible misfortune you know little of our Torah, you would be well advised to master at least nine of its sentences. These constitute the first nine verses of Exodus 23 which is included in the Scriptural reading for this Sabbath. I quote them in full:

"Thou shalt not utter a false report; put not thy hand with the wicked to be an unrighteous witness.

"Thou shalt not follow a multitude to pervert justice.

"Neither shalt thou favor a poor man in his cause.

"If thou meet thy enemy's ox or his donkey going astray, thou shalt surely bring it back to him again.

"If thou see the donkey of him that hateth thee lying under its burden, thou shalt forbear to pass by him; thou shalt surely release it with him.

"Thou shalt not wrest the judgment of thy poor in his cause.

"Keep thee far from a false matter; and the innocent and righteous slay thou not; for I will not justify the wicked.

"And thou shalt take no bribe; for a bribe blindeth them that have a sight and perverteth the words of the righteous.

"And a stranger shalt thou not oppress, seeing ye were strangers in the land of Egypt."

*

What do you see here? I'll tell you what *I* see. I see summarized herein all the necessary principles for the Society of Justice. We might state them as follows:

Alef: The foundation of any just society can be none other than truth — truth in its particulars as well as in its sum, truth in the individual as well as in the mass. Truth is not *ipso facto* the decision of the majority. Where such decision is false, it is incumbent upon the dissenting minority to hold its ground steadily until such time as truth will prevail.

Beth. Justice is not to be equated with the right of the underdog. The welfare of the proletariat, for example, must not be attained at the expense of truth and morality. *The end, be it ever so worthy, does not justify unworthy means.* The majority is only a rule, not a deity.

Gimmel: Mutual assistance is indispensable to the survival of a just society. Mutual assistance should not be a matter of volition; it must be a matter of duty.

Daled: Any religion and any god invoked in the cause of oppression is a false religion and a false god. *Religion is not to be rendered the opiate of the subjugated.*

Hay: Though love for all men, regardless of description, cannot be legislated, a superstructure of law whose substructure is devoid of human love and compassion, cannot be the superstructure for the Society of Justice.

*

All this is implied in the nine sentences quoted above. Passages such as these are Judaism's guarantors of immortality.

V

SUICIDE THROUGH HYPNOSIS

"Thou shalt not follow a multitude to do evil." — Exodus
23:2 — This statement in our Torah reading for the Sabbath
must rank with the most precious of teaching. It is applicable
in so many ways and charged with so much significance that
it remains ever fresh, ever timely.

Man is a gregarious animal, to be sure, but his opinions are
even more so. They tend to cluster together and to conform
to a prevailing pattern. Few are the people with the courage
to go out on a limb and give utterance to a view which dissents
from that of an erring majority. Few are those who venture
even to question the validity of majority judgment. The urge
to be *au courant* applies, it would seem, not only to such things
as clothing and catering but also to the realm of ideas.

This must be deemed most regrettable. An idiotic fashion in
hats may not lead to catastrophic consequences but an idiotic
fashion in thoughts may — and often does. And it is precisely
in the arena of thought that man's penchant for imitativeness
is most rampant. People can be mesmerized by the barbaric,
antedeluvian mumbo-jumbo of a madman like Hitler and no
reasoning in the world is capable of restoring their sanity. The
contagion of distorted thinking can spread faster than the plague
and before it is somehow stopped it may often leave a trail of
bloody destruction, as horrible as it is senseless. Most of the
wars of mankind must be attributed to such distorted thinking
and to the failure of that brand of courage which alone might
have stemmed it.

Do you remember that fine film called "The Ox Bow Incident"? It was the story of the lynching of three innocent men,
a horror brought on by the blind persistence of ordinarily decent
people in refusing to question an impulsive, spontaneous *feeling*
that the three victims were guilty of a murder. Only after the

innocent men were hanged did the body of their presumed victim show up — alive. And it was too late for tears.

Now today there is something in the air suspiciously like mass hypnosis with respect to our ideas about Russia's intentions. It is universally assumed that everytime Russia talks disarmament and peace what she really has in mind is a treacherous assault upon our helpless shores, that Russia *cannot* be sincere in any of her pretensions of concern for the weal of civilization and the survival of mankind.

Such thinking is servile and unwholesome. It may indeed bring about the very disaster against which it presumes to alert us. The time has come for courageous minds to get off this defeatist bandwagon and to venture on the refreshingly original idea that perhaps Russia is as unenthusiastic about the devastation of its people as we are about ours. That's something to think about, isn't it?

TERUMAH • תרומה

I

THE ART OF PRAYER

It isn't easy to pray. Prayer, as a matter of fact is enormously difficult to achieve. Prayer is obviously a function of the heart — not of the lips nor of the mind. To pray is to feel, and feeling is not mechanically engineered. To pray is to communicate with God. Communication at best is an art. Communication with the Creator is art at the highest level.

To attend a service in the synagogue does not yet constitute prayer. To be passively attentive as prayers are chanted and recited from the pulpit is still a state short of prayer. To recite and to chant the service along with the Rabbi, Cantor, and choir is not quite prayer yet. To rise to a mood of inspired devotion, to experience a sense of identity with that which is deathless, to attain the ecstasy of nearness to God, to achieve the degree of a spiritual concentration that obliterates all physical images, to live through that priceless moment of the soul's exaltation which purges our being of everything base, prosaic and commonplace — that is prayer.

To scale these heights is a privilege and a blessing not often given to us and far from easily negotiated. Prayer above all is induced by a particular state of mind — a condition which is psychologically receptive to the Great Idea of God. One simply cannot expect to enter the synagogue and to find God there. To find God in the synagogue, He must first of all exist within the heart of the individual. A man takes out that spiritual treasure from the synagogue which he brings into it with him. The synagogue is the spark for prayer. The fuel thereof is — or is not — in the human heart.

"And let them make Me a sanctuary that I may dwell among them", (Exodus 25:8) is a beautiful verse from our Torah reading for this week. Upon this verse our rabbis of old made the highly significant comment that God resides not within the sanctuary but within every individual.

Unless, of course, the Great Tenant is dispossessed.

II

BUY BONDS!

"And the Lord spoke unto Moses, saying: Speak unto the children of Israel, that they take for Me an offering...". — Exodus 25:1-2 — That is how the section of the Torah for this Sabbath begins.

*

Now the expression to "take an offering" has bothered students of the Torah for a long time. Is it not a contradiction in terms, they have asked? Should not the phrase read to *give* an offering, since an offering is that which *leaves* a person's pocket, not that which comes into it?

*

The difficulty has been answered by some homiletically-minded commentators with the observation that there are some kinds of charities to which giving represents receiving as well. If you feed a hungry man or cure a sick man, for example, what is involved is giving pure and simple. Nothing is received in turn except the joy of having done something decent. On the other hand when one gives to a Synagogue as an example, one is a receiver as well since he benefits directly from what the Synagogue has to offer.

*

I have a better and, certainly, more current example. I have reference to the purchase of State of Israel Bonds. Very literally, this signifies the *taking* of an offering. The offer is made by the Jewish State to all takers. Those who accept the offer and buy the bonds are making an immense contribution to the future of our spiritual homeland. At the same time, they are making a sound and profitable investment which pays a handsome rate of interest. Is this not literally "taking an offering"?

*

Israel is the miracle of modern times. It is the very embodiment of the Rabbinic belief in Resurrection. In the face of colossal odds and in defiance of both history and logic, the land of Abraham and David and Jannus Alexander and Bar Kochba is once again — after the intervention of two millenia — in the hands of their descendants. What is more, it is being brought back from the dead by those whom many have long pronounced dead. This is a miracle unparalleled anywhere at any time.

*

In this enormous and celestial experience every Jew all over the world is being given the opportunity, nay, the rare privilege, of participation. That there may be Jews who would turn their backs at so glorious an offering would seem to be an inconceivable thought.

III

ALL OF ONE PIECE

"And thou shalt make a candlestick of pure gold: of beaten work shall the candlestick be made, even its base and its shaft; its cups, its knops and its flowers shall be of one piece with it."
Exodus 25:31

*

The Menorah, construction of which was described in the above verse, has become the symbol of the Jewish religion and the Jewish people. It is part and parcel of almost every synagogue pulpit, it is the central figure in the seal of the modern state of Israel and it figures conspicuously among the spoils of the Temple as depicted upon the Arch of Titus in Rome.

That being the case we ought perhaps to pay more careful attention to the central plan of the classic Mosaic Menorah. It had to be "of beaten work" which means that it had to be hammered out of one piece. This, it seems to me, is of the most crucial significance. The people of Israel must be of one piece if it is to survive. A unity of idealistic purpose overriding everything else must be the *sina qua non* of Jewish living. The moment Israel is not of one piece as to the mainstream of its spiritual direction, disaster lurks very close by. Indeed schism within the ranks of Israel was responsible for the fall of both the First and the Second Temple. Conversely, it has been *the indomitable will to survive as Jews* that has united us in all parts of our dispersion and has kept us in life through a two millenial *galut*.

Now to be "of one piece" does not mean that we must accept a monolithic way of life which permits of no differences in thought or in practice. This, indeed, has never been true in the history of our people. There has always been divergence in opinion and in outlook from the days of Hillel and Shammai, those great ideological adversaries, down to the present. But these divergences have been *le'shem shamayeem,* idealistically motivated world-views which shared the common purpose of Jewry's spiritual welfare.

For certainly the Menorah of Judaism has room within it for variegated elements: base and shaft, cups and knops and flowers. The personality and the function of the base is different from that of the shaft as both differ from the cup or the knop or the flower and as any of the latter differ from each other. Were this not so the Menorah would be a drab piece of metal indeed. Yet with all these differences, the individual elements were designed to be "of one piece" insofar as each in its own way contributed to that which counted most: the light and the radiance which the Menorah was to shed.

*

There is a sermon here somewhere, don't you think?

IV

THE SYNAGOGUE IS A TASKMASTER

The last part of the Book of Exodus which we are currently engaged in reading from the Torah is concerned almost entirely with the blueprints for the first Jewish House of Worship — The Tabernacle in the Wilderness. A prodigious amount of work went into the making of that Tabernacle. The intricate and exacting specifications for everything connected with it — from the sacred Altar to the Priest's Breastplate — are truly staggering.

A multitude of people was engaged in the holy work —
carpenters, goldsmiths, artists, engravers, diamond cutters, tailors,
toolmakers — and the success of the project was the product
of uncompromising devotion and unmitigated toil.

All who worked for the House of Worship were volunteers
who were impelled by a through cognizance of the spiritual
exigencies which dictated the construction of the Tabernacle.
The high degree of enthusiastic cooperation which marked the
great work from its inception was simply the natural result of
shared spiritual experience.

No temple since has been able to do without unstinting labor
— freely and generously given; without the solid measure of
brotherliness and cooperation vital to its set of ideals; without
great quantities of human energy and strength, readily made
available for its altar.

It was last week that one of our board members complained
to me that the synagogue was monopolizing too much of his
time, that there were too many meetings to attend, too many
campaigns and projects, et cetera. I told him then that I would
respond to his statement by means of this essay, and this is my
response:

Dear Friend: I'm sorry that I cannot offer my sympathy.
Your statement reflects a pitiful lack of understanding of the
responsibilities of a Jew towards his synagogue. The synagogue
is a stern taskmaster which expects and demands a maximum
of work and energy and effort from you. If your attachment to
the synagogue is real and not perfunctory, your labors in its
behalf too, must be real and not perfunctory. The synagogue
wants you to give to its service everything you've got — even if
it means three, four or — when necessary — five nights a week.

For if you have accepted the sacred trust of a Trustee, you
have presumably indicated thereby your understanding of a
basic fact:

The synagogue is a life and death matter to the Jewish people.

Upon its survival and health depends your own survival and health as a Jew.

So stop muttering, uncross your knees and get to work!

TETSAVEH • תצוה

THE ETERNAL LIGHT

"And thou shalt command the children of Israel, that they bring unto thee pure olive oil beaten for the light, to cause a lamp to burn continually. In the tent of Meeting — — — Aaron and his sons shall set it in order, to burn from evening to morning before the Lord; it shall be a statute forever throughout their generations on behalf of the children of Israel."

Exodus 27:20-21

This is the passage at the beginning of our Torah reading for this Sabbath. It should be at the beginning and the middle and the end of everything which pertains to our religion.

For if anything is true of Judaism it is its obsession with perpetuation. As a people we have been perpetuated against seemingly insurmountable odds because the soul of our people is indentifiable with perpetuation.

We are the most history conscious faith the world has ever seen. Every vital aspect of our past has been incorporated into our present as every vital part of the present will become a part of our future.

When we pray to our "God of Abraham, Isaac, and Jacob" we are not merely mouthing a formula; we are expressing a philosophy. We *are* a people today precisely *because* we have linked ourselves with Abraham, Isaac and Jacob — *and* with Moses and Samuel, Isaiah and Ezekiel, Ezra and Hillel, Akiba and Saadia, Maimonides and Caro, the Gaon of Vilna and the Iluy of Rogatchev.

Like the plant that blooms and grows, Judaism has ever sucked life-giving sustenance from its roots. Yet Judaism has not been parasitic. The Judaic plant of any given generation justifies itself not only by imbibing from the past but by infusing into the future. The Eternal Light concept described in the Torah quotation above embraces this most critical idea of perpetuation through the simultaneous process of giving and receiving — just as the wick draws its vitality from the oil while suffusing its environs with light.

No generation of Jews can afford to rest comfortably upon the laurels of the past. To do so would be to snap the process of perpetuation and to snuff out the hitherto Eternal Light (*hass ve'halila*). The prophets took from Mosaic teaching and transmitted to the Scribes of the early post-exilic centuries. The teachings of these Scribes became the basis for the towering creative efforts of the Tanaim and the Amoraim who were the architects of the Talmud. The Talmud was the fresh-water spring from which the great codists of the 12th, 14th and 16th centuries fashioned the monumental *Shulchan Aruch,* inspired by the earlier efforts of the Geonim who thrived during the 8th, 9th and 10th centuries. And the gigantic centers of European Jewish learning like Volhodzin, Slabodka, Mir, Telz and Lubavich to name but a few were the most recent great contribution of "pure olive oil" for the Eternal Light of Judaism.

In the greatest catastrophe of our history these centers have been wiped off the map and we are faced today — we the Jews of the world — with an acute shortage of "pure olive oil" for our Eternal Light.

And who is to make good that shortage if not the most populous Jewish community on earth?

KI SEESAU • כי תשא

I

TORAH-VISION

"They shall give every man a ransom for his soul..."
Exodus 30:12

The soul is the divine within each of us, the image of God in which we were created. It is that which sets us apart from salamanders and hippopotomi. True we eat, drink, sleep and procreate just as they do. But we are capable of looking up and away from our food, heavenwards. We have the potential to prevent bodily desire from becoming obsessive and all-consuming by remembering that in the beginning the Lord created heaven as well as earth.

But the peril of joining the hippopotamus as generic kindred confronts men constantly. And many are they who succumb. Such are the people who become enslaved by the wants of the body and utterly neglect the wants of the soul. Like unused muscles, the unused soul too can suffer atrophy. When that happens the metamorphosis is complete — from man to hippopotamus. And the soul is committed to cruel bondage.

"What is life," I heard a citizen of this community say once, "but food and sex. Now let's be honest, fellows, and admit it." I have small doubt that the citizen was very honest with himself. I should, however, be reduced to utter despair if I thought that this definition of life was valid for all of us. To desire food and enjoy the facts of biology is no sin in the eyes of Judaism. But to elevate these natural cravings to the summit of all meaningfulness in human life is to descend to the hippopotamic cesspool — a place infested with stench and degeneracy.

"They shall give every man a ransom for his soul". If to be called man is our desire then we must liberate our soul from atrophy by activating it. Judaism is the greatest and truest of all religions because its heart — *the mitsvoth* — really constitutes the activating medicine of the soul. Judaism demands constant spiritual exercise through its regimen of commandments, rules, practices and ordinances. To be a good Jew is to practice the laws of the Torah — no more, no less. It is hardly conceivable for a good Jew to choose Aladdin's Magic Lamp on channel four over the Eternal Light on channel infinity.

For the good Jew TV means Torah-Vision!

II

THE SABBATH

...*"wherefore the children of Israel shall keep the Sabbath to observe the Sabbath throughout their generations for a perpetual covenant. It is a sign between Me and the children of Israel for ever"*... — Exodus 31:16-17

The Sabbath is a corner stone of Judaism. Upon it rests a major share of our ritual, ethics, history, culture, philosophy, psychology, literature, art, music — in a word, our way of life.

Eliminate the institution of the Sabbath from our midst and you have cut away the heart of our religion. No synagogue of whatever denomination would abide for as much as a week without the Sabbath. No Jewish education is conceivable without the Sabbath. No spiritual values can stand without the Sabbath.

And, I wish to add: No Jew is much of a Jew who makes no personal contribution to the collective observance of the Sabbath. This is as valid as saying that no American is much of an American who makes no personal contribution to the operation of the American democratic system.

There are Jews who utilize the Sabbath for shopping expeditions downtown. They are the Sabbath Saboteurs.

There are Jews for whom the Sabbath is "Family Entertainment" day. They are the Sabbath Assassins.

There are Jews for whom the Sabbath is the grab-bag for a miscellany of appointments which include everything from high finance to low comedy, everything except an appointment with the spirit of Sabbath. They are the Sabbath Spitters.

To these Jews the Voice of the Sabbath calls as with the voice of conscience:

"Remember me? I am the Fourth Commandment. I am the beloved of your Creator and the pride of your ancestry. Through me Israel has lived through ages of devastation, by me was his soul sustained, for me did he often fall a martyr. I am human dignity. I am eternal truth. I am beauty and balance. I am poetry and piety. I am the belle and the bride. I was affianced to Israel and Israel to me in solemn and (I had hoped) inseverable bonds. Will you now give me a bill of divorcement? If so, you will have divorced yourself from "Klal Yisrael" as well.

III

A LONELY, LONELY TENT

Poor, pathetic lonely figure of a Moses — a figure above and apart from the masses to whom he dedicated his life. The agony of the call to duty, the heartbreaking shafts of a double-dealing Pharaoh, the frustration of a lethargic response from those whom he arrived to liberate — all this and the Golden Calf too! It would seem entirely too much for one man to endure!

*

Poor, pathetic, lonely figure of a Moses — speaking to Israel of God and of Heavens and of the Infinite and then to find that his audience had an ear only for raucous, idolatrous music-making and a stomach only for the fleshpots of Egypt. He — echoing the divine word "I am the Lord Thy God who brought you out of the land of Egypt;" they — prancing in deomoniac style before the idiotic image of a young cow and imputing to it feats of incredible grandeur.

*

Poor, pathetic, lonely figure of Moses — dreaming of a promised land flowing with the milk and the honey of a new and emancipated spirit in man, only to be assailed with endless complaints about the good old days of blissfully irresponsible Goshenite thralldom. He proclaiming the sweet music of the noble vision "And when thou shalt come unto the land which the Lord, Thy God giveth unto Thee"; they — shouting with rabble-roused hoarseness the dissonance of the endless refrain "Get us a new leader and we will return to Egypt".

*

Poor, pathetic lonely figure of a Moses — enchanted by the splendor of a Day apart from all other days, a Sabbath liberated from the tentacles of toil and turmoil and given over unto the spirit and soul of man, only to be disenchanted by the greediness and the avarice of acquisitive hands, hands powered by insatiable salivary juices. He — "Remember the Sabbath day to keep it holy!". They — "And it came to pass on the seventh day, that there went out some of the people to gather..." Gather, gather, gather, gather. Eat, drink, sleep, drink, sleep, eat, sleep, eat, drink — ceaseless, endless, bottomless round of emptiness, a whirl of frenzied futility round-about the Golden Calf.

*

"And Moses took the Tent and pitched it outside the camp, afar off from the camp...And it came to pass when Moses entered into the Tent the pillar of cloud descended and stood at the door of the Tent..." — Exodus 33:7-9

*

Poor, pathetic, lonely figure of a Moses.

IV

SOLILOQUY, MONOLOGUE, CONVERSATION

"And the Lord spoke unto Moses face to face as a man speaketh unto his friend" — Exodus 33:11

In the verse above which appears in our Torah reading for this Sabbath is summarized the essence of religious faith. If the Lord becomes so real and so vital to a man that He almost seems within his conversational orbit — the man so favored is a man of religious faith. No voluminous or scanty theological dissertation on the nature of God and man can say more about the meaning of Faith — nor can it say less without being meaningless.

*

Prayer is the supreme expression of faith in God since it is essentially the act of conversation with God. Now here is a point to understand: the very word *conversation* implies mutuality. It means two parties talking with each other. If talk is limited to only one of the parties, there is no conversation. There is only monologue.

*

But even monologue implies talking with an audience. A person engaged in monologue while not allowing for rejoinder from his audience nevertheless addresses his words to an audience and obviously believes the audience to be there. If there is no audience or if he believes no audience to exist and still he talks, then he is engaged in a soliloquy or in a talking to one's self.

*

Conversation, monologue, soliloquy — these are the three levels of religious expression through worship. At the very lowest state is soliloquy. A man recites a prayer nominally addressed to God, but he does not *really* believe that there is a

God who hears. All too sadly, many are the "worshippers" in
this category. They occupy seats in synagogues and in churches
and when they "pray" they might just as well be talking to
themselves. Their prayer is soliloquy.

Above this there is the much higher level of monologue. In
this situation the worshipper truly believes that he has an
audience in God and it is to this exalted audience that he
addresses his prayer. But though he believes "that his redeemer
liveth," God seems very, very remote — too far away to be
real, too ephemeral to be vital. This conception of God precludes
the possibility of conversation with Him. The prayer is a monologue.

*

At the apex of religious faith there stands conversation. This
is prayer which is the epitomization of harmony and union
between man and his God. Man speaks to God as one would
speak to a living *presence.* This can only be if man's faith is so
powerful, so pervasive, so persuasive as to give him the feeling
of God's omnipresent proximity to him at every moment of the
day and especially through the long intervals of the night.
This is Prayer with a capital P. This is Faith triumphant. This
is Glory transcendant.

*

*"And the Lord spoke unto Moses face to face as a man
speaketh to his friend."*

VAYAKHEL • ויקהל

I

THE END DOES NOT JUSTIFY THE MEANS

The beginning of the Torah reading for this week is an
injunction against the violation of the Sabbath through labor
and the kindling of fire. The rest of the portion is a detailed

account of the actual construction of the Tabernacle in the wilderness.

The juxtaposition of those two seemingly unrelated topics led our Rabbis to comment that even so sacred a cause as the building of the Tabernacle could not justify the desecration of the Sabbath. Herein is lucidly demonstrated the Judaic view that the end does not justify the means.

Rebecca persuaded Jacob to disguise his identity in order to obtain a blessing which she regarded as his due. But Jacob was punished ultimately by a marriage which involved a disguised identity.

Samson married a Phillistine woman against his tradition and over the protests of his parents because he thought that by this means he could more effectively harass his Phillistine enemies. In the end Samson's downfall was wrought by a Phillistine woman.

Solomon married alien princesses with the idea of cementing and strengthening his kingdom. The ultimate product of these marriages was a weakening of the ramparts of his state to the breaking point and beyond.

Moses struck the rock in his great anxiety to supply the people with water. In this he countermanded God's command to use no violence upon the stone because he thought that the important thing was to get the water *by any means*. For this Moses was penalized by being denied entry into the Promised Land.

Elijah wished to stamp out the idolatrous worship of Ba'al from the midst of Israel. With vindictive cruelty he caused four hundred of the priests of Ba'al to be slaughtered. Shortly thereafter he was sternly rebuked by the Lord in the unforgettable scene within the Cave of Horeb (see Kings I, 19).

The biblical incidents refuting the doctrine of justification of bad means by good ends are easily multiplied. It seems to me that the advocates of "the end justifies the means" lose sight of a basic truth, to wit: an originally "good" end which is reached through base and treacherous means ceases to be "good" upon being reached because it is grasped by hands which have already become contaminated with baseness and treachery.

The road to the Good must be a good road! Else it can lead only to the blind alley of evil. You cannot fight a war to make the world safe for democracy because *war is the incarnation of evil and it will never lead to permanent good*. You cannot build a socialist state upon the mutilated bodies of its opponents because no just structure can rest upon a bloody foundation. You cannot "save Judaism for the modern age" by draining it of its content because no well was ever filled by being drained and no congenital drainer can be a filler. You cannot build much of a church through the proceeds of bingo, poker, or "Monte Carlo" because religion is not a game of chance.

And so on.......

II

ISRAEL: A TABERNACLE IN THE WILDERNESS

"The people bring much more than enough for the service of the work which the Lord commanded to make". — Exodus 36:5

Can you imagine that? The builders of the Tabernacle in the Wilderness were faced with a serious problem. The funds for building the structure were oversubscribed. The people were contributing too much material. There was too much gold in the treasury.

Whatever faults the generation of the wilderness may have possessed, it certainly was a people capable of rising to occasions of great need. It responded to the call of the hour with a fervor and an eagerness unsurpassed in the annals of religious achievement. The men and the woman of the Exodus comprehended that great effort was needed for building a House of God under the best circumstances. To build a House of God in the *wilderness* required superlative effort. And that is precisely the sort of effort which they summoned to the construction of the Tabernacle in the Wilderness.

*

A Tabernacle in the Wilderness has been under construction in the Middle East since May 14, 1948, when Israel was born. It is the first Tabernacle since the year 70 for the Jewish people. Its erection from the very first has been fraught with the most painful difficulties and has encountered the most spiteful opposition. It is an architectural project that has been waited upon through 2,000 years of ghastly terror.

The effort required for the successful completion of the Tabernacle called Israel is of a superlative order. The Jews of the world — like the generation of the wilderness — must rise to the occasion or they shall forever remain in the wilderness. Our effort thus far has been far from adequate and astronomically remote from superlative.

Ought we not to invest all the material we can in a cause in which incalculable investments in blood and marrow have already been made? Well, now, ought we or oughten't we?

PIKUDAI • פקודי

I

THEY SAID IT COULDN'T BE DONE

The Tabernacle was finished. The immense workmanship and mammoth labor that went into its construction was at an end. "And Moses reared up the tabernacle, and laid its sockets, and set up the boards thereof, and put in the bars thereof and reared up its pillars. And he spread the tent over the tabernacle and put the covering of the tent above upon it; as the Lord commanded Moses." — Exodus 40:17-19

The new Temple was no longer a dream of visionaries, an hallucination of impractical prestidigitators, a mirage in the wilderness. It was hard and fast and vital reality. It was a reality which the multitude of the entire Congregation of Israel helped to achieve. It was tangible. It was beautiful. It was there. And the people who struggled so selflessly to build it were justifiably saturated with pride.

A magnificent cathedral in the desert of Sinai it was — and it belonged to *all* the children of Israel. It was not the handiwork of Moses alone, nor yet of that most inspired of architects, Bezalel, son of Uri. It was, in essence, the heart and the soul and the muscle and the sinew of *all* the people. They had come, "both men and women, as many as were willing hearted...and brought the Lord's offering...And all the women that were wisehearted did spin with their hands...And the leaders brought the onyx stones and the stones to be set...Every man and woman whose heart made them willing..."toiled and brought to the Tabernacle and for the Tabernacle.

Undoubtedly there must have been some among the children of Israel who had scoffed at the entire idea from the start. "A Tabernacle in this wilderness by the sea!" — they must have sneered. "What for? Isn't the Tent of Meeting large enough? It was good enough yesterday. What's wrong with it today? And do you seriously believe that you can amass the vast contributions required by so ambitious a structure as the Tabernacle? And say, hey, did you ever consider what a huge Tabernacle in our midst would do to our privacy? We'll just have to fold our tents and move on to Edom or Phillistia or Phoenicia and other unincorporated villages whose modest tabernacles are hard by the market place, not by hearth and home?"

But the dreamers and the visionaries and the prestidigitators had rolled up their sleeves in the glare of the hot and hostile sun of the wilderness and had responded to the unbelievers with the one commodity which even unbelievers can understand — achievement. One obstacle after another was shattered in the face of the industry of the laborers on the Tabernacle. The site for the structure was staked out, the building materials were amassed, the manpower levy was realized — and behold, the Tabernacle in the wilderness by the Sea!

"Then the cloud covered the tent of meeting and the glory of the Lord filled the Tabernacle." Exodus 40:35

"Eben ma'asu ha'bonim, hay'tah leh'rosh pinah." (Psalms 118:22) . . .

II

A JEW WITHOUT A SYNAGOGUE?

The Book of Exodus ends with the completion of the first Temple in the history of the Jewish People.

I like to regard that as a symbolic fact. For it is my considered conviction that the personal "Exodus" or "Exile" of every Jew is terminated only with his entry into the Jewish Temple, the Synagogue.

A Jew has not found his people unless he has found his way into the synagogue. And, a Jew cannot find himself before he has found his people.

The soul of the Jewish people is its religion and the soul of that religion is the synagogue. A Jew cannot belong to his people, cannot become integrated with it, cannot partake of its essence unless he identifies himself with the synagogue.

A Jew can be a member of B'nai B'rith or American Jewish Congress or Hadassah or the Community Center movement and still not be truly identified with the essence of Jewishness. And such Jews as may attempt to salve their Jewish consciences by limiting their Jewish "belongingness" to such activity alone are deluding no one more sharply than themselves.

Jewish identification begins with the synagogue. Any other interpretation is untrue to the very nature of Judaism which is *primarily* a religious force.

Outside the synagogue is the wilderness of Jewish anomaly.
Inside of it is the "glory of the Lord".

Whoever would share in that glory, let him enter!

III

CHAZAK!

The Book of Exodus the reading of which is concluded this
Sabbath is the very heart of the Torah and hence the very
essence of our religion.

Two basic components are prominent in its wealth of narrative
and exposition:

A. — Freedom and B. — Law.

Freedom is concerned with human rights while law is concerned with human duties.

Freedom is a concept born of the conviction that God created
all human beings in His image and that only He deserves to be
called Master.

Law is a concept born of the conviction that the boon of
God's image exacts the price of obligation to Him and to His
other creatures.

Before Judaism could be fashioned it had, therefore, to hurdle
two obstacles: The Red Sea of physical bondage and the wilderness of moral anarchy.

Both hurdles were difficult and, really, interdependent.

Only the ideal of a Sinai could have succeeded in breaking
the yoke of a Pharaoh and only the emancipation of the slaves
could have attuned their ears to the voice of Sinai.

The motivation for meaningful freedom must be the desire
to accept responsibility; responsibility can be assumed and discharged only by free men.

Judaism is the inspired compound of the democracy of mankind and the Lordship of God.

Judaism does not believe that the Society of Free Men car
come into being in an atmosphere of Godlessness.

Therefore Judaism must reject a Communism which is athe-
istic as evil and hypocritical.

On the other hand Judaism does not believe that God's will
can be served in a society of social and economic injustice.

Therefore Judaism must reject a Capitalism which exploits
pious platitiudes for the justification of an unjust *status quo.*

The key idea of Exodus is embraced by the number One:
One God and one people.

One God created us all; in His eyes we are all as one.

This, in fact, has been, is, and shall continue to be the whole
of the message of Judaism: *"And the Lord shall be King over
all the earth; in that day the Lord shall be One and His name
One."*

ויקרא

•

VAYIKRA

VAYIKRA • ויקרא

J'ACCUSE!

Chapter Five of Leviticus condemns as heavy sinners those who maintain silence when evil is done and do not call out in testimony against it.

Indeed there is no greater sin than silence in the midst of injustice; it is worse evil than the evil being done.

Even the inanimate earth was forced to cry out against the murder of Abel because there was no one else (besides God) to witness the horror.

The erasure of evil is everybody's business and it is not optional but mandatory.

For no condition is more favorable to the prosperity of evil than a soil which is silent in the face of it.

The youthful Herod, twenty five years old and already rotten to the core was guilty of a crime which required him to appear before the highest tribunal of Judea, the Sanhedrin.

Arrogantly he appeared, sworded, swaggering and sneering, and at the menacing sight of him seventy of the members of that august body looked down at their feet in sheepish confusion.

But the seventy first, a man called Shammai, stood up on his feet and thundered at his colleagues: "Judge this man now or you will live to be soaked with the blood he will spill."

Still they were silent and the next forty years were the bloodiest in the history of the land called Judea and the people called Israel.

"Non-intervention!" cried America and Britain as Francisco Franco devastated Barcelona.

"Peace in our time!" cried Neville Chamberlain as he stepped off a plane on his return trip from a city called Munich.

"America First!" cried the Lone Eagle, Charles A. Lindbergh, as Hitler's wehrmacht roared across Poland, France and the Low Countries.

"Hands off!" cried everybody in sight as seven Arab armies invaded tiny Israel with the idea of pushing its people into the Meditteranean Sea.

"A bas les juifs!" cried the rabble as an innocent Captain Dreyfuss was condemned to Devil's Island and "liberté, égalite, fraternité" were trampled in the dust.

*

But in the last instance there *was* a man who throughout the farcically-tragic rape of justice and emasculation of truth shouted from the rooftops:

"J'accuse!"

Men like him, rare in this world, will yet save the world if, indeed, it is not beyond saving already.

II

THAT GOOD OLD GUILT FEELING

Every so often I hear the complaint of a congregant to the effect that a certain sermon has left him with a guilt-feeling. The implication almost invariably is that this is an undesirable and unhealthy effect. "I come to the synagogue for solace and serenity", one gentleman put it, "and what do I get instead but an agitating scolding from the pulpit which sends me away unhappy and disturbed".

A generation or so ago this kind of reaction could never be. But in between Mr. Freud appeared to initiate a climate in which "guilt-feeling" became a dirty phrase, something to be exorcised from the human personality because it is a symptom of malady and aberration. Witness in our own day the long chain of best-sellers of the Peace-of-Mind—Peace-of-Soul—Power-of-Positive-Thinking genre. This soothing, sweet, smooth literary ointment has been matched by a like outpouring of myrh and frankincense from many a pulpit of all denominations. Men of the cloth have increasingly substituted saccharine and vegetable-oil for substance and vinegar. Jeremiah's words twenty-five hundred years ago have never been more pertinent than they are today: "From the prophet even unto the priest every one dealeth falsely. And they have healed the hurt of the daughter of my people lightly, saying: 'Peace, peace' when there is no peace."*

I submit that guilt-feeling is the most necessary ingredient in the moral personality. .I submit that guilt-feeling is *the* prime requisite for improvement. I submit that the role of religion is to accentuate the guilt feeling, not to attenuate it. Witness the horrible nightmare of our own generation. The smoke of Auschewitz and Bergen-Belsen has not yet evaporated but Germany is already among the most prosperous nations on earth and its aged head-of-state comes to Washington blustering demands all over the Capitol and acting for all the world like a man who had nothing to live down. Jeremiah had a phrase for that, too. "The forhead of a whore", he called it, a forehead which for all its unspeakable iniquity is oblivious to the Mark of Cain so heavily etched into it.

This is the generation of bromides, sedatives and tranquilizers. The diagnosis does not call for these at all. It calls for radical surgery. *The pain-killer is our worst enemy.* It sweeps our faults under the carpet, as it were. It makes us oblivious to the wrong and hence stands in the way of amelioration, of constructive and lasting therapy. From the macrocosmic ailments in our universe to the microcosmic aliments of our own individual selves, the missing therapeutical agent is the guilt-feeling. An ounce of prevention may be worth a pound of cure but a pound of remorse is worth a ton of anaesthesia.

And this is what our Torah lection this week is all about. It is about guilt-feelings and guilt-offerings in every classification: the guilt of the political leader, the guilt of the priest and the

*Jeremiah 6:13, 14

guilt of the plain people. Guilt, guilt, guilt—yes! We are all
guilty of deliberate self-deception. We are all conspirators in a
gigantic plot of pulling the wool over our own eyes and thus
stripping the lamb—which is ourselves—for slaughter.

Oh, Jeremiah!

*

TSAV • צו

SOME MYSTERIES SHOULD NOT BE SOLVED

*"And the fire upon the altar shall be kept burning . . . it shall
not go out."*—Leviticus 6:5—

The service of God as symbolized by the sacrifices demands
constancy. All too often, religious expression on the part of many
people comes in spurts of enthusiasm followed by protracted
periods of inertia. The extreme example is, of course, that "High-
Holiday" Judaism which is so characteristic of the majority of
our people in this land. Barmitsvaitis is another of the spiritual
ailments which is widespread. The pageantry of the lad's religious initiation—its pomp and circumstance—is much more often
than not the very final offering upon God's altar. So many people
become "interested" and "active" in the synagogue only to fall
away and drop out with the passage of time for reasons good
and bad. Judaism, properly conceived, rejects "Grand Openings"
and dismal follow-ups. . . . *"the fire upon altar shall be kept
burning . . . it shall not go out."*

*

*"But the soul that eateth of the flesh of the sacrifice of peace-
offerings . . . having his uncleanness upon him, that soul shall be
cut off from his people."*—Leviticus 7:20—

The peace-seeker and the peace-advocate must not be soiled with the blood of violence. .Only the man of peace can labor towards a viable peace. The man of war does not belong at the peace table with his blood soiled hands. The iniquity of the twentieth century is reflected in the fact that so often those who were clamoring for peace were simultaneously in the process of digesting the victims of their rapine. Hitler devoured Czechoslovakia and proceeded *the very next day* to bark-out a three hour harangue in which he called for world peace. . .

The disarmament talks of our own day will continue to breed naught but discord if the people sitting round the table will have just completed the "successful" testing of yet another Intercontinental Ballistic Missile.

*

"And he placed the breastplate upon him; and in the breastplate he put the Urim and the Tumim.—Leviticus 8:8—One of the great mysteries of the Pentateuch are the Urim and the Tumim which were apparently an integral part of the ceremonial breastplate worn by Aaron, the first High Priest of Israel and all of the High Priests thereafter. What were they? What was their function?

We do know that some sort of Oracular or divining procedure was associated with the Urim and Tumim; that they were employed to determine major yes or no decisions for the entire people of Israel. (cf Numbers 27:21; I Samuel 28:6; Ezra 2:63; Nehemiah 7:65). Still, beyond a vague, intuitive kind of conjecture regarding the precise nature of the Urim and Tumim we have not been able to go.

Perhaps that is as it should be. Perhaps the High Priest should be left his tiny refuge of mystery and privacy. After all, every other detail of his priestly paraphernalia is a matter of public knowledge, and hence of public comment. Regard with what elaborate detail every vestment and every furnishing of

the High Priest's garments are described in the Torah reading
for the week! Observe the minute reportage of his going out
and of his coming in, of his standing and sitting, of his ablutions
and ministrations! Consider the painstaking definition of his
physical qualifications and disqualifications, of the role of his
family and clan, of the innermost layer of his very clothing!
Heavens above, hath the High Priest no privacy at all?

And yet this has ever been the lot of "High Priests" and
spiritual ministers. They have ever lived in glass houses, they
have always been subject to the closest scrutiny, they have never
ceased to be the targets of even the meanest (meaning least considerable) of their flock. It is always open season on the "high
priest" and his family. Even Caesar's wife was not so vulnerable.
This, of course, is psychologically understandable, being, in a
sense, of the very nature of public office.

And yet the excesses of familiarity can jeopardize the efficacy
of the "high priest's" (read Rabbi's) ministry. It is not well that
an I-thou relationship should exist between him and individual
members of the congregation. Certainly he should not be aloof
and forbidding. But neither should he descend to the level of
conviviality with one and all. He is, after all, the spiritual leader
and as such he must perforce be insulated to a degree from the
banalities of common associations. "Hail-fellow-well met" is for
the social director; emphatically not for the spiritual leader.

The "high priest" should be permitted his sanctum-sanctorum.
He should be clad in the mystery of "Urim and Tumim." Else
the much-touted and overly extolled "common touch" will render
him only common.

*

SHEMINI • שמיני

I

ALIEN FIRE

"And Nadab and Abihu, the sons of Aaron, took each of them his censer, and put fire therein, and laid incense thereon, and offered strange fire before the Lord, which He had not commanded them. And there came forth fire from before the Lord, and devoured them, and they died before the Lord."—Leviticus 10:1,2—

This passage from the Torah-reading for this Sabbath is of the utmost significance to the theory and practice of Judaism. It speaks out plainly, for those who would hear, against the grafting of alien elements upon the body Judaic. In a world whose Jewish element is quantitatively microscopic, the temptation to overlay the structure of our faith and practice with ingredients borrowed from other religions and cultures can in the long run lead only to the complete erasure of Judaic identity. But apart from this negative, albeit, decisive reason Judaism is of itself a conception and way of life so profoundly original and beautiful that no foreign elements are required for its enhancement. The attempt to "ennoble" and "beautify" Judaism —both on the theoretical and experimental levels—by appending to it the "fashionable" appurtenances of majority churches is vain delusion. It bespeaks lack of understanding or lack of faith or both. It is servility, poorly disguised; self-deprecation, thinly concealed.

This is not to say that Judaism should not strive for ever higher norms and forms or that the process of evolving contemporary vocabularies for the expression of Jewish values should not be diligently pursued in every generation. Not at all. The vitality of our faith has consisted in its remarkable creative and developmental powers. But these norms and forms, this creativity and development shoud be actuated *from within ourselves as*

Jews and should not consist of the arbitrary behavior which is
the result of the desire to conform. Such behavior is propelled by
forces *outside of ourselves* and can lead us only to the banks of
that river of forgetfulness and perdition called Lethe.

The introduction into our synagogues of the practices of
Christian churches which began about 150 years ago and which
was instigated by the powerful desire to *conform* (rather than
to reform) is precisely the kind of "strange fire" which ought
not to be brought to the altar of the Lord. And it is high time
indeed for the tendency to be eradicated that we may once again
plow, seed and reap the harvest of our own Jewish soil. The
sermon in the synagogue should be *Jewish* to the core, to the
hilt, to the utmost. The tendency of many contemporary Rabbis
to shy away from preaching Judaism as one shies away from the
plague would be grotesquely comical if it were not so painfully
tragic. They will talk about the drama, the arts, international
affairs, social action, fictional and fictitious best sellers, meta-
physics, Yoga, and philately—but not about the six hundred and
thirteen commandments of the Torah. They will talk about
Kirkegard and Jean Paul Sartre but not about Israel Salanter or
the Rabbi of Berditchev. They will invite a Max Lerner and an
Eleanor Roosevelt to speak at their Institutes of Adult Studies
but not a Salo Baron or an Abraham Newman. They will talk
tennis, TV and Turkey but they will not talk Torah.

Is this or is this not a farce? You tell *me*. And if one should
say: "Well, this is what the people want", I would answer: That
is a dastardly calumny against the children of Abraham! If they
want "strange fires" they know where to go for it. They certainly do not have to come to the synagogue to get it.

*

II

ELOQUENT SILENCE

It is difficult enough to be articulate when one has something to say. It is infinitely more difficult when one has nothing to say.

Nothing is more false than the adage "speech is silver; silence golden". When speech is called for, silence is out of place. When silence is called for, speech is out of place.

The art of the matter is to know precisely *when* speech is called for and *when* silence is indicated.

Most of us talk when we shouldn't and are silent when we shouldn't be.

The classic category of misplaced talk is gossip. Gossip is gratuitous and frequently leads to calumny and character defamation.

The classic category of misplaced silence is tolerated injustice. The cowed silence that frequently prevails in the wake of criminality is the soil in which violence and catastrophe flourish.

McCarthyism was a product of loose talk. Hitlerism was a product of loose silence.

Had the Sanhedria had the courage to speak the one word "Guilty!" when young Herod appeared before it, there would never have been a King Herod to inundate an emaciated Judea with innocent blood.

A teacher of mine told me once. "If you have nothing to say, don't elaborate on it." Sound advice, indeed, for politicians, orators and preachers!

The corrolary is, however, equally true. If there is something to be said and it is worthwhile hearing, failure to say it is an act of moral abortion.

Just think how often we find God commanding Moses: *"Speak unto the children of Israel!"*

Yet one of the most eloquent statements in the Bible was made by a *silent* Aaron. (See Leviticus 10:3 for the details).

Eloquence is a matter neither of speech nor of silence. It is a matter of timing. The crowing of the cock at sunrise is the epitome of eloquence. At high noon the same sound is redundant and meaningless.

Both speech and silence are commentaries. Misplaced silence is as hard to undo and fully as devastating as misplaced speech.

We have a *b'racha* over food and wine and lightning. I propose a b'racha more important, perhaps, than all others, to be recited every morning upon awakening:

"I pray to Thee O Lord My God to teach me what to say."

TAZRIA-MEZORA • תזריע-מצורע

QUARANTINE!

An evil tongue is just about the most deadly weapon in the world. It can rend families asunder, disrupt the bonds of mutual trust, poison the atmosphere and annihilate the foundations of peace.

I shall never forget Guy de Maupassant's classic tale, "A Piece of String". It recounts the slow death of a tragic victim of character assassination. It exposes graphically the diabolical effects of malicious rumor and vile innuendo. It is a stark and terrifying story because it is basically not fiction at all.

"Whosoever delighteth in life and loveth days of good: keep thy tongue from evil and thy lips from speaking deceit."* Those are the words of our Psalms. Conversely, our Great Rabbis of blessed memory believed that leprosy is the punishment of God which He visits upon rumor-mongers and purveyors of sinister gossip.

Metaphorically, if not literally, the latter view is perfectly tenable. For just as leprosy is contagious and just as one leper may

* Psalms 34

disease an entire community, so can an evil tongue contaminate the whole of society. Loose talk gratuitously dispensed by people of loose morality can unleash the fury of Sheol upon any association of men. And the result is violence, terror and perdition.

What can be done, nay, what *must* be done to avert catastrophical contamination by the mendacious?

Our Torah reading for this Sabbath, dealing as it does with lepers and leprosy, has the answer:

"The leper in whom the plague is...he is unclean...outside of the camp shall his dwelling be."—Leviticus 13:45—

Quarantine!

ACHARAI MOS • אחרי מות

THE EARTH CAN VOMIT

"And the Lord spoke unto Moses, after the death of the two sons of Aaron, speak unto Aaron thy brother, that he come... etc."—Leviticus 16:1, 2—

Remarkable! Aaron has just buried two of his beloved children who died under extremely shocking and tragic circumstances. He has hardly caught his breath and already he is being ordered back to the gruelling routine of his work.

Truth to tell, this was not cruelty but an act of real kindness. The alleviation of sorrow will not be attained by abrupt retirement from one's duties. Quite the contrary! Constructive, creative, meaningful work holds out the best hope for triumph over one's personal tragedy. Activity in behalf of others constitutes the best therapy for the malady of being sorry for one's self.

*

"And Aaron shall present the bullock of the sin-offering, which is for himself, and make atonement for himself and for his house."—Leviticus 16:6—

"Do as I say, not as I do" is a well known witticism which takes cognizance of the frequent failure to practice what one preaches. The Torah will have none of that. It will not permit anyone—be he ever so august—to proceed to the purification of others before he has purified himself. Even the great Isaiah was not ready to go out and preach to the people of Israel until he himself was thoroughly cleansed: *"Then flew unto me one of the seraphim, with a glowing stone in his hand, which he had taken with the tongs from off the altar. And he touched my mouth with it and said: 'Lo, this hath touched thy lips, and thine iniquity is taken away, and thy sin expiated'."** Only then was the prophet ready to respond to the call of prophecy with the words: "Here am I; send me!" Jewish liturgical tradition has been in the spirit of this idea in affixing the moving "Hineni" preface to the service of the cantor about to plead in behalf of the congregation. The burden of this prayer is the fearful sense of inadequacy experienced by the "sheliach tsibur" who is so mindful of the adage "Physician, heal thyself!"

In the modern maelstrom of materialistic mire, the spiritual leader must above all beware of the treachery of the ground underfoot. For if he be sucked in by it, how can he ever hope to extricate others?

*

"And the land was defiled, therefore I did visit the iniquity thereof upon it, and the land vomited out her inhabitants."— Leviticus 18:25—

A powerful, significant metaphor is herein employed by the Torah. God's world is good and true and beautiful. The corruption within it is induced by man. God intended all of his creation and all of his creatures to perpetuate the pristine purity which obtained "In the beginning." By its very nature the earth is full of kindness and bounty. It freely offers up to man and

Isaiah 6:6,7

animal the fullest supply of sustenance and comfort, receiving
absolutely nothing in return. The earth is the very epitome of
unselfish generosity and in that sense is an extension of the
nature of God. When man perpetrates evil on earth, he is grafting upon it something alien and hostile to its character, something thoroughly indigestible. *"And the land vomited out its
inhabitants."*

Perhaps we are headed for this ultimate denouement. Perhaps
the evil we have sired on earth has just about overfilled the cup
of its endurance. Perhaps the emetive being fiendlishly brewed
by ourselves is the thermonuclear eradicator—deadly and final.

KEDOSHIM ● קדושים

I

THE ESSENCE OF JUDAISM

Excerpts from *Kedoshim*—Leviticus 19:20—
Ye shall be holy; for I the Lord your God am holy.

*

Ye shall not steal; neither shall ye deal falsely, nor lie one to
another. And ye shall not swear by My name falsely, so that thou
profane the name of thy God.

*

Thou shalt not oppress thy neighbor nor rob him; the wages
of a hired servant shall not abide with thee all night until
the morning.

*

Thou shalt not curse the deaf nor put a stumbling-block before
the blind but thou shalt fear Thy God. (Though you may have
nothing to fear from the deaf man or the blind man.—My
parentheses).

Thou shalt not walk about as a talebearer among thy people;
neither shalt thou stand by idly over thy neighbor's blood.

*

Thou shalt not take vengeance nor bear any grudge against
the children of thy people, but thou shalt love thy neighbor as
thyself: I am the Lord.

*

And if a stranger sojourn with thee in your land, ye shall not
do him wrong. The stranger that sojourneth with you shall be
unto you as the native among you and thou shalt love him as
thyself; for ye were strangers in the land of Egypt: I am the
Lord your God.

*

Ye shall not pervert justice in meteyard, in weight or in
measure. Just balances, just weights, a just ephah, and a just
hin shall ye have.

*

Sanctify yourselves therefore, and be ye holy; for I am the
Lord your God.

Just a Thought: In the Jewish way of life Godliness and humanity are inseparable. Decency and human love can grow only
from the roots of sanctity and Godly love. There is no secularism
in our faith. All of our life, our being, our essence must be
steeped in holiness if it is to be Jewish life, Jewish being, Jewish
essence.

A good Jew must be God-conscious.

II

A GOOD JEW IS GOD-CONSCIOUS

Leviticus chapter nineteen which is read in the Torah this
week is a masterful synopsis of the morality of Judaism. Let us
look into it with some sensitivity.

"Ye shall be holy for I the Lord your God am holy."—The
supreme purpose of human life is the perpetual effort to emulate
the moral perfection of the deity. *That* man's life has meaning
whose mind's eye is forever focused upon the image of God. A
ladder set up on the earth and with its top reaching towards
heaven—that is the ideal which ought to inform the dreams of
all Jews.

*"Ye shall fear every man his father and his mother and ye
shall keep my Sabbaths: I am the Lord your God."*—A moral
society must hold its elders in reverence and must create for
itself an island of spirituality in the roaring, materialistic universe. The Sabbath is precisely such an island and its spirit is a
light tower amidst the darkness of human doubts and fears. The
Sabbath can impart balance to biased living and perspective to
distorted views.

*"And thou shalt not glean thy vineyard, neither shalt thou
gather its fallen fruit; thou shalt leave them for the poor...I am
the Lord your God."* The desire for material increment should
not become an all-consuming obsession. To "corner the market"
on the bounty of the earth is to violate the precept "that thy
brother may live with thee", expounded elsewhere in Leviticus
(25:36). Communism of property is not advocated by the Torah.
But the capitalism whose holy motto is "rugged individualism"
is roundly condemned by Moasic teaching.

*"And ye shall not swear by my name falsely so that thou pro-
fane the name of thy God: I am the Lord".*—God is the perfection of The Good. Anything associated with His name that is
evil, any use of His name to justify any hurt inflicted upon man
or woman is a dastardly desecration of the Spirit of God. The
ghastly Inquisitions of Spain and Portugal, the earlier butcheries
that masqueraded as Crusades, the witch-burning in the Salem of
yesterday and in the Washington of today and Francisco Franco's
Catholic "piety" are all examples of perjury by God's name.

*"Thou shalt not curse the deaf, nor put a stumbling block
before the blind, but thou shalt fear thy God: I am the Lord."*—

Power should be the province of those who take no advantage. To exercise self control when no other controls stand in the way is to achieve indubitable strength.. The lively ears of the hearing and the unobstructed eyes of the seeing will temper discordant voices and treacherous feet. But the only tempering influence in the presence of the deaf and the blind is the still, small voice from within us.

That is the heart of the matter: the still small voice within us. For that still, small voice is the voice of God.

And it can only then be heard when there are not too many distracting sounds to drown it.

III

CURSING A DEAF MAN

"Thou shalt not curse the deaf."—Leviticus 19:14—

This simple sentence from the Reading for this Sabbath is of extensive significance. Obviously it was intended to embrace more than its literal connotation. It was meant to warn against the abuse of a person who is not in a position to defend himself.

The case of cursing a deaf man is only the dramatic classical example of the immorality involved in a situation which is basically unfair. It is an established principle in law that an accused party has the right to confront his accusers. A verdict of "guilty" brought in without such a confrontation is patently a mockery of justice.

Everyone seems to appreciate the rightness of this with respect to any defendant in a court of law. The trouble with most people, however, is that their definition of "a court of law" is extremely narrow and limited.. A court of law is not only an arm of statecraft with such trappings as judge and jury and the power to impose sentence upon offenders. This is the narrowest of possible constructions. Actually every human being is a court of law insofar as every human being is capable of formulating a

judgment in his mind with respect to any other human being.. If
any of us forms a certain impression, opinion or attitude concerning somebody else, the effect is of a microcosmic court of
law sitting in judgment..

If this is true, *and it is true,* then abusing someone behind his
back in the presence of another is tantamount to denying a defendant the essential right of confronting his accuser. It is a clear
violation of the Torah law "Thou shalt not curse the deaf."

Yet this is what many of us do much of the time. Nary a conversation springs to life between two people than the abuse or
severe criticism of a third (and absent) party emerges on the
verbal arena. Reputations are often sullied or ruined behind the
back of some innocent soul who, since his ear is deaf to the
sound and the fury of his assailants, is powerless to defend himself.

The person who while innocent of behind-the-back calumny
himself does not however refrain from lending an ear to it, is
equally guilty for he is encouraging a wrong and cooperating in
its execution. The irony of the whole situation consists of the
fact that in an atmosphere of this kind the very people who
abuse or villify are themselves especial targets of villification
behind *their* backs. It is a fact that they do not add to their
popularity as they become known for their habitual denunciation
of others.

EMOR   •   אמור

CHILLUL HASHEM

*"They shall be holy unto their God and not profane the name
of their God".*—Leviticus 21:6—

This passage from the weekly Pentateuchal reading is among
the most basic in the Torah. *Kiddush Hashem* means "Sanctifica-
tion of the Divine Name" and "Chillul Hashem" is the reverse:

desecration.. Now the former is a level very difficult for the ordinary human being to attain. Indeed *"Kiddush Hashem"* in Jewish tradition is most frequently applied to those martyrs of our people who laid down their very lives for sacred Jewish ideals. To be able to rise to that spiritual altitude is a privilege that is not accorded to many.

But the converse side of this concept, that of refraining from *"Chillul Hashem"*, is a demand that can be made of every Jew. Even the least gifted among us is commanded to engage in nothing that will lead to the desecration of the name of God. And there is no excuse whatever for any Jew worthy of the name who fails to abide by this commandment.

Just what is *"Chillul Hashem"?* Tersely defined, it is an act committed by an individual Jew in the full glare of public attention which brings disgrace to other Jews and to Judaism.

A Jew committing murder is guilty not only of homicide but also of *"Chillul Hashem"*. And thus for theft and thus for violence.

A Jew whose synagogue manner and attitude falls short of the utmost sense of reverence is guilty of "Chillul Hashem". I would say that conversation during services and such habits as "lounging" in the pews or slovenly dress are manifestations of "Chillul Hashem".

A Jew who is habitually loud and indecorous is guilty of "Chillul Hashem".

A Jew who publicly violates Jewish tradition in the presence of these to whom it is sacred is guilty of *"Chillul Hashem"*. In this category is the act of smoking on the Sabbath directly in front of a traditional synagogue.

A Jewish group which holds public business conferences and meetings on the Sabbath and other Jewish Holy Days is guilty of *"Chillul Hashem."*

A Jewish group whose membership embraces Jews of all religious persuasion and which holds a *trefe* function for said membership is guilty of *"Chillul Hashem"*.

Resort hotels which advertise holiday services side by side with night club acts and golf tournaments are guilty of "Chillul Hashem". (Paranthetically I may add that "Days of Awe" services in lush hotels are a *"Chillul Hashem"* to begin with.)

Monte Carlos and "Cafe society" entertainments sponsored by synagogue affiliates upon synagogue premises are demonstrations of *"Chillul Hashem"*.

Elmer Berger and Lessing Rosenwald casting malicious aspersions at "Klal Yisroel" before the forum of American public opinion are past-masters of the "art" of *"Chillul Hashem"*.

*

We were created in the image of God. *"Chillul Hashem"* is the plastic surgery undergone by those who would efface that image.

BEHAR • בהר

"GIVE ME LIBERTY..."

Liberty and tyranny can never reach *a modus vivendi* in the long run. One or the other must die.

Liberty is not the privilege of the few but the God-given right of all.

Liberty cannot breathe in an atmosphere of fear. Truth— unhampered, unshackled, uncowed—is the very soul of liberty.

Liberty cannot function in the spheres of injustice, for injustice is predicated upon the doctrine of power. Power is the implacable ememy of liberty.

Liberty cannot flourish upon the soil of economic inequity. Freedom to starve and to ail and to suffer is not freedom at all but the very essence of bondage. Economic inequity is moral iniquity.

Liberty is not a statue but a living thing. It is not a word but a condition. It is not an abstract concept but a vital reality. To

possess   liberty is to possess food and clothing and shelter and
dignity and self-respect.

Liberty without these things stands exposed as the sham catch-
word of the oppressors, the exploiters and the demagogues.

Liberty is freedom *from* violence, not freedom to do violence.
Violence is the instrument of tyranny. Peace is the handmaiden
of liberty.

Liberty is in total harmony with law. Tyranny is intimately
allied with lawlessness.

Liberty is the daughter of God, betrothed by Him to all men.
Tyranny is the creature of the devil who prostitutes her dubious
charms for the price of men's souls.

The great utterance of the Torah portion this Sabbath (Leviticus 25:10) reads: "Proclaim liberty throughout the land unto
all the inhabitants thereof."

A truer observation on the nature of liberty has never been
made. Liberty cannot be delimited, either geographically or
numerically.

Liberty is a commodity which can neither be imported nor
exported. It must be home grown. It is the most precious of all
the resources of a nation.

BECHUKOSAI   •   בחוקותי

I

"AND GIVE THEE PEACE."

"And I will give peace in the land and ye shall lie down and
none shall make you afraid."—Leviticus 26:6.—

Peace is at the pinnacle of Judaic idealism. The passion for
peace in Israel has been surpassed only by the passion for justice, and with good reason. Without a foundation of justice no
structure of peace can stand. So that the quest for justice has
really been the quest for peace.

I should like to bring to your attention some of the hundreds of passages in the Bible which attest to the exalted place occupied by the ideal of peace in the hierarchy of Jewish values.

"The Lord lift up His face to you and give you peace."—Numbers 6:26.

"And Gideon built there an altar and he called it: The Lord of Peace"—Judges 6:24.

"And ye shall say: May it thus be throughout thy life: and peace be to thee, and peace to thy house and to all that thou hast be peace"—1 Samuel 25:6.

"Unto David and unto his seed and unto his house and unto his throne may there be peace forever from the Lord."—I Kings 2:33.

"If he but take hold of my strength, make peace with me; make peace with me."—Isaiah 27:5.

"And the work of righteousness shall be peace and the effect of righteousness, quietness and security forever."—Isaiah 32:17.

"How beautiful upon the mountains are the feet of the messenger of good tidings that publisheth peace, that announceth tidings of happiness."—Isaiah 52:7.

"Peace, peace to him that is afar off and to him that is near, saith the Lord."—Isaiah 57:19.

"For thus hath said the Lord: Behold I will extend to her peace like a river."—Isaiah 66:12.

"Greater will be the glory of this latter house than that of the former, saith the Lord of hosts; and in this place will I give peace."—Haggai 2:9.

"These are the things that ye shall do: speak ye the truth every man to his neighbor, with truth and the law of peace judge ye in your gates."—Zechariah 8:16.

"Who is the man that desireth life, loveth many days that he may see happiness? Guard thy tongue from evil and thy lips from speaking deceit; depart from evil and do good, seek peace and pursue it."—Psalms 34:13-15.

"Observe the perfect man and regard the upright for there is a happy future to the man of peace."—Psalms 37:37.

"I am for peace."—Psalms 120:7.

"Pray ye for peace of Jerusalem: may those that love thee prosper. May there be peace within thy walls...For the sake of my brethren and my friends, let me now speak: Peace be within thee."—Psalms 122:6-8.

"Peace shall be upon Israel."—Psalms 125:5 and 128:6

"Her ways are ways of pleasantness and all her paths are peace."—Proverbs 3:17.

"For the counsellors of peace there is joy."—Proverbs 12:20.

"He maketh peace in His high places."—Job 25:2.

"And he sent letters to all the Jews to the hundred and twenty seven provinces of the Kingdom of Ahaseurus, words of peace and truth."—Esther 9:30.

"Fear not, O man, greatly beloved, peace be unto thee; be strong, yea be strong."—Daniel 10:19.

*

O God, King of Israel: When?

II

MY GOD

I regard myself as a religious man because my mind is never devoid of the consciousness of God. God is not a matter of speculation or conjecture for me. He is not even an object of faith with me. God is for me reality because I am conditioned and motivated, governed and actuated, moved and stimulated by my conviction of His being and His uniquity.

There are many variables in my life, as is the case indeed with all human beings. If there is one rule which is always operative in the life process it is the rule of change. Biologically and organically all matter is in constant flux, never retaining its sameness for even the fraction of a second. As Zeno put it: "You can't step into the same river twice".

In all of this perpetual motion, unsteadiness and disequilibrium there is for me one constant, in any event. That constant is God. In a wildly whirling and mercurial setting, He is The Unfailing Pillar, The Rock, The Eternity by Whose being alone reality is established and stability retained.

To me God is a necessity, the most vital of all necessities, for without cognizance of Him, I can find no anchorage. He is the Great Stabilizer of my personality, the Restorer of Equilibrium, the Imparter of Meaning. I fully understand David's allusion to Him as a "rod" and a "staff" and I can fully appreciate David's exalted outcry: "Yea though I walk in the valley of the shadow of death I shall fear no evil for Thou art with me". To the *homo religiosis* this is not poetry. It is truth. It is The Truth.

In our faith, the faith of Abraham, Isaac, Jacob, Moses, David and Jeremiah, God is not only the Creator of the Universe, the King of Kings but the God of Man, "the God of the Spirit of all flesh", the personal God of all who believe. He is not remote and not aloof and not abstract but He is near, He is here, He is dear.

Thus speaks Jeremiah in the Prophetic reading this Sabbath:

"The Lord is my strength and my stronghold and my refuge ...Blessed is the man that trusteth in the Lord and whose trust the Lord is. For he shall be as a tree planted by the waters and that spreadeth out its roots by the river and he shall not see when heat cometh. But its foliage shall be luxuriant; And shall not be anxious in the year of drought, neither shall cease from yielding fruit."—Jeremiah 16:1; 17:7,8—

III

HOLINESS AND THE MAN

The Book of Leviticus will be concluded with the Torah reading for this coming Shabbos. This third of the Five Books of Moses is notable in several respects. For one thing it embraces some of the most difficult concepts of Judaic ritual practice. For another it presents a rich and multi-faceted picture of the ancient Temple cult of the Hebrews as well as a comprehensive compendium of Priestly and Levite regulations. No section of the Torah offers a more rewarding insight   into the marrow and sinew of early Judaism than does this book of Va'yikro.

The recurrent theme of the Book is "Holiness". Again and again is this idea stressed and in every conceivable context. Witness the following random examples:

"Ye shall be holy for I the Lord your God am holy;" "Sanctify yourselves and be holy;" "Thou shalt sanctify him for he offers the bread of your God"; "And they shall not profane the holy things of the children of Israel"; "For it is a jubilee; it shall be holy unto you"; "All that any man giveth of such to the Lord shall be holy"; "Through them that are near unto me will I be sanctified".

What is this thing called "holiness" or "sanctity"? It is, good people, nothing more nor less than the soul of the Jewish Religion. It is the conscious and deliberate effort of the human being to come closer to God. It is the incessant and systematic striving for moral perfection through a prescribed regimen of behavior, a regimen calculated to ennoble the personality, refine the character, and distill the pettiness of the individual—a regimen, moreover, so all-inclusive as to confront its practitioner with perpetual reminders of his established goal—proximity to God.

Jewish ritual is a spiritual diet designed to safeguard the well-being of the soul in much the same fashion as gastronomic diets are designed to safeguard the well-being of the body. This is the basic significance of Kashruth. This is the *raison d'etre* of the Sabbath. This is the inner meaning of the laws of familial purity. This is the concept of "holiness" and the core of Judaism. For Judaism there is no dichotomy in the realm of human life as between the "earthly" and the "heavenly", the "ethical" and the "religious", the things that are "unto Caesar" and the things that are "unto God". Judaism—as a teacher of mine once put it—is co-extensive with life. "Holiness" is not a word restricted to the vocabulary of Temple and Worship. In Judaism it is as fully applicable to honesty in the market place, to justice in the law, to decency in personal relationship, to love of one's wife, to sympathy with one's neighbor. There are no "Holy Men" as a caste in Judaism. The entire congregation of Israel is holy in the sense that it is dedicated to the ideal of approach to God.

"And ye shall make holy the fiftieth year and proclaim liberty throughout the land to all the inhabitants thereof."—Leviticus 25:10—There you have it in a word: *To be holy is to be free.*

במדבר

•

BAMIDBAR

BAMIDBAR • במדבר

NUMBERS IS A WRONG TRANSLATION

This Sabbath the reading is begun of the Fourth Book of the Torah, *Bemidbar,* which is translated into English as The Book of Numbers. Now the word Bemidbar doesn't mean numbers at all. It means "In the Wilderness." Pondering the discrepancy in the Hebrew and English rendering, the thought occurs that there is an interesting commentary here on the nature of American Jewish civilization.

There has been much talk in recent years of the resurgence of Jewish interest, Jewish feeling, Jewish culture and the like within our American community. Those who view the picture with cheerful optimism point to the phenomenal growth of congregations and membership and organizational strength in the past decade or so. They speak of the many millions of dollars that have been spent in our generation on the construction of new synagogue buildings and community centers. They point to the fact that young suburban communities in particular are mushrooming forth in every Jewish direction. Young married folks, they say with pride, are leading the vanguard of the return to the Synagogue as well as to other important spheres of Jewish interest.

I don't want to put a damper upon this enthusiastic acclamation of an American Jewish renaissance. But I must express serious doubt as to whether or not the optimists in our midst are not permitting themselves to be intoxicated by the magic potion of Numbers; as to whether or not they are substituting a purely misleading quantitative phenomenon for the truer image of qualitative development. It seems to me that substantial increases in Synagogue membership, for example, ought not to be equated necessarily with a corresponding intensification of loyalty to Jewish precepts and to Jewish tradition. The fact of the matter re-

mains that despite the undoubted increase in the number of Jews
affiliated with Synagogues, attendance at the Sabbath Services
of most American congregations has increased very little and in
many cases not at all. If someone were to produce a reliable
statistic, for example, to the effect that there is a greater proportion of Jews observing the laws of kashruth today than there
was in the past, I should be impressed. If someone were to produce
evidence of a larger measure of Sabbath observers amongst American Jews than there has been in the past, I should be delighted.
If someone were to demonstrate that Jewish literacy amongst the
younger adult generation of our American communities is on the
increase, I should be overjoyed. If someone were to testify to the
fact that more Jewish books in any language are being bought
and read today than in the past, I should be thrilled. But the
sadness of the statistical situation lies in the fact that all of the
many Numbers cited, quoted, imagined or alleged are just that:
Numbers pure and simple, if I may be pardoned the tautology
involved, numerical Numbers.

They are Numbers involving people, structures, membership
cards and the like. They are not Numbers involving ideas, ideals,
principles and everything that pertains to the heart rather than
to the "capita." Until such time as the quality of Jewish belongingness is improved, the number of Jewish "belongers" will remain relatively insignificant and the expression "In the Wilderness" will continue to be mistranslated.

NASO • נשא

SAMSON: A HERO WITH CLAY FEET

The reading from the prophets this Sabbath is all about
Samson, a figure as fabled and as legendary as one may find in
the Bible. When I was a little boy, the Samson stories were my
delight, fully the equivalent of the Superman-type tales swal-

lowed so hungrily by present day children. Samson was my glorious hero, my knight in shining armor, my invincible idol triumphing over the forces of evil, trouncing the "bad guys" with inexorable finality.

How in my grieving heart did I curse Delilah, the sorceress, who engineered my hero's humiliating defeat! The tears of my chagrin and frustration flowed all the more freely at the conviction that the dowfall of my idol was so *unnecessary,* so much the result of fate's mere whim. How shall I explain the feeling? Let me perhaps put it this way. Your team is ahead by a run in the last half of the ninth inning. The enemy has two men out and men on second and third. Your pitcher delivers a beautiful throw from which the hitter tries to pull his bat away. But accidentally the ball hits the bat and pops over second base in sickly fashion as two runs score and all is lost. Now you could have borne up under a solid, deliberate line drive hit. But to suffer the pangs of defeat through so capricious and *unnecessary* a stroke of fate — ah, that is more than the human heart can bear. A Samson beaten fair and square on the honorable field of battle would be a heartbreaking sight to behold. But a Samson crushed beneath the blades of a harlot's scissors—fie, fie, ye gods!

I have to some extent grown up since my childhood adoration of the son of Manoah. Nostalgia still belabors me with sorrow as I reread the saga of Samson. But my grief is considerably mitigated today by the sober thought that *far from being capricious and haphazard, Samson's downfall was necessary and inevitable by the very nature of the Bible's weltanschaüng.* Samson is the most atypical hero Jewish lore has produced. Indeed Samson is not a Jewish hero at all. He is all muscle and might. He is as earthy as the guts of the lion from which he licked up honey. He is as unspiritual as the jawbone of the ass with which he licked thousands of the Phillistines. Indeed, if the irreverance will be pardoned, Samson *is* a phillistine, sharing their passion for the exercise of brute force and their orgiasmic dedication to the pleasures of the flesh.

Samson's victories are the functions of sheer physical power. They may be gratifying to infantile minds. They must be galling to those who think of meaningful victory only in terms of the triumph of superior ideas over those which are inferior. And the whole of Jewish history testifies to the fact that this is the only kind of victory that can have any meaning or value. If Samson's weapons are physical, he will ultimately have to pay the price of defeat by physical means. And Delilah, the harlot, is the perfect embodiment of the physical—naked, incarnate, unadorned.

No, sir, Mr. Menahem Beigin, I can't buy your Samsonite luggage.

B'HA'ALOSCHA • בהעלתך

I

ZECHARIA CALLING!

"Not by might, nor by power, but by My spirit, saith the Lord of hosts."—Zecharia 4:6—

This great utterance from the prophetic reading of the coming Sabbath ought to be inscribed in bold letters on the walls of the Conference Rooms in Geneva for all the delegates to see. I mean *all* the delegates, American as well as Russian, British as well as Chinese.

For it is clear that the impasse at Geneva is the direct outgrowth of power-powered thinking. The West and the East are apparently bent upon equating justice with force and truth with violence. Justice is *not* the interest of the stronger, Socrates said at one time and the statement remains absolutely true today.

Indeed, the statement is more true today than it ever was, for it should be quite obvious to any thinking mind that since the advent of the thermonuclear bomb the concepts of the strong and the weak have largely perished. *All* nations today are on the weak side in the face of the Invincible Weapon of universal destruction. All nations and all peoples today are actually arrayed against only one enemy: The Angel of Death, who even now lurks ominously over our shoulders and breathes his malodorous breath in audible and grotesque gasps.

The issue is not Korea or Laos or Cuba or the Congo or Communism or Capitalism. The issue is specifically and indubitably *life or death,* life or death for *all concerned,* regardless of geographical or ideological demarcations.

The time for the imposition of the will of one nation upon another—be that will benevolent or malevolent—is long since past. All nations must now be left free to choose their way of life no matter how unwise that choice is likely to be. A way of life once chosen can yet be altered. The door is not slammed with irretrievable finality. But should we allow stupidity and pettiness to catapult us into a Third World War, we shall be slamming the door forever upon all of us who live here on earth.

Let the spirit of the Lord prevail over the anachronistic concepts of might and power. Let the spirit of the Lord hover once more over the waters, bringing order into chaos and light into darkness.

Let there be light!

II

THE VOICE OF THE BAGEL

Several people can *look* at the same object without *seeing* the same thing. The image retained in the mind is a function of two factors: (a) the matter observed (b) the mind that does the observing. Obviously while factor (a) is a constant, factor (b) is a variable and it varies from person to person.

I once attended a concert recital in Chicago's orchestra hall with two acquaintances, a high-school teacher of literature and a man who made a mint in bagels. The soloist was a world-

renowned tenor who that night was in exceptionally fine voice.
After his first number, a meticulously executed German *lied,* the
teacher exclaimed "What delicacy of phrasing!" the bagel man
said "Cheez what a fat son of —that croaker is!"

When I delivered my first sermon in my first congregation
back in 1942, two unsolicited reactions were brought back to my
ears by a solicitous usher. He reported one man as saying: "This
young fella will make a terrific speaker one day." And the other's
comment: "This kid's no Stephen Wise!"

Throughout life one encounters the eternal conflict between
the voice of the sensitive, feeling, perceptive man and the voice
of the harsh, crude and boorish creature which, with your per-
mission, I shall describe as the voice of the bagel. It's an old,
old story and our Torah-portion for the week offers a striking
example.

The children of Israel marching through the Sinai wilderness
have just been witness to a series of sublime phenomena unheard
of ever before. A powerful enemy was destroyed for them, a Sea
was divided before them, the thundering word of God from the
Creator Himself came to them, and manna-food from the heavens
was rained upon them. Inspiring! you would say, feeling at the
same time the utter failure of the word to do justice to the
events. But hearken to the voice of the bagel: "And the mixed
multitude that was among them fell a-lusting; and the children
of Israel also wept on their part, and said: Would that we were
given flesh to eat! We remember the fish which we were wont
to eat in Egypt for naught, the cucumbers and the melons and
the leeks and the onions and the garlic. But now our soul is
dried away; there is nothing at all; we have naught save this
manna to look at."—Numbers 11:4-6.

Pharaoh is subdued and the murmurers remember the fish!
The Red Sea is divided and the grumblers talk of cucumbers!
Water is drawn from a rock and the rabble shouts "Melon!" The
Celestial Soloist proclaims: "I am the Lord thy God...thou shalt

have no other Gods before me!" And the Voice of the Bagel
responds in chorus "Leeks! Onions! Garlic!"

A glory-saturated event has befallen our Judaic generation.
The rebirth of Israel is a fact so stupendous as to belong to the
same order of Sinaitic events above cited. The sensitive Jew, he
of ever the slightest sense of history and of the slightest tinge
of poetry in his heart is overwhelmed with the magnificence, the
splendor, the miraculousness, yes, the very divinity of it all.

Yet even here the Voice of the Bagel is not to be silenced.
Like flying saucers some of these bagels take whirlwind trips to
the Jewish State and then return to their American fleshpots and
announce that they are "disillusioned" with Israel because
("grumble - mumble - bumble") and also because ("bumble -
mumble- grumble") and that therefore they are "not yet ready"
to announce their UJA pledge for this year (or, for that matter,
to redeem their pledges of yesteryear).

If we could only learn that the Bagel has a big hole in it!

SHELACH • שלח

A MAN IS TEN FEET TALL

Some years ago I witnessed a very fine television play entitled
"A Man is Ten Feet Tall." I thought the message was exceptionally moral and beautiful. In graphic dramatic terms it illustrated
the great heights to which a human being can attain if he
possesses an inner dignity and a measure of deep respect for the
humanity within him. Now self-respect is not to be equated with
scornful pride or arrogant egotism. It means simply that a man
recognizes that he partakes of divine attributes, that he was
indeed created in the image of God and that, therefore, it is
his sacred responsibility not to descrate this nobility within him.
If he does, then he sinks to the level of the members of the
lower echelon of the animal kingdom.

*

The incident of the spies whom Moses sent to explore the promised land—a story beautifully told in our Torah reading for the week—is evidence of the chronic failure of many human beings to appreciate the divine potential within them. These spies came back utterly crestfallen. They were overwhelmed by the huge barriers they had to surmount in order to win the land of Canaan. They were reduced to a state of paralytic fear when contemplating the enormity of the task. They saw only impediments, obstacles, snags. They failed to see the goal which should have rendered all of these difficulties relatively meaningless.

"Howbeit," said they in their report, "the people who dwell in the land are fierce, and the cities are fortified, and very great; and moreover we saw the children of giants there. Amalek dwelleth in the land of the South; and the Hittie and the Jebusite and the Amorite dwell in the mountains; and the Canaanite dwelleth by the sea and by the side of the Jordan."—Numbers 13:28,29.

Giants, Hittites, Jebusites, Canaanites, fortifications—all "reasons" why *not* to go forward. Such "reasons" are the easiest things in the world to find. But all of them must pale into insignificance alongside of the human will *yes* to go forward. This is the will and the spirit that makes a giant of man, that makes a man Ten Feet Tall.

Such a man was Caleb who, along with Joshua, constituted the minority opinion among the spies. Note carefully that in his dissenting opinion Caleb does not deny the existence of any one of the enumerated obstacles. What *does* he say? He says simply:

"We shall go up *at once* and possess it, for we shall certainly overcome it!"—Numbers 13:30.

What made Caleb so sure? It was the irresistible spark of divinity within him which (he knew) when exercised would reduce all obstacles to ashes.

A man is Ten Feet Tall—but only if he rises to the full measure of his stature.

KORACH • קרח

THE RABBI AND HIS CONGREGATION

At the recently held convention of the Metropolitan Council of the United Synagogue one of the several interesting seminars was on "The Rabbi and His Congregation". It was the best attended of all the seminars, as might be expected, and it featured in turn a congregational president and a Rabbi, not, and wisely so, of the same synagogue.

I did not participate in the discussion because I was more interested in hearing than in being heard. However I do have some observations to make on the subject and I should think that you are entitled to read them.

alef: Goodwill is the most necessary item in a healthy Rabbi-congregation relationship. If that obtains then the congregation's criticism of its Rabbi is honest *and* acceptable since that goodwill preclude personal axe grinding. Where goodwill is lacking there is frequently a tendency to camouflage anti-Rabbi animosity behind a facade of "principle" or "idealism".

beth: Conversely, a Rabbi's criticism of his congregation must be suspect if he is actuated by bitterness or frustration. It is as the Rabbi of Berditchev once shouted after he heard an itinerant magid pour fire, brimstone and all hell upon the heads of the worshippers: Don't believe a word of it, God. Poor penniless fellow has four grown daughters to marry off!"

gimmel: A Rabbi cannot afford to be "rabbit eared". Human nature being what it is, people will always fire shafts of criticism at convenient and conspicuous targets. The Rabbi qualifies on both grounds. If he takes to heart every report of adverse comment brought back to his ears, he can never be happy nor is he likely to live long.

daled: *A Rabbi should not play favorites.* He should not concentrate on cultivating the favor of the affluent or the influen-

tial in preference to the not-so-affluent and the not-so-influential.
To do this may be politic (though I doubt even that) but it is
certainly not Jewish. Korach is legendarily reported to have been
enormously wealthy yet Moses made no attempt to curry any
special favor with him though, if Moses had done so, Korach
might not have started his Moses-must-go rebellion.

hay: The Rabbi must not attempt to dictate. He must rather
do everything in his power to *teach* what he sees as the truth.
This is not to say that he must capitulate to the will of the congregation if he regards it as religiously wrong. It does mean that
he ought not to pound a table and say: "Gentlemen, this is the
way it has got to be, take it or leave it!" Rather ought he to say:
"Gentlemen, this is the right and the religious thing to do in my
opinion and let me try to show you why." If the gentlemen agree
—fine! If they do not, the Rabbi's challenge to teach becomes
that much greater. If ultimately he fails in obtaining a course of
religious action or procedure which is to him of *paramount*
moment, why, then, he and his congregation ought to part
company amicably.

Vav: Every Rabbi, being human, likes to be held in the high
esteem of his congregation. But no sensible Rabbi, it seems to me,
would relish being exalted to the level of saint or angel. The air
on that level is much too rarified even for a Rabbi and no sound
is more shattering and jarring than that of a fallen angel. (See
Genesis 6:1-8)

Zayen: It would be very helpful if a Rabbi made the congregation feel that when he preaches, he includes himself in the
preachment and where he doesn't always practice what he
preaches it is not hypocrisy but frailty.

Heth: The Rabbi should respect his people as human beings
deserve to be respected. The Congregation should respect its Rabbi
on two grounds: a) as a human being b) as a symbol of Torah.
The symbol will never be perfect as long as flesh and blood
embody it. But the honest "symbol" always tries. And, please
remember, being a "symbol" isn't easy.

If you think it is, please to consult once again the Torah lection for this Sabbath which begins with the assault of "layman" Korach for no visible reason upon "Rabbi" Moses, son of Amram.

CHUKAS • חקת

THE OLD ORDER CHANGETH...

An aura of sadness pervades the Torah reading of the week as all at once the three central personalities of the Exodus and the trek through the wilderness are doomed to death on the very threshold of the Promised Land. The deaths of Miriam and Aaron, children of Amram, are in fact recorded in the twentieth chapter of Numbers, and the fatal edict for their illustrious brother is pronounced in between. One dares say that no more distinguished a triumverate ever trod the corridors of history, certainly none that left so indelible an imprint upon the destiny and the aspiration of man.

Like the blows of a sledgehammer and with the suddenness of lightning the three leaders of their people are removed from the scene they had dominated for forty years. There seems to be an air of arbitrariness, of willfulness and caprice about the sentences so rapidly pronounced. Wherein lay the guilt of the three? Wherein did Miriam, Aaron and Moses so fearfully transgress as to merit consignment to a desert tomb along with the riffraff and rabble of the generation of the wilderness? And even allowing for some grave though well-concealed iniquity on their part, surely their colossal contributions easily overwhelmed it, indeed nullified it! It is quite understandable that our midrashic sages were at a loss for a satisfactory answer to these gnawing questions. The very best they could do is to come up with transparently weak "reasons" such as failure to *talk* to rocks instead of smiting them, and others similarly anemic..

Yet perhaps the truest answer is on the rather obvious side. No, the children of Amram were guilty of no significant sin. Among the righteous they shone "with the brightness of the firmament." Towering titans of the spirit, no reward would have been too rich for them and certainly not the reward to which they were most logically and clearly entitled: admission to the inheritance of that land of milk and honey the passage to which was lined with their own tears of anguish. If anyone earned his way into the Land of Promise, it was these three.

But they were denied admission into Canaan because even the most illustrious leadership on earth must ultimately give up the reins. There is nothing so pathetic as a once glorious and mighty master attempting to carry on as though his legs have not begun to buckle, as though his eyes have not begun to dim, as though his hands have not begun to tremble, as though his voice has not begun to quaver and as though his flock has not begun to chaff at his bit. A shell of his once commanding self, such a *past-master* dwells on the irretrievable strands of his yesterdays and as long as he persists in his stubborn, desperate clutches at a power he no longer really possesses, he—like the proverbial dog-in-the-manger—will defy the dictates of usefulness and deify futility. He will become a positive menace to progress. He will, given the chance, succeed in submerging his own youthful, efficacious image beneath the debris wreaked by his tottering ineptitude.

Moses in his prime was peerless. Moses in his decline was no match for Joshua. For years on end, the devoted disciple attended his master, imbibing mightily at the Fount of his strength and his wisdom. Now the master was grown old in the service to which he gave his marrow and his life's blood. Joshua was ready willing and able. Joshua's time had come. It was time for Moses to go.

And in this connection the Midrash, still preoccupied with the pathos of Moses' demise, offers a brilliant flash of insight into the human — all - too - human — condition. It depicts Moses as arguing with God against his cruel fate, pleading with Him to relent and to allow the forty-year-long shepherd to enter Canaan along with his erstwhile flock. Yes, erstwhile! For in his anxiety to come into the land, Moses is even willing to yield his leadership to Joshua. God consents, but only upon the condition that Moses experience a sampling of subservience to Joshua before he makes up mind that this is indeed what he wants. It is not long before Moses pleads with the Lord to take his life, for to play second-fiddle after a lifetime of being the maestro is entirely too awesome a punishment for a man to absorb.

Precisely, is what the Creator must have mused.

BALAK • בלק

IN DEFENSE OF BALAAM

Few characters in the Bible are as intriguing as that of the pagan prophet Balaam. It is he, it will be recalled, who was engaged by the Moabite King to cast a curse upon the children of Israel in the hope of arresting their seemingly irresistable progress towards the conquest of Canaan. In the end he wound up blessing the people in terms which for sheer grandeur and inspiration are unequalled in the Holy Writ.

Balaam emerges in ugly colors from the homiletical treatment accorded him by our traditional exegetical literature. He is castigated as a malevolent, spiteful, sadistic man whose wholly evil purpose was frustrated only by divine intervention. He is depicted as having pronounced the blessings upon Israel under duress and contrary to the designs of his innermost heart.

No doubt there is much in the scriptural tale that can be used to advance this image of Balaam. He did after all consent to essaying a malediction upon the Israelites. He *did* pursue devious and occult tactics in the hope of implementing King Balak's desire. He *was* most cruel toward his stubborn and wayward animal, smiting it fiercely with his whip. And finally the Bible

informs us elsewhere that years later Balaam was slain in battle
by the very same children of Israel who were the beneficiaries
of his exalted blessings.

And yet, I am fully persuaded that a grave injustice has been
done to the son of Beor named Balaam. I see him as one of the
genuine heroes of the Bible. I see him as that rarest of individuals
who will not permit preconceived prejudices to obscure the truth,
once that truth emerges before his eyes. Nothing dies harder than
fully-formulated opinion. People are loath to scuttle it on two
grounds. First, reorientation and readjustment to new ideas require
immense effort. Often they call for nothing short of a total
mental housecleaning and refurnishing. Intellectually and ideol-
ogically people are lazy, a fact fully appreciated by the demagogues of history. They will therefore stubbornly, often desperately, resist the mandate of a new sphere of reference. They will
shut their minds tight against an invasion of a new tenant who
will not easily fit into the bag and baggage of ideas already
housed therein. Second, a strange notion of pride vigorously
militates against the probability of a man's rising to say that
for all of his life up to a particular moment—*the moment
of truth*—he had been wrong. And particularly so if the matters
in which he had been wrong constituted the very philosophy
upon which his life was predicated.

Balaam was a prophet of paganism, idolatry and sorcery. He
was a vested interest in these spheres, using modern terminology,
he was a paid professional. He was a "doctor of the evil eye",
a past master in the art of demonology, voodoo and witchcraft.
He enjoyed an international reputation as *the* man in his field
and was sent for by kings far and wide to serve as the instruments of their ante-bellum machinations.

And suddenly Balaam is face-to-face with the shock of his life.
He arrives to curse—i. e. to practice his craft—and behold, he
is witness to a new phenomenon: a people who cannot be cursed
because it rejects the very premise upon which the efficacy of
curses is based, the premise that there exist esoteric and demonic

forces and formulae by means of which the initiate may exercise
the prerogatives of a deity. Israel is a monotheistic people which
rejects the theory that interference with the divine purpose is
possible. And Balaam exclaims: "How shall I curse, whom God
hath not cursed? And how shall I execrate, whom the Lord hath
not execrated?"—Numbers 23:8.

What great heights of courage were scaled by Balaam to have
uttered such a thought! What even greater heights did he attain
when the shattering new Revelation asserted itself *immediately*
within his consciousness and there flowed from mind, heart and
lips a veritable torrent of sublime benedictions upon that same
people for whom he had contemplated such different treatment!

*Who hath counted the dust of Jacob or numbered the stock of
Israel? Let me die the death of the righteous, and let mine end
be like his!"*—Numbers 23:10.

From an enemy of Israel, Balaam is so transformed as to yearn
for nothing more than a complete identification with that people.
Balaam is a new man, a man who has allowed his hitherto
unseeing eyes to be opened. "And he took up his parable and
said:

*"The saying of Balaam the son of Beor, And the saying of the
man whose eye is opened: The saying of him who heareth the
words of G-d. Who seeth the vision of the Almighty, Fallen down
yet with opened eyes. How goodly are thy tents, O Jacob, Thy
dwellings, O Israel."*. . .—Numbers 24:3-5.

Bravo, Balaam!

PHINEAS • פנחס

THE STILL, SMALL VOICE

Those who would justify war as an instrument of peace advance the argument that violence can be successfully met only
by counter-violence, that "you must fight fire with fire" and that
"you cannot reason with a madman".

I suppose that there is an abundance of evidence in history to support these contentions and we need go no farther back than Adolf Hitler to find it. Still I remain unpersuaded of the long-run efficacy of violence as a means of putting an end to violence. It is not theoretical teaching which fashions attitudes and ways of life. *It is the way of life itself which conditions behavior.* For example, a charitable tendency is cultivated by the *practice* of charity, a democratic orientation is fashioned by democratic institutions in operation, a love for good literature is nurtured by the *reading* of good literature and so on, of course.

Now it is very difficult for me to see how the practice of its opposite can lead to the cultivation of some notion or ideal. It seems clear that only that which is practiced becomes ingrained into the pattern of human behavior. If violence is practiced—be its justification adduced on any ground whatever—service is being rendered to the perpetuation of violence, and naught else. It is sheer folly to anticipate that peace can be attained by its opposite for above all the desideratum for peace must be the demonstration that it need not be and must not be disturbed. The phenomenon of a Hitler is in itself the offshoot of long centuries of the application of violence toward the resolution of problems. The antidote plainly lies in snapping the vicious cycle of violence, of scrapping false mottos on the order of "wars to make the world safe for democracy", of doing what seems so logical and elementary: practicing peace as a means of perpetuating peace.

The little doggerel of Chad Gadya at the end of the Seder service has always impressed me as a magnificent sermon on the futility of violence as a means of rectifying wrong. The crime which is perpetrated upon the innocent little kid by the rapacious cat sets off a chain reaction of terror which simply does not end, at least not this side of heaven. Because the hound saw fit to teach the cat a lesson by treating her to a dose of her own medicine, all hell is unloosed in a grotesque cacophany of bloody reverberations which involve slashing canes, consuming fires, tor-

rential waters, gulping bovine, growling executioners—all urged
on to demonic frenzy by the Angel of Death himsef—for, after
all, it is his party.

Now, I ask myself, what would have happened if the dog had
not lost his temper? Is it not reasonable to suppose that all the
bloodletting might have been averted? Is it not at least conceivable that a better, more peaceful approach to the cat-problem
could have effectively checked violence in its incipient stage?

*

These thoughts all come to mind as a result of the character
of the two men who are respectively the heroes of the Torah
and the Prophetic readings for this Sabbath. Indeed the Talmudic
sages sensed an identity of spirit animating both of these men in
stating that Phineas is Elijah. (Yalkut, Phineas 771). Both were
impassioned idealists. Both were confronted with severe challenges
to their ideals by nefarious practitioners of evil doctrine. Both
reacted violently to this challenge, the response in both cases
being a flaming sword. Both have been acclaimed heroes of the
spirit in the Bible itself and in Jewish tradition.

Yet, I believe, that both were gently but firmly rebuked for
their methodology. The third verse of this Torah lection seems to
me most significant in the "Citation of Merit" to Phineas: *"wherefore say: 'Behold I give unto him my covenant of peace'."*—
Numbers 25:12. Your zeal, Phineas, the Torah would seem to
be saying is commendable; your tactics are not. It is highly to be
hoped that henceforth you will invoke God's covenant of peace
in combating evil. And as for the fiery, tempestuous Elijah,
slayer of the four-hundred false prophets of Ba'al, he is involved
in one of the true pinnacles of biblical narrative. Standing upon
the mount of the Lord, Horeb, he reviews an unusual parade: in
rapid, dramatic procession there pass before his eyes first a great
and strong mountain-rending, stone smashing wind, then an
earthquake, then a fire. In none of these is the Lord to be found.

But after the fire there came a still, small voice. And the message of God to Elijah came out of the still, small voice.

No, Phineas-Elijah, violence is no deterrant to violence. Only the still, small voice offers any hope of permanently silencing the cacophany of terror.

MATOS-MASAI ● מטות-מסעי

ENOUGH OF TENT FOLDING!

The Tabernacle is the symbol of transient living and as such it is an admirable comment upon the history of our people.

*

"And they journeyed and they camped" is an expression used dozens of times in the Torah with reference to the Odyssey of Israel. It is the *leitmotif* of this week's Torah lection.

*

This was not only true of the desert itinerary of the Israelites; it has been a dominant fact of our existence from one age to the next.

*

Paraphrasing, the historian might say: "And they journeyed from Jerusalem and they camped in Babylon; and they journeyed from Babylon and they camped in Jerusalem; and they journeyed from Jerusalem and they camped in Baghdad; and they journeyed from Baghdad and they camped in Fez; and they journeyed from Fez and they camped in Cordova; and they journeyed from Cordova and they camped in Warsaw; and they journeyed from Warsaw and they camped in Buchenwald; and (some very few) journeyed from Buchenward and they camped in Jerusalem.

*

The Tabernacle has been the curse but also the blessing of the Jewish people, for a home that is anchored is lost when destroyed but a home which is, as it were, portable can be lifted and put up elsewhere.

*

The boxer whose jaw stands steadfastly in the way of the on-coming fist is a candidate for the knockout punch but a fighter who, in ring parlance "rolls with the punch" will be up again when the bell heralds the next round.

For two and a half thousand years, or since the days of Assyrian Tiglath-Pileser (circa 722 B.C.E.) we have been absorbing mighty punches and have been rolling with them; we have suffered smashing *technical* K.O.'s while amassing a long string of "moral" victories.

*

The wolf has huffed and has puffed but hasn't been able to blow our Succah down.

*

But an endless diet of "moral victories" can lead to a sick stomach and a sicker heart. Ask the Boy Scout and he'll tell you that living in a tent ceases to be fun after a while.

*

And is not two and a half thousand years a long enough while?

*

It is, I say, it is! An end with this "journeying and camping and journeying and camping life!" An end to "moral" victories and technical defeats! An end to the rocking and the rolling and the swaying and the tottering! Down with the portable Tabernacle!—Up with Zion! and let's keep it up!

ד ב ר י ם

•

DEVARIM

VA'ESCHANAN • ואתחנן

THE GENERATION OF JUVENILE DELINQUENCY

"And thou shalt teach them diligently unto thy children"—
Deuteronomy 6:7.

Juvenile delinquency has been much in the news of late. As a result there is a sense of genuine anxiety in the air, shared by parents, educators and members of the Fourth Estate alike. That the increased incidence of delinquency is a measure of the instability and uncertainty of the nuclear era cannot be seriously questioned. Certainly, an age over which a Sword of Damocles is suspended is hardly capable of inspiring that sense of security which is indispensable terrain for the growth of standards of justice and morality. Under the impact of grave psychic stress, general breakdowns of socially acceptable patterns of behavior are common phenomena. A minor instance in point some years ago was the "its a riot" battle-cry of mentally overtaxed Columbia students—punch drunk with final exams—as they hurled water filled paper bags at passing pedestrians from their dormitory windows. In the course of my military service as an Army Chaplain, I saw soldiers from perfectly good homes behave in a manner which they themselves would have deemed unthinkable under normal conditions.

The generation of present day Juvenile delinquents has been reared between the years 1939-1955. They were born into a world engaged in ruinous war. They have been raised in the poisoned atmosphere of fear, bitterness, malice and distrust prevalent on a massive scale and encompassing the breadth and width of the earth. All of the media of communication which reach them—television, movies, newspaper headlines—reflect a deep-rooted panic, clearly discernable even when not clearly articulated. And in the background there lurks the monstrous image of the mushrooming clouds of Yucca Flats—a nameless horror which by now must have penetrated the subconscious recesses of even the least porous gray-cells.

In such a climate, amoral and criminal behavior is inevitable. What can be done to remedy the situation? Patently, the only real answer to this question is the obvious one that the poisonous climate of schismatic suspicion existent in our twentieth century planet must be permanently dispelled. That is a goal towards which all people of good will must strive indefatigably and hero-ically. It may, however, take years—perhaps beyond the span of our own lifetime—to bring about this fundamental change. In the meantime the microcosmic family unit must attempt as best it can to supply the anchorage of security and morality which is so tragically lacking on the macrocosmic scale. This is the real reason why it is so vitally important for parents to foster love and harmony, patience and understanding, within the four walls of their domestic universe. Any manifestation of strife or violence or deceit or wrong is an injection of the deadly virus of discon-tent and disillusion into the inhabitants of the home.

In the great task of cementing the bonds of unity, decency and principle within the family unit, the Synagogue can play a cen-tral role. The tenets of our religion are perennially noble and true. They transcend the uncertainties of time and place because they partake of the immortality of the Creator. A family for whom the Synagogue is an integral part of its way of life will bask in the life-giving rays of Jewish spirit—rays unimpaired by the Stygian darkness of our own day. It will find strength and fortitude and permanence and meaning and direction within the strong, sturdy, loving arms of a structure permeated by the spirit of God, a spirit which hovers even above the waters of chaos.

"And it shall be righteousness unto us, if we observe to do all this commandment before the Lord our God."—Deuteronomy 6:25.

This passage from our Sidrah is the peroration of the answer to the questions of a perplexed child, seeking anchorage in a world he never made.

II

DOES JUDAISM NEED A CODE?

I had the pleasure about a week ago of attending a conference of the Metropolitan Council of the United Synagogue with five of the loyal members of our Congregation. The conclave was an all day affair during which plenary and seminar sessions were dedicated to a discussion of the manifold facets of the work of the Conservative Synagogue. Most of the one hundred twenty-five Conservative Congregations in the Metropolitan area were represented and warm, lively discussions on any theme and every theme were the order of the day.

My role, as I envisaged it, consisted of listening. Believe me, I discharged this role faithfully, resisting the temptation to say even one word for a full day. I was sorely tempted—you may well believe that too. But with stoic patience, I conquered. My theory was that this was one day for the *ba'aly batim,* the so-called laymen and that I would not invade their forum for anything.

I adhered to this principle tenaciously even on the trip back to Manhattan Beach, on which trip I found myself in the same car with three of our men. The discussion was still lively and, if anything, even more hectic, which is, of course, all to the good

Most of the argument centered about one main point. It seems that at one of the Seminars the proposal was made to enact a code of religious procedure for the Metropolitan Council which was to govern its member synagogues. This code was to cover such matters as Kashruth enforcement within the synagogue precincts, gambling activities as fund raising devices and several other matters within the area of religious observance. One of our men, an intelligent and articulate citizen, I may add, registered heated objection to any kind of code, any kind of regimentation which, to quote him directly, "will tell me how I ough* to conduct myself religiously. That's my own business and I want no codes regulating my own mind and my own thoughts."

I maintained my policy of silence and allowed the debate in the car to proceed without my intervention. Frankly I was curious to see precisely to what lengths such a point of view could be stretched and to what extent the other passengers were in accord with it.

I wonder if you can see the obvious fallacy in this point of view carried to its logical conclusion. It simply means that all codes of Jewish living—the Torah included—should be nullified forthwith in the interests of individual freedom and the abolition of regimentation. It means that Jewish principle and Jewish practice are variable functions of individual mood or caprice. It means that such institutions as Sabbath, the Dietary Laws, Synagogue Prayer, Kaddish, Kiddush and in fact anything you could think of should be thrown out the window. After all they are integral parts of the "Code of Jewish Religious Practice" which our friend finds so objectionable. How then can they be sustained?

Fact is that Judaism itself cannot be sustained without its code of practice. No one denies that such codes require—and in fact do undergo and have undergone—revision from time to time. But such revision is the result of an orderly and disciplined approach by qualified students of the Torah to the manifold problems of the viability of our religious practice. Revision itself is bound by order and system. If every Yussel and Beryl and Mottel could tamper with the venerated and proved tenets of our faith and the application of those tenets which we call *Mitsvoth,* the result would be nothing less catastrophic than the death of Judaism. Are these not precisely the thoughts of the Great Lawgiver in the sidrah for this Sabbath: "And now, O Israel, hearken unto the statutes and unto the ordinances which I teach you to practice *—that ye may live."*—Deuteronomy 4:1.

AIKEV • עקב

POOR, LITTLE JEWISH GIRL

"And ye shall teach them unto your children"...—Deuteronomy 11:19.

A little girl has just left my study with the result that I am setting aside the essay I had already written for this sidrah and am writing another instead.

In the confidential file that I keep, wherein are recorded accounts of Counseling Interviews I have had over the years with many hundreds of people, my just departed young visitor will henceforth occupy a very important place.

With the conversation still very fresh in my mind, I'm quite sure I can recount it almost verbatim with a high degree of accuracy.

"I hate to disturb you Rabbi, I know you have a lot to do. But could I talk to you a few minutes, please?"

"Come on in, sweetheart. I'd love to talk to you anytime. Just sit down and make yourself comfortable. Now, what's on your mind?"

"Gosh, Rabbi, I'm a little bit mixed up about something and its bothering me an awful lot the last few weeks and gosh, I just don't know what to think."

"What is it, sweetheart? Go right ahead and tell me. I'll listen and maybe I can help."

"Well, I want to ask you something first. Is it important to come to the Synagogue to pray? Of course I know your answer but I want to hear you say it just the same."

"Very well, I'll say it. It's important to come to the Synagogue to pray."

"For who (sic) is it important?"

"Why for everybody, sweetheart! For me, for you, for everybody who is a Jew."

"For grown up people, too—or just for children and the Rabbi? I mean—is it important mainly for children—just like Hebrew school is important for children—and the adults, well they really don't have to come but they can just drop in once in a while when they feel like it, like when some grown-up's friend's boy becomes Bar Mitzvah and the grown-up comes to hear him do his part in the Service. So that day he doesn't sleep till eleven but sets the alarm for nine."

"Why do you think that there is a difference, sweetheart? Is there a reason for all this that you're saying?"

"Well, *of course* there's a reason, Rabbi (with a snapping, chagrined quality to the voice)—it's my father, that's who it is. Every Saturday after I've had my breakfast and start out for the Synagogue he calls me from his bedroom and says: My Baby isn't going to leave her old father without a goodby kiss, is she now? And I go in and there he is in pajamas smoking a cigarette and reading the paper in bed. And I kiss him and say goodby daddy and he waves at me with a smile and that happens every Saturday. Rabbi, (impulsively and with deadly seriousness) if it's important for me to go and I really love to go and all that, shouldn't my father go, too? Well, now shouldn't he?"

"Yes, sweetheart, (very uncertain quality to my voice) he should."

"Well, now, why doesn't he then, Rabbi, why doesn't he?"

"Why don't you ask him that question yourself, honey?"

"But I shouldn't *have* to ask him, Rabbi! (snapping, chagrined voice quality returned). Isn't he old enough to know himself? Isn't he supposed to show *me* things. I just don't understand it." (A moment of silence during which I'M thinking on all rickety cylinders.)

"Tell you what, angel. I'll make a deal with you. You do me a favor and ask him tonight. Maybe you'll get a good answer. And Thursday when you come for classes again, come in to talk to me some more and we'll see if we can't figure this one out, okay?"

(Suspiciously and unhappily) "Okay."

*

What shall I say to my little sweetheart Thursday?

RE'AI • ראה

WHAT GOES INTO THE MOUTH *IS* IMPORTANT

Far and away the most telling characteristic of a Jewish home is its *Kashruth*. The observance of the dietary laws immediately endows a home with a predominantly Jewish spirit. Since the most regularly scheduled item in a family's daily routine are the meals, the rituals of Kashruth are the most effective and most constant symbols of a home's Jewishness. A Kosher home is the most positive contribution a Jewish woman can make towards the religious inspiration of her husband and children. A Kosher home is the life-blood of its Jewish essence. A Kosher home is the spiritual bond which connects the domiciles of Israel from the Tents of the Wilderness to the split level luxury homes of our own generation; it connects the homes of the Jewish people over the space of three thousand years in inseverable fashion, justifying the ecstatic praise of the pagan Balaam: "How beautiful are thy tents, O Jacob, Thy dwelling places, O Israel".

A Kosher home refines, elevates, enobles and enriches. It gives tangible dimensions to the ideas of our faith. It substantiates the ephemeral. It captures the elusive. It embodies the ideal. In the most literal sense, it makes the conscious Jew feel at home.

All that blarney to the effect that "it isn't what goes into the mouth, it's what comes out of it that is important" to the contrary notwithstanding, what goes into the Jewish mouth generally bears a direct correlation to what comes out of it. The Jew who practices the care and the concern with regard to what he eats in the same religious spirit of his ancestors is *Jewishly* more articulate than the Jew who has no concern whatever with Kashruth.

It is no accident that our Torah reading for this Sabbath, after establishing the basic categories of kosher and un-kosher food dramatically proclaims:

"For thou art a holy people unto the Lord thy God."—Deuteronomy 14:21.

SHOFTIM ● שופטים

THE TELEPHONE GAME

"...if the witness be a false witness, and hath testified falsely against his brother..."—Deuteronomy 19:18.

You may have seen a game children often play that goes by the name of "Telephone". It begins as one child whispers what he thinks he heard into the ear of his immediate neighbor. The process is continued until the child at the end of the line has heard the whisper from the one before him, at which point he pronounces the word aloud with frequently funny results. More often than not, and especially if the number of participants is large, the word as heard by the last child bears not the faintest resemblance to the originally transmitted word.

This sounds like an amusing game for children, as indeed it likely is. But in our own lives in an adult world this process is constantly in operation, though it isn't a game at all and it is far from amusing. I shall never understand what it is that gives people itchy tongues and why it is that said tongues are in a state of perpetual oscillation. The fact remains, however, that a substantial and pestilential number among us love to lick up and expectorate multi-masticated morsels of lacerated, mutilated and evaporated misinformation. The consequences of such verbal promiscuousness are never happy and often tragic.

I have always been acutely distrustful of the man or woman who begins many sentences with "I understand that" or "there'e a rumor making the rounds" or "I got this straight from the horse's mouth" (if that's true, incidentally, the animal thus identified was a jackass, not a horse).

Of such people I try to steer clear. Their proximity is contaminating and demoralizing. Unfortunately, they cannot always be readily identified, and especially is this identity submerged when they are in the presence of a Rabbi. The only foolproof method then would be utter silence.

I ask you now: can a Rabbi manage utter silence and still do the work of the Lord?

KE SAITSAI • כי תצא

MORALITY IN THE FLESH

"If a man have a stubborn and rebellious son . . ."—Deuteronomy 21: 18—is one of the many important problems with which the Torah reading of this Sabbath is concerned. This is a strikingly timely question in light of the great stir occasioned by the public discussion of juvenile delinquency now taking place in our great metropolis. The Torah gives a considerable amount of attention to the matter of child-rearing and child-education. It can be safely said that the expression *"and thou shalt tell thy child"* is one of the most commonly seen in the Pentateuch. The Torah was keenly aware of the peril of youth's delinquency and its prescription for it was on the proverbial "ounce of prevention" level. Only conscientious dedication of parents to the gravest of all responsibilities—the healthy education of the child, academic as well as empirical—can in the long run minimize the scourge of juvenile delinquency. Mayors and Police Commissioners please take note.

*

"Thou shalt not see thy brother's ox or his sheep driven away, and hide thyself from them."—Deuteronomy 22:1—So many people are vocal and emphatic about the sanctity of *their* private property. But the private property of others is of no concern to them at all. They seem to feel that as long as they withstay their hand from damaging or stealing then they have fulfilled the respect demanded of them for the property rights of others. This is a narrow and a dishonest attitude. As the Torah sees it, regard for the rights of private property must be expressed in positive terms. Deliberate averting of the eyes when our neighbor's property is in jeopardy is the most damning evidence of selfishness at its worst. Because Czechoslovakia's private property in the Sudetenland was gobbled up before the very (averted) eyes of Messers Chamberlain, Daladier and Roosevelt, the world paid the horrifying price of World War number two. And should said world avert its eyes as Nasser makes sport with the property *of any nation* at Suez, then as sure as darkness World War number three will end it all.

*

"A woman shall not wear that which pertaineth unto a man, neither shall a man put on a woman's garments; for whosoever doeth these things is an abomination to the Lord thy God."—Deuteronomy 22:5—What our Torah emphasizes here is that every human being must be true to his nature. The attempt to pass oneself off for that which one is not is the basest treachery. Playacting is permissible only as entertainment from a stage. But when one play acts in the dead-seriousness of life situations, one is perpetrating malicious deceit upon one's fellow man and perpetuating an aura of sham and hypocrisy within his environment. This is, indeed, an abomination in the eyes of God. Our Rabbis have said: "Truth is God's seal." Anything which would tarnish that seal is EVIL, writ large.

KI SAUVO • כי תבא

MOUNT GERIZIM AND MOUNT EBAL

At the very beginning, God gave man a choice. He said to Adam: I advise you *not* to eat the forbidden fruit, but whether you do or not is up to you—and *because* it is up to you, you will naturally have to bear the consequences.

At the very beginning, God determined the course of nature—planets, vegetation, winds, waters, volcanos, everything—everything, that is, except *human* nature. Human conduct He left deliberately to man himself.

"Behold," says Moses, the man of God, "I set before you this day a blessing and a curse." And nothing more. They—blessing and curse alike—are lying prone before you. Take your pick.

There is a mountain called Gerizim. It is the symbol of all that is good and true, noble and beautiful in human aspirations. It is the mountain whose climbers are blessed.

There is a mountain called Ebal. It is the symbol of all that is evil and false, base and ugly in human strife. It is the mountain whose climbers are cursed.

Israel is the chosen people, to be sure, but only if it makes the proper choice. To be chosen is *not* to be automatically saved, as Monsieur Jean Cauvin would have had it. To be chosen is to be paid the compliment of being *given* a choice. The beasts of the jungle are not chosen for they have no choice. They are as little to be blamed for being carnivorous as lightning is to be blamed for dispensing sudden death.

With man it is different and only by virtue of this difference can we at all speak of morals or ethics or justice or, indeed, of God Himself. For what is God if not Will Unlimited, Power Infinite, Choice Boundless? And to speak of man as partaking of God's image means nothing at all if it does not mean that man, too, has been granted an area of decision. In this wise is man God-like for it is within the limits of his power of option that he most nearly shares the attributes of the deity.

So many times has it been said: "We stand today at a crossroads." Truth of the matter is that we are *always* standing at a crossroads. .Opting for good or for evil, for life or for death is a perpetual process. It goes on and on for the individual to the day of his demise—and thus is it for that aggregate of individuals whom we call peoples or nations. Whatever immense geological agitations may have changed the topography of the earth, whatever massive upheavals may have sired mountains and canyons, two peaks have always been there, are here with us today, and (be it said with less certainty in this thermonuclear age) shall always be with us: Mount Gerizim and Mount Ebal.

(Note: For more detailed information on the subject, study the week's Torah lection, Deuteronomy Chapters 26, 27 and 28.)

NITZAVIM-VAYELECH • נצבים־וילך

"THEREFORE, CHOOSE YOU LIFE!"

The Man of God is keenly aware that he is living out his last few days on earth. He is feverish with a passionate desire to communicate Eternal Verities to his people before the icy fingers of the Angel of Death grip his own and lead him on to the beyond, to the road from which no traveler returns. (See Deuteronomy 31:27-30).

One can almost hear the desperate urgency in his voice, worn thin from forty years of expostulation with a stiff-necked people but rising nonetheless to that sublime crescendo which is the essence of all that is said in the name of God:

"Ye are standing this day (says Moses) all of you, before the Lord Your God; the heads of your tribes, your elders, your

officers all the men of Israel. Your little ones, your wives, and the stranger in thy midst, from the hewer of thy wood, unto the drawer of thy water."—Deuteronomy 29:9, 10.

Ah, my people, (the Man of God must have mused) can you not see that before God there can be no rank, that this hierarchical game, this caste system with which we amuse ourselves and abuse ourselves in this our life is utterly hollow in the presence of heaven? For if the God-idea,—this matter called religion,—does not begin with the premise that *all* life is *equally* sacred then it begins not at all. Yet when the glorious opportunity of absorbing divine revelation came for all of you, you spurned it, saying unto me: "Speak *thou* with us, and we will hear, but let not God speak with us lest we die". And ye stood afar off.

*

"And not with you alone do I make this covenant and this oath. But with him who is standing here with us this day before the Lord our God and with him that is not here with us this day."—Deuteronomy 29:13, 14.

A sense of history, my people, a sense of history. Live only for the "today" and you have lived uselessly. For if religion is close identification with God (as it must be) and if God is Eternal (as He must be) then you must banish narrow egoism from your soul and regard yourself as one link in the chain of eternity which is the handiwork of God. And what is a link which is not joined both to the "before" and to the "after"? It is a ridiculous and meaningless piece of I-don't-know-what.

*

"And the latter generation... when they see the plagues of the land AND its sufferings with which the Lord hath smitten it, that the whole soil thereof is brimstone and salt and a burning waste... like the overthrow of Sodom and Amorah, Admah and

Zeboyim which the Lord overthrew in his anger and in his wrath:
—Even all the nations will say: Wherefore hath the Lord done
thus unto this land? Whence the heat of this great anger? Then
shall men say: Because they had forsaken the covenant of the
Lord, the God of their father!"—Deuteronomy 29:21-24.

Brimstone and salt and a burning waste! Sodom, Amorah,
Admah and Zeboyim! Hiroshima, Nagasaki, Bikini and Nevada!
ICBM or "I am the Lord thy God"! Hydrogen, or Adonoy! God
or Satan! Peace or perdition. Life or death. . . .

. . . The Man of God reaches his peroration and his words
thunder with majestic undeniability:

"I call heaven and earth as witnesses against you this day that
I have set before you life and death, the blessing and the curse;
therefore choose you life, in order that thou mayest live, both you
and thy seed: to love the Lord thy God, to hearken to his Voice,
and to cleave unto him; for He is thy life and the length of thy
days."—Deuteronomy 30:19, 20.

How clear! How plain! How simple!

Holy Moses!

ימים טובים

•

FESTIVALS

CHESHBON HANEFESH

The period beginning with the *Slichoth* and ending with *Yom Kippur* is often referred to as a time for *Heshbon Hanefesh,* a Hebrew phase meaning approximately "taking stock of the soul."

In this highly developed commercial civilization the process of stock-taking is commonly recognized as indispensable to the very life-blood of business.

A merchant who fails to take regular, periodical inventory is almost certainly headed for bankruptcy.

Yet in that storehouse of commodities of which moral values constitute the entire array of stock—the human soul—more likely as not the bookkeeping system is faulty, if not non-existent.

Our life of the spirit generally represents a hand-to-mouth operation—without plan, without purpose, without analysis, without introspection.

Modern man is physically health conscious; it is unthinkable for him not to visit his physician for a complete check-up at regular intervals.

But his health consciousness does not extend to the well being of his soul; the efficiency of the soul is left to chance.

It is at best permitted to gather rosebuds where it may.

So that symptoms of ulcerous, even cancerous growths within the soul remain unseen by the eyes of their victim.

And the need for either adding or subtracting certain elements within that soul toward its better health remains buried in the folds of the unknown.

The result is spiritual bankruptcy at best; complete deterioration of character at worse.

*

Along comes the High Holyday season in the calendar of Israel to remind every blessed one of us that the time has come for *Heshbon Hanefesh.*

221

It is the equivalent of a doctor's reminder to his patient to drop in to his office for his annual check-up.

And a beneficial *Heshbon Hanefesh*—check-up administered by the soul's physician (which must perforce be our own conscience) will contain the following questions among others:

Have you radiated love all about you during the past year—towards family, towards acquaintances, towards employees, toward all whom you chanced to meet, the love of *deed,* not merely of word?

Has G—d's presence filled your mind, your heart, your home, the atmosphere in which you walked so that it has been impossible to dismiss Him from any of your serious calculations?

Do you believe that there is method and plan to this Universe, that you are an important cog in its complex mechanism, that you are called upon to perform your chores within it honorably and faithfully and that finally you will be held accountable by the Lord of the Universe?

As a Jew, are you glad of it and if glad have you shown any appreciation of it?

In the multifarious correspondence you have conducted during the past year, have you corresponded with G—d too? Have you known the experience of prayer (not mere attendance at the synagogue, but *prayer?*)

If being a Jew is important to you, have you done anything about making it important for your children as well?

If the immense culture and tradition of Israel is something which you cherish and of which you are proud, have you done anything during the past year to absorb some of it into yourself thus helping to ensure its survival?

Have you loved the Lord, Thy G—d, "with all your heart, with all your soul, with all your might?"

A perfect *Heshbon Hanefesh* score is one which will find all responses to the above in the affirmative.

What's the score?

THE DAY AFTER YOM KIPPUR...

We are about to open the Book of 57—in the Jewish calendar year. It is my earnest prayer that the reading of it will be meaningful and edifying and that the readers will include all of the families of our congregation, without exception.

You see, we have been known for a long, long time as "The People of the Book." All of our reputation as a people rests upon the Great Book, the Book of Books, which we published for the benefit of all mankind several thousand years ago. It would be ironic now, would it not, if we, of all people, were derelict in our responsibilities as publishers?

And those responsibilities are twofold: We must know the Book. We must observe the Book.

Some people have been held together by a land. Some have been held together by a language. Some people have been held together by a color. We have been held together by the Book. Our Tree of Life has been the Torah. Should we forsake the Book, we should be committing collective suicide. Should we become ignorant of its contents, we should be courting collective amnesia.

Once upon a time in the not-so-long-ago there was no question but that we were indeed "The People of the Book." The most ignorant of us studied Torah on his own level. The least learned of us was a practitioner of its contents. Jewish illiteracy was simply non-existent. Physical indigence was paralleled by spiritual opulence.

And now, unfortunately, the same cannot be said. We are become more people of the flyleaf than a people of the Book. Superficiality has supplanted depth. Form has dislodged content. The High Holidays has for many become a substitute for year-round Jewish living.

Rosh Hashanah is only the flyleaf. It is only the prelude to the composition of our religious life. That composition is in 365 movements, Jewish music for every day of the year, music of a spirit deathless and timeless.

The day *after* Yom Kippur, will The Book be with you yet?

THE UNIVERSAL MOMENT

We are living in a fragmented world. It is a world worn with tension and torn with dissention. It is a faithful replica of The House Divided Against Itself. It is a world of fission in more senses than one. Atom and Adam alike are subject to the explosive force of that fission, and the most delicate of threads would seem to be the anchor-line of mankind's survival.

The call of the hour is for the cosmopolitan and the universal, not the sectarian and chauvinistic. For the lot of all men of all countries and climes has been thrown together—whether or not they will it so—and very literally, the realization of this fact is a matter of life and death for every one who lives here on earth.

It is against this all-enveloping background that we Jews gather again for the prayer of Rosh Hashannah and Yom Kippur. Of all significant days of the Jewish calendar, these Days of Awe are most dramatically universal in spirit. We shall pray:

"Now, Lord our God, put Thy awe upon all whom Thou hast made . . . let all Thy creatures worship Thee; may they all blend into one brotherhoood to do Thy will with a perfect heart . . . Iniquity shall be stilled, and wickedness shall vanish like smoke, when Thou wilt abolish the rule of tyranny on earth . . ."

And further:

"All shall come to serve Thee and bless Thy glorious name, Throughout the continents Thy truth they shall acclaim."

And the truth is, as the Ancient Mariner put it:

"The Good God who loveth us,
He made and loveth all."

*

ROSH HASHANNAH • ראש השנה

I

"WE, THE DEFENDENTS"

Rosh Hashannah is a Red Light which orders us to stop, to look and to listen.

To stop upon the road we have been travelling and to consider whether it is the right road after all.

To look around us and relate ourselves to the people and to the world of which we are a part; to see if the vehicle we are driving does not infringe upon the right-of-way of others or jeopardize their safety.

To listen to the whistle of the policeman or, if you will, the blare of the Shofar, and to consider whether it is we who by violating a law of traffic set off the sound.

*

Rosh Hashannah is a crossroads and an opportunity.

Only the traveller himself knows as he reaches that crossroads which direction he is going to take.

Nobody else knows.

"Nobody but nobody",as the advertisers say—nobody knows, not even God.

For the one thing that God chooses *not* to know is the road which an individual mortal will choose to travel.

The decision rests with man alone and with no one else and he and no one else must bear the consequences of that choice.

The crossroads point to no joyride; whatever the direction opted it is dead serious business.

*

Rosh Hashannah is a court of law with no defense attorney, no prosecuting attorney and no jury—only a defendant and a judge, *The* Judge.

For the defendent is also his own prosecutor and his own champion.

What he did during the year past which was wrong condemns him; what he did which was right commends him.

And there is no need for words; the actions have already spoken.

By Rosh Hashannah all the evidence is in, The Judge knows it all, and if commendation outweighs condemnation—why, all is well.

But if the reverse is true, no brilliant Darrow or Steuer can do a blessed thing about getting the defendent off.

Only the defendent himself can do something to save himself —he can plead guilty, promise to mend his ways and throw himself upon the mercy of the court.

But—caution of cautions!—no defendent can pull the wool over the eyes of the Judge, for the Eyes of God see into the human heart. (See I Samuel, 16:7)

Therefore let those who must plead guilty on the Day of Judgment (meaning *all* of us) plead with their hearts and not with their mouths.

And let the defendents take heart at the thought that The Judge is a great liberal.

For it is written (Isaiah 55:7): "Let the wicked man give up his ways and the evil man his designs; let him turn back to the Lord who will have pity on him, to our God who pardons abundantly."

*

Rosh Hashannah, finally, is a summons from on High!
Who be he that dare disregard it?

III

REVEILLE!

A world of thought and meaning is contained in the concept of Rosh Hashannah, a Jewish holiday of powerful dramatic

impact. Indeed, the literature on Rosh Hashannah is so profuse
and prolific that to master it alone would involve a life time of
arduous study. But of all the shades and nuances, the highlights
and sidelights, the symbols and the signs and the portents of
this unique time, one central idea towers majestically above the
rest: The Lord God enthroned upon the Seat of Judgment dispensing sentences of life or death to the myriad of his creatures
on earth. The most concise expression of this idea is best evidenced, perhaps, in the Mahzor itself: "On the First Day of the
year it is written—Who shall live and who shall die."

But to conceive of Rosh Hashanah in a narrow sense of individual salvation or damnation is to sadly misconstrue its spirit.
For the very soul of Rosh Hashannah resides in its universality,
in a panoramic sweep and breadth that encompasses a world and
its continents and its people in thoroughgoing disregard of petty
and paltry demarcations along racial, national or even religious
lines. The epic reverberations of the blasts of the Shofar, inter-
mittently punctuating the solemnity of the synagogue service,
are followed three times by one telling and revealing paragraph:
"This day the world was called into being; this day all the creatures of the universe stand in judgment before Thee as children
or as servants." The image thus evoked is of One World standing
in quivering anticipation beneath that celestial canopy whence
must proceed the Divine pronunciation of survival or destruction.

A more magnificent idea than that suggested by Rosh Hashannah, thus conceived and thus comprehended, is impossible to
imagine. For to declare, as Rosh Hashannah does declare, that
the fate of mankind is one, that the destiny of life on earth is
indivisible, that all sons of flesh stand alike before the Lord in
the role of children and servants is to express in theological terms
the most profound essence of democracy and fraternity. As children of the One God we inhabit the One World which ultimately
will share One Destiny. What that destiny is to be will be determined by the degree to which we grasp the implications of the
One-ness fo God. Properly digested, the One-ness of God dictates

the unity, the brotherhood and the solidarity of all mankind. For "have we not all one father? Hath not one God created us?" Failure to assimilate this basic idea points either to atheism or to idolatry—and the cause of human salvation lies with neither of these.

The world and its children have been struggling for many millenia to rise above the sanguinary morass of atheism and idolatry towards that brave new day when "the world shall be perfected under the kingdom of the almighty and all mankind shall call upon God's name...When all the children of earth shall perceive and know that unto God every knee must bend, every tongue avow loyalty..." It has been a bloody struggle. And there have been many whose throats have ejaculated the pessimism of disillusion and defeat. The Jew has never been among these, though, perhaps, he had better cause for heartbreak than anyone else. Adamant, unabashed, undefeated, supremely courageous, indefatigable, undaunted and erect—he has come year after year into his synagogue in every country and in every clime carrying with him the crooked little unmusical instrument with the message more musical than the symphony of the spheres:

"On that day a great Shofar shall be sounded; and they shall come who were lost in the land of Assyria, and they who were cast away in the land of Egypt; and they shall bow down to the Lord, on the holy mountain at Jerusalem."

YOM KIPPUR • יום כפור

I

THE ROAD BACK

There is no day quite like *Yom Kippur* in the calendar of any religion. This is because the central idea of *Yom Kippur* is basically and intrinsically Jewish and would not properly fit into the pattern of any of the other major faiths of mankind.

❋

What is this central idea? It is that salvation is within the grasp of any man at any time and without any need of auxiliary or intermediary agencies. The purgative, the cleansing, the regenerating force lies not outside of but *within* every human being. In Judaism, no one can be borne to salvation on the wings of some occult, mystic, demigodly power. The vehicle must be self-propelling and the mechanism for this locomotion is a built-in affair, residing in the heart of all human flesh.

*

The key word of the entire Yom Kippur day ritual is the word *te'shuvah* which—rather inadequately—is rendered into the English *penitence*. Penitence is a word with passive connotations. *Te'shuvah* is a noun cut from a very active verb, the verb "to return", to retrace. Therein lies a profound, two-fold meaning. First is the implication that penitence cannot be merely a state of mind. It must entail doings and action—or, as put by that magnificent Hebrew phrase, *ma'asim tovim,* good deeds. To say, as so many do: "I'm a good Jew at heart" is to say something quite meaningless. Judaism is a heart religion, yes. But its heart is kinetic and active, not inert and passive. Of all extant religions, Judaism has stressed doctrine least and *mitzvoth,* Judaic-deeds, most. Our ritual, our law—though at times anachronistic and antique—has by and large served as a truly marvelous vehicle for the revelation of the heart of our religion. Judaism stripped of its ritual, of its cultus, is not Judaism at all.

The second implication of *te'shuvah* comprehended as an act of returning is that basically *man is originally good.* He is *not* born in a welter of red ink. He is *not* dominated by a satanic penchant for evil. He is *not* mortgaged to some atavistic "Original Sin". On the contrary, man, the supreme achievement of God's creation is good, fine, noble, sublime—indeed fashioned in the very image of his Creator. One of the most beautiful prayers of our morning service, the Sha'harith, begins with these words:

"O My God, the Soul which Thou hast set within me is pure. Thou hast created it, Thou didst fashion it, Thou hast breathed it into me and Thou preservest it within me". Judaism, to modify an Aristotelian phrase, believes that man is an *ethical* animal. If, then, a human being commits sin he is abasing his innate Godly nature and detouring from the road of decency plainly laid out by his soul. To redeem himself, therefore, the sinner quite literally must return to the road of rightness and decency which for him is the only true road. All other roads are dead ends.

The road of *Te'shuva* is a long road and a lonely road and an uphill road. To those who have departed a great distance from the Great Highway of Judaism, the trip back to it along *te'shuva* road may seem discouraging at the best and well nigh impossible at the worst. For these especially is *Yom Kippur* designed as a radiant and inviting Lighthouse on the horizon. The difficulties of the Return are many—but the reward is stupendous. Said our Rabbis on the thirty-fourth page of the Talmud's first tractate: "Where those who have travelled the road of *te'shuva* stand, not even saints are privileged to stand".

II

THE BLUEPRINT

The key word for the most sacred day of the Jewish year is *te'shuva* or Penitence. Obviously if the Day of Atonement is to live up to its name it must be accompanied by penitence on our part. It is clear, is it not, that one cannot atone for a wrong in which he intends to persist? One cannot kick a person accidentally and in the process of saying "I'm sorry" kick him again.

Yom Kippur has no meaning at all without *te'shuva*. The word is one of the most recurrent in the *Machzor*. The whole of the spirit of the day is one of Penitence. What we come to say to God on Yom Kippur is basically this: "Lord, I did wrong in this respect or in that or in both and I am sorry for what I did. I come here today to ask your forgiveness and to pledge the mending of my ways."

Now a Jew who believes he has absolutely nothing to be sorry for, who sees nothing in his pattern of life requiring improvement, is wasting his time in the Synagogue on Yom Kippur. Further, a Jew who has not the slightest intention of striving for improvement within his moral and religious life — Yom Kippur or no Yom Kippur — has no business to perform in the Synagogue no that day.

As to just what in the life of each one of us calls for betterment that is something that only God and the individual concerned can tell. To God, all is an open book. To the individual all *should* become an open book at least on Yom Kippur Day. The torn pages, the frayed edges, the disfigured paragraphs, the crumbling binding — all these should be thoroughly scanned *for the purpose of being set to rights.*

What we accomplish on Yom Kippur, if we accomplish anything at all, is a blueprint. The construction of the edifice is a task for the whole of the year and every blessed day thereof. Beautiful as a blueprint may be, one cannot enjoy the shelter of its roof or breathe the fresh air from its windows. The blueprint is the necessary idea. The building makes that idea live. But the blueprint needs the building even more than the building needs the blueprint.

Yom Kippur and its central idea of penitence is the blueprint. What we do as Jewish human beings the rest of the year is the very structure of the lives of which we and only we, are the architects.

This coming year of 57 : how many of us will it see emerging from the blueprint stage?

SUCCOS • סוכות

I

HUMBLE LITTLE HUT

A humble little hut it is, a wobbly, weak, sickly bit of a thing with tree branches for a roof and patchwork bits of board and cloth for walls — and yet it has survived the ill winds and torrents of several thousand years. For it has been cemented by the stuff of which immortality is bred — the faith and the spirit of a people.

Has not the life of our people been the very picture of the Sukkah? Has not our physical position through the centuries been as precarious as that of the Sukkah? Has not Israel folded and unfolded his tent in the long and tragic saga of settlement and exile and exile and settlement from the days of the Mosaic Exodus to the days of "Festung Europa" and "Iron Curtains?"

And yet during all this time nations have emerged and been submerged — mighty nations whose physical establishment was steel and granite; but the Sukkah of Judea, like Noah's Ark, has ridden the crests and the eddies and the whirlpools of time — undaunted and unafraid.

How beautiful are the tents of Jacob? As beautiful as the spirit that dwells therein — no more, no less. Walls do not a prison make; neither do they guarantee the permanency of an abode. That will abide which is animated by spirit and buttressed by faith. The unpretentious tent of Jacob, the humble little Sukkah has withstood the ravages of time because of its indomitable spirit. It will continue to stand as long as that spirit endures.

II

QUARTET

Succos is a holiday rich in imagery, laden with meaningful symbolism, and saturated with poetry. But the imagery must be seen to be appreciated; the symbolism must be studied to be understood; the poetry must be felt to be loved. All these things cannot be accomplished anywhere but in the Synagogue and in the Succah itself....

*

The *Esrog* is the Heart of the Matter, said our sages of yore. It casts its lovely fragrance all about it — and that is the essence of all goodness. To impart good and well being to all those about us — that is the heart of the matter.

The *pittum* or stem of the Esrog must be undamaged, else the Esrog is ritually unfit. Were we as industrious in applying this rule to our own progeny — the children who stem from us — the world would be well on its way to salvation.

*

The *Lulav* represents the spine, say the very same sages. Certainly it is tall and upright. That is as it should be, for the dignity of man demands no less. But the Lulav is not inflexible. It will bend — sometimes forward, sometimes backward, sometimes sideways. It will not allow its upright dignity to harden into unbending, uncompromising, senseless pride.

*

Esrog, Lulav, Hadas (Myrtle) and Arava (willow) constitute the "Four Specie" — the quartet of the Succos ritual. They are so unlike each other — botanically and structually. Yet it is a *sina qua non* of the service that they must be held together and used together. What a wonderful object lesson to the species which goes by the name of *Homo Sapiens!*

*

Among the first words which are uttered in the Succah prior to the commencement of the meal are words of invitation to "Ushpizin", the Aramaic word for guests, to enter and partake of the hospitality within. There are no locks — visible or invisible — on the Succah, no McCarren-Walter Acts to bely the love which radiates from this humble little, human little, hearty little hut.

*

A happy, happy, happy Succos to all of you. May you be more than occasional Ushpizim in God's Succah.

III

WHAT'S HAPPENED TO THE SUCCAH?

"If you'll be a good lad," an old Yiddish expression has it, "then you'll eat in the Succah". In the yesterday of our Jewish life, this promise was the ultimate of the child's Utopia. "To eat in the Succah" — along with the adult kingdom — was to be admitted into the inner circle of the initiated and the privileged; to have made one's mark in the world; to have arrived in the society of the elite.

*

Most Jewish children do not eat in the Succah anymore. This is not because they have not lived up to the requisites of being good lads. It is because there is no Succah in the backyard to eat in — as simple and as heartbreaking as that. No, there is no Succah to eat in, be it for children *or* for adults.

*

What happened to the Succah? Well, it went the way of most of our glorious traditions. It has been swept away by the first hurricane of assimilation, the hurricane called apathy. The Succah has appeared anachronistic to most American Jews. In this age of split-level luxury homes, what foolishness it would be to dwell in a straw-thatched shack! Even if it is only a symbol, the symbol, too, has lost its meaning in the maze of deep wall-to-wall carpeting and gadget lined, all-electric kitchens.

And yet for those who would only take the trouble to see and to discern, the Succah is even richer in meaning and in purpose today than it ever has been in past. Of the matzoh, called a bread of affliction, the Torah declares; "And thou shalt remember that you were once a stranger in the land of Egypt." Strangers and slaves were our ancestors in the land of the Pharaohs and our very peoplehood is inextricably interwined with the idea of human emancipation. Similarly, no understanding of the soul of the Jew is possible without constant reminders of his role as a wanderer, a career-wanderer, one may say, whose travels to the four corners of the earth have had a spiritalizing effect on all mankind. The Succah is the most eloquent badge of Israel's mission among the nations.

*

The Succah is also a most eloquent symbol of the Jew's duty towards himself. It should remind us of the humble, pastoral, nomadic life of our Patriarchs and of the great legacy they transmitted to us. It should remind us of the days of our youth as a people in the wilderness of Sinai which was pierced by the voice of a God who revealed himself to the world through his people, the children of Israel. It should serve as the perpetual voice of Jewish conscience inveighing against that abdication of spiritual responsibility which often is the result of physical prosperity.

*

Above all is the Succah — like most of the other symbols of our ritual a powerful psychological instrument in the Jewish education of our children. The little lad or the little lass who has been in the Succah and has eaten of its provision and has feasted upon its humble beauty and has breathed deeply of its botanical aroma — that child has imbibed some of the essence of our tradition, an essence that is likely to stick to the ribs.

*

Alas, alas, alas! The American Jewish landscape is Succah-less, as the American Jewish home is Mitsvah-less and the American Jewish atmosphere is Torah-less. In the mournful words of one of our morning prayers: "What can we say, what can we speak, how can we justify ourselves?" The question *is* however followed by an answer: "Let us examine our ways, search our souls, and return to God." Israel must return to the God of Israel — as he already has returned to the land of Israel. Statehood will not guarantee our survival. The permanent home is fine and eminently to be desired. But the Jewish people cannot live by a permanent home alone. They must have their Succah in addition.

Gut Yom-tov!

IV

AN EMBARASSMENT OF RICHES

The holiday season comes to an end with this week end's completion of Succoth. With regard to the first Jewish month of Tishrai, it can certainly be remarked that some months have all the luck. Tishrai begins with two days of Rosh Hashannah, absorbs Yom Kippur in its tenth day and envelops the nine days of Succos holiday in the folds of its fifteenth through twenty-third day.

*

Yes, indeed, some months have all the luck. Take the month immediately after Tishral, the month called Heshvan. Poor Heshvan has no holidays at all to grace it excepting, of course, the ubiquitous Sabbath. It just doesn't seem fair at all. Yet it should not seem too strange to us humans. For in this respect, at least, months are like people. Some have it all and some have it not at all.

The well known Hebrew-Yiddish word *Mazel* represents an important concept in the understanding of the imbalance of many things. *Mazel* means chance, coincidence, fortuitous accident. In its characteristically cryptic and illuminating style the Zohar has observed, "Everything depends on *Mazel* to some extent; even the holy scroll of the Torah in the ark." Take a holy scroll, for example (I sure wish you would). Every scroll contains the same Five Books of Moses. Yet — as *Mazel* or chance would have it — one or two scrolls get to be read from constantly, while the others lie in one corner of the *Aron Hakodesh* like spiritual wallflowers.

We could go farther and say that within the Torah itself which contains 613 mitzvoths or ordinances, some have the Mazel to rank high in frequency of observance while others — fully as important and even more so — languish in the limbo of neglect, disdain or forgetfulness. In American Jewish life particularly can be observed the oft-mentioned but nonetheless weird phenomenon of minute observance of the laws of death and reckless disregard of the laws of Life. The same people — and their number is legion — who would never dream of missing Yizkor do not give a second thought to puffing on an obese Havana on the Sabbath. Yet, oddly enough, the act of smoking on Shabbos constitutes the most violent of conceivable violations of Jewish ritual while *Yizkor* — with all due respect to its reverential nuances — is a custom not even mentioned in the Torah and of comparatively recent origin. *Mazel,* all right! No element of logic is discernible here.

The case for *Mazel* could easily be extended both *ad infinitum* and *ad nauseum*. One could, for example, point to relatively untalented men who occupy the best and the finest positions in their fields while men who are immeasurably their superiors are buried in the morass of virtual anonymity. (Why is it — to take a minor example — that nothing can happen on NBC television without Dave Garroway? Is he that good?) But to return to the beginning of this essay and to the amply endowed month of Tishrai, just a thought occurs to us, namely: Isn't it possible that the Jewish Calendar makers deliberately stocked Tishrai with an abundance of spiritual bounty in order to plant a maximum of inspiration in Jewish hearts at the very outest, that the enthusiasm for Jewish living be carried through all the way to Elul?

Very possible, indeed!

PESACH • פסח

I

EXODUS, 20th CENTURY

Pesach will occupy our homes for an eight day period beginning Saturday night. The prize question, more important than the classic Four Questions is simply this: Will Pesach this year occupy our minds and hearts as well?

In the spirit of soul-searching self-interrogation we *must* put the following questions:

1. — Are we to assume that with our exultation over the redemption of Israel from Egyptian bondage several thousand years ago our Pesach spirit has had its full outlet, or are we to realize (as we *must* realize) that Pesach is meaningless unless we continue to pursue the cause of Israel's redemption until it is finally and conclusively achieved?

2. — Are we to understand the words of the Haggadah that "in every single generation an individual must consider himself to have been personally liberated from Egypt" in their true sense, which is to say: "There, but for the grace of God might I have languished; there, but for the grace of God might I have been cremated; there, but for the grace of God might I have been entombed"?

3. — Are we to settle back in the plush luxury of our television dens, cigars in mouth, mixed-drinks in hand, candytrays on side, slapping our well-fed stomachs contentedly and persuading ourselves that our token (and for the large part, ridiculously inadequate) contribution to the United Jewish Appeal has neatly absolved us of all responsibility to the broken, beaten and emaciated of our people?

4. — Are we to rise to the great privilege of having been the witnesses to the greatest event in the 2500 years of Jewish history since 538 B.C.E. or are we to allow the indescribably magnificent achievement of the rebirth of the Jewish State and of Jewish self-respect to be annulled by colossal stupidity and callous myopia?

5. — Can we get it through our heads that — the Good God forbid it! —if Israel should collapse it may well mean the end of the line for all of us as Jews?

EREV PESACH

Nothing of lasting good can happen without preparation for it.
Preparation is the foundation of any solid structure — — — else it is reared on quicksand.
A good architect spends many, many hours on a blueprint even before the first shovel is turned in the the ground.
A good teacher spends the lion's share of this time in studying and a far smaller share teaching.

A good boxer spends months in training and minutes in actual combat with his adversary.

A good composer sends hundreds of scraps of music paper to the waste basket before he sends the one sheet of finished copy to the publisher.

And so on, of course.

*

Everything vital in Jewish history was the result of long and laborious preparation.

Monotheism itself went through the crucible of trial, error, defection, retrogression and progress between the days of Moses and Ezekiel when it achieved its final triumph.

The Bible was easily nine hundred years being hammered out in the anvil of Judaic genius.

The Talmud was the end product of another nine hundred years of titanic Jewish scholarship.

Nineteen Hundred years of single minded purposefulness preceded the fifth day of Iyar 5708 — — and throughout that long stretch of time Israel *in its very exile* was on the Road to Jerusalem.

*

This is the week before Pesach and the coming Sabbath is the overture to Pesach.

Shabbat Hagadol — The Great Sabbath — is its title, for Pesach can be no greater than Erev Pesach; freedom can be no more tangible than the eve in which it is conceived.

The period of preparation for the Exodus involved blood and hailstorm and darkness and death.

Without these there could have been no Exodus.

A journey of a few short days extended into an Odyssey of forty long years before the children of Israel were ready for the Promised Land.

*

Judaism can be reached by no "short-cut". It is a long, a hard, a demanding journey.

Those who desire Judaism in capsule form, sugar-coated or saccharined had best step out of The Great March altogether.

Those who would blossom forth as savants of Israel's lore on the basis of pamphlets, digests, book reviews and frothy forums are literally living in a fool's paradise.

Those who think of Bar Mitsvah as the culmination of "Bar Mitsvah" lessons (whatever that may mean) are preparing children for an exodus from Judaism.

Those who would boil down the substance of Judaism to "Love Thy Neighbor" are not Jews but pagans.

Pesach is not puffy kneidlach and sweet Haroset.

More than anything else Pesach is sacrifice and hard matzoh and bitter maror.

Rabban Gamliel said so.

II

FREEDOM IS A TYRANT

Freedom may be an abstract concept. But the pursuit of freedom is a very concrete matter, fraught with very real and tangible obstacles. Therefore: Those who cherish freedom must embody within themselves the vision of poetry and the practicality of prose.

Moses, the greatest of all champions of freedom, saw The Burning Bush, but he also saw the stern and obdurate visage of the Pharaoh.

*

To penetrate the bleak darkness of Egyptian servitude, Moses availed himself of the inspirational light from The Burning Bush. Others may have seen the phenomenon before him, but were probably repelled by the burning process. Moses was attracted not by the fire but by the indestructability of the bush. Such a bush — Moses mused — is worth fighting for.

*

The greatest foes of freedom are those who lull the slaves' restlessness with false promises of its imminent realization. Mark Twain said that giving up smoking was easy since he had done it a thousand times. Pharaoh found it extremely expedient to offer guarantees of freedom any number of times. Hollow words constitute the bread of affliction with which despots feed their oppressed.

*

No one can qualify as a fighter for freedom who cannot digest a diet of steady setbacks. The road to bondage is a down-hill road — easily and rapidly negotiated. The road to freedom is an uphill road — painfully and laboriously ascended.

*

Fire and water and blood and tears are the four indispensable elements in the composition of freedom. No short-cut of long duration has yet been devised. Tyranny is a curse which has been blessed with longevity.

*

The most difficult obstacle in the pursuit of freedom is not at all the stony-hearted stubborness of the tyrant but the empty-eyed indifference of the slave.

*

Vigilance is the password of freedom, even after freedom is won. "A Night of Watching" — that marvellous phrase in the story of the Exodus — is the finest expression of the nature of the struggle for liberation ever devised. Yet — and this is the most tragic fact of all — when freedom finally came, the children of Israel were caught unprepared.

*

And, that is why we eat Matzoh, the bread of affiction, to the present day.

III

THE ANGEL OF DEATH IS STILL ABOUT

Dear Friends and Gentle People:

You and I and all the members of the House of Israel are standing today at the crossroad of our destiny.

We are facing one of the gravest crises in the long history of our people and our faith.

We are confronted by the question of all questions on the eve of this Holiday of Questions: It is simply: Do we live or do we die?

The question was almost tragically answered for us by one Adolf Hitler more than a decade ago but God wrought a miracle and granted us a reprieve.

That reprieve is the State of Israel, the Third Jewish Commonwealth in 2,900 years.

The ruins of Zion were rebuilt, Phoenix-fashion, out of the ashes of six millions of our cremated brothers and sisters.

The year 1948 was a glorious one in our annals because it threw into the teeth of a hostile world the ageless defiance of our people: "We shall not die but live."

Our brothers achieved the face-saving feat of the ages against literally impossible odds by rebuilding once more the land of our fathers and raising thereon the banner of our independence.

Satan was humiliated in defeat but Satan was not silenced.

His raucous, venomous voice has resumed its call for the blood of our people and its land.

It is the modern incarnation of the eerie screech of the Angel of Death as he whirled by the hearth and home of the people of Egypt.

Then, the ghastly terror by-passed the homes of our ancestors as the Providence of our God stood guard over the houses of Israel.

Today the Angel of Death is once again loose in Egypt but this time he has no intention of passing over the Collective House of Israel.

Indeed the House of Israel is his prime target.

My brothers: the hand of this nocturnal monstrosity must be stayed or night will fall.

We must fight him with all of the means at our disposal and we must cast him back to the pit whence he emanates.

We must fight his legion of hatred on every front, for his demonic emissaries are scattered over the face of the earth.

He has headquarters, has Satan, in all places; he has head-quarters in Washington, D. C. too.

My brothers: this is our last chance: there is little likelihood of another.

My brothers: rise out of your complacency to the call of the Critical Hour.

My brothers: gird your loins and keep your shoes on.

IV

THE NATURE OF A MIRACLE

Miracles do not just happen. The stage must be carefully set for them first. As I see it, a miracle represents the intervention of Providence after the human element has been exerted to the utmost in an heroic effort to bring that miracle about.

The story of Pesach is, I believe, a case in point. It is illuminating to observe that at the very beginning of the developments which led to the redemption of the children of Israel, the first act of Moses — an act which set the ball of freedom rolling — was to preach to the elders and leaders of the Jewish people

and to sell them, as it were, on the idea that the whole business
of the struggle for freedom was worthwhile and desirable. Going
to Pharaoh was only a second step. There would have been
absolutely no use approaching Pharaoh and showering Ten Plagues
upon his recalcitrant neck if the Jewish people would not have
wanted to be free to begin with. It was the will of the people
of Israel to achieve their own salvation which was the chief
ingredient in the great miracle of the Exodus.

*

A study of the Rabbinic tradition revolving about the miracle
of the Crossing of the Red Sea will serve as further elucidation
of the nature of miracles. As our Rabbis reconstruct the tale,
here is what happened: the children of Israel have arrived at the
shore of the Red Sea. Pharaoh and his pursuing army are closing
in from behind. The Israelites raise an hysterical voice in helpless
anguish. Moses turns to God with a question: What next?
God responds: tell the children of Israel to move forward,
meaning, of course, forward into the Red Sea. This advice
is regarded as outlandish by a good many of the people. What!
After all our troubles are we being asked to commit collective
suicide by drowning? Let the Almighty perform a miracle right
now. Surely this is the time for miracles. But there was a
handful of courageous, farseeing men who understood the
true nature of the advice to move forward. So long as it was
still possible to wade, swim or float forward, why then it was
up to them to do it. So they rushed forward into the torrential
waters until they were in it up to their necks. The limit of
their own capacities having been achieved, enter the miracle!
And the waters of the Sea were parted and all the children
of Israel marched on dry land through the heart of the Sea.

*

Pesach is a seven and eight day holiday, not, a one day
holiday. You see, the miracle of freedom is not achieved in

one day. After the Exodus there is still the Red Sea and after
the Red Sea there is still the wilderness and after the wilderness there are still the Canaanites and after the Canaanites
there is still a land to be consolidated and after the consoli-
dation there is still a land to be held. The holding process
never comes to an end. As someone has said: eternal vigilance
is the price of freedom. Thus was it in the days of Pharaoh.
Thus is it in the days of Nasser. Those among us descendants
of the children of Israel standing by the waters of the Red
Sea who fear to get our feet wet, are unworthy of the freedom
that lies ahead. The call of this critical hour in the history
of our people is the call for swimmers, waders and divers.
Should we fail to recognize this supreme truth, we shall be
guilty of the drowning of our hopes and the submerging fo our
dreams.

V

HAGADA VS. KNEIDLACH

Pesach is possibly the holiday with the richest content of all.
One never seems to exhaust the fountain of teaching and inspi-
ration to be found in it. Why the Seder table alone is so laden
with significance that the hour or two or three around it can
never suffice for the absorption of its variegated implications.
This doubtless is the thought behind the statement of the
Hagadah that "the more one discusses the Departure from
Egypt the more is he to be praised".

*

But — as with so many things — people will see in the
Seder what they want to see in it. Herman Wouk, for example,
chose to see the Seder as an extravaganza of tawdry epicurean-
ism, and thus does it emerge in "Marjorie Morningstar". Myron
Kauffman treated the Seder as a round table for boors and shrews

in *his* magnum opus "Remember Me to God". Yet I shall never forget the comment of the Protestant Post Chaplain at Fort Bragg, North Carolina who turned to me at the dais of the G.I. Seder as we were finishing "Had Gadya" and said: "Never before have I been at a sumptuous banquet which it seems silly to describe in terms of food".

*

The Seder is almost like Caesar's wife in being so many things to so many people. Some place heavy emphasis on the "kneidlach", boiling the Hagadah down to a microscopic foot-note. These belong to the same group who in the concept "Bar Mitsvah" conjure up a representation of the first word, (in its English meaning) to the virtual exclusion of the second. Others regard the Seder as a great big family gathering whose significance is predominantly social. Still others exploit the Seder for purposes of conspicuous consumption designed to impress the invited guests with the hosts' affluence or liberality. And, of course, there is the alarming proportion of our people who view the whole business of the Seder as expendable.

*

Yet for all the world to see, to study and to *feel* — — there is the Hagada, big as life and clear as the morning sun rising over the hills of Canaan. *What* is Pesach? "We were slaves of Pharaoh in Egypt and the Lord our God brought us out of there"......

"Blessed be God who keeps his promise to Israel. For God ended the bondage just as he told Abraham our father in the Convenant of Sacrifices..."

"This promise made to our forefathers holds true also for us. For more than once have they risen against us to destroy us; in *every* generation they rise against us, but the Holy One, blessed be He, saves us from their hands...."

*

What is Pesach? It is the triumph of spirit over matter, of redemption over Galut, of Sinai over the Pyramids, of Moses B. Amram over Cecil B. De Mille, of Truth over Mendacity, of Israel over the pagans, of the Mitsvah over the Bar, of the synagogue over the gymnasium, of *inner* space over outer space, of light over darkness, of Torah-vision over Television, of Theology over Thingology, of "We" over "Me", of Hagada over Kneidlach.

*

Its all in the Hagada. Leastwise that's how Eliezer, Joshua, Elazer ben Azariah, Akiba and Tarfon saw it as they sat around one Seder table in B'nai B'rak.

VI

POST—PESACH PROBLEM

So there we are. Pesach is over. The Jews have been redeemed from slavery. They have even managed to cross the Red Sea. And where do we go from here? Ah, that is the prize question that even the interrogative Hagada does not think of putting.

Many were they who must have congratulated themselves when the opposite shore was reached and their feet were once more on *terra firma.* In their moment of intoxication with initial triumph they must have lost all sight of the vast and foreboding wilderness that lay ahead — a wilderness that had to be negotiated before the promise of the Promised Land became reality.

*

Indeed, sobering elements were not belated in their realization of inherent difficulty of survival in fairly barren and unproductive land. Immediately, the problem of water arose and close upon its heels naturally followed the problem of bread and vegetation, not to mention meat and spices. The Crossers-of-the-Red-Sea were thirsty and hungry and uncomfortable.

*

And then the "Mixed Multitude" problem began to assert itself. The weird conglomeration of refugees from Egypt who had hopped on the Exodus bandwagon was not easily assimilable by the children of Israel. This motley aggregation of multifarious peoples was an enormous obstacle on the road to Canaan. Yet, since it was an integral portion of the Ingathering of the Exiles, its burden had to be borne with patience and equanimity.

*

And, what do you know — the enemy had not really been left behind. Out of the hot blue sky there came Amalek — fierce, barbaric and unreasonable. He was out to kill and he had to be dealt with. And then there were Sichon of the Emorites and Og of the Bashanites and Balak af the Moabites all members to the "Stop-Israel" league and all hell-bent upon the destruction of the Hebrews.

*

Allies — there were none, that is, allies of the Hebrews. Diplomacy and sweet talk to the Edomites and to the Ammonites — whose civilization had descended from the Hebrews — were a dismal failure. Nobody was enthusiastic about Israel except the children of Israel.

*

So it was blood and sweat and tears ahead. It was labor and toil and diligence and strife. It was not only the entrance into Canaan; it was the Conquest of Canaan. And the process of that conquest was slow and tedious and laborious and — at times maddening and frustrating and exasperating. It took three hundred years before the historian could speak of men sitting under their own vines and under their own fig trees.

*

So there we are. Pesach is over — Pesach *circa* 1250 B.C.E. and Pesach, 1948.

Pesach is over but the long road to the Promised Land still stretches far, far ahead.

SHAVUOT ● שבועות

I

TIME AND TIME AGAIN

Shavuoth means Weeks and it is one of many instances of the fact that Judaism is the most Time-conscious of religions.

The Jew has always been keenly, even painfully, aware of the dimension called Time. In his daily prayers is included a specific psalm for the particular day in the week and it is prefaced: "This is the (second, third, etc.) day of the week, on which the Levites in the Temple used to recite..."

*

The transition from one month to the next is not permitted to take place without a punctuated notice. The blessing of the New Month is a very significant element of the Sabbath Service preceding it. The first day of each month, Rosh Hodesh, is in the nature of a semi-holiday and the order of prayers on that day differs from that of the ordinary day.

The pattern of life in ancient Israel revolved about cycles of time. There was the Sabbatical cycle of seven years and the

Jubilee cycle of seven sabbatical cycles. Not only the ritual
aspect of Israel's life but the economic and sociological aspects
as well were governed by these cycles, and effected by them.

Our Bible is filled with passages testifying to the enormous
part which the element of Time played in the thinking of our
illustrious forbears. Indeed the very beginning of the Torah is
Time-permeated. "And there was evening and there was morning a second day...and there was evening and there was morning a third day," and so on. The Psalmist speculated very often
on Time, both absolute and relative. In the Ninetieth Psalm,
for example: "For a thousand years in thy sight are like a day
that passes, like a watch in the night." And in the same chapter:
"The length of our life is seventy years, or, by reason of
strength, eighty years; their pride is only toil and futility for
it is speedily gone, and we fly away." And, immediately there
follows that veritably sublime statement: *"Teach us how to
number our days that we may attain a heart of wisdom."*

Therein lies the clue to the Judaic intoxication with Time:
"Teach us how to number our days"! Life is so fleeting, our
days on earth are so few — how can we make each day count?
How can we justify the expenditure of Divine attention upon
the business of creating us in the first place? How can we leave
an imprint behind us which will defy our bodily mortality?

*

Ah Time, Time, Time — moving on and on and on, in-
exorably, relentlessly, uncontrollably — an ever present gadfly
of conscience, a ubiquitous, perennial rebuke to slothfulness
and futility. "Rabbi (Judah, the Prince) wept and said: 'There
are those who gain their world in the fleeting space of a
moment and there are those for whom even a lifetime does not
suffice.' "

*

What Time do *you* have?

II

AN OPEN LETTER TO NINETEEN YOUNG LADIES

Dear Audrey and Carol and Karen and Linda Z and Myra and
Robin and Ruth and Susan L and Ellen and Helen and Judith
and Leah and Linda K and Linda S and Lydia and Nedda and
Rhoda and Susan S and Vivian,

I love you all. That is the first thing I want to say to you,
if you don't already know. I have worked with you and talked
with you and argued with you for two years and I know everyone of you very well — much better than you may think. We
have spent many hours together talking of many things more
important than shoelaces and ceiling wax and cabbages and
kings. We have spoken of Moses and of Ezekiel and of Ezra and
of Miriam and of Deborah and of Hannah. We have tried to
look together into the souls of an anguished Samson, a tortured
Saul, an angry Nathan, a confused Ahab, a storming Elijah, a
blundering Jonah an epic Isaiah and a heartbroken Jeremiah.

We have paid visits to such varied places as the palace of
Pharaoh, the Tent of Jael, the attic of Eli, the mountaintop of
Gilboa, the cave of Adulam, the vineyard of Naboth and the
River Chebar. We have wondered about so many things —
where God can be found and what makes a man good and
what really happened at Sinai and whether Joshua wasn't too
cruel and how kosher meat is supposed to make a better Jew
and what good is ritual and what's wrong, if anything, with
shopping on Shabbos and how can you pray when you don't
feel like it and what's this business of winding leather around
your arm and what makes a Jew a Jew and whether you can
cure antisemitism and if Jesus wasn't a great man and what's
wrong, if anything, with sending Christmas cards and why we

Americans have to bother with Israel at all and who cares about the Ten Plagues anyway.

You listened and I listened and we all tried very hard to see if we couldn't get just a wee bit closer to the mountain called Sinai. And now, after all this talk and argument and questions and answers you are going to stand on the pulpit this coming Shavuoth and you will receive white covered Bibles and certificates of Confirmation and a blessing from the Rabbi. You will all look beautiful in your white caps and gowns and flowers and your folks will be proud.

But I come now to the most important question we have ever raised together: What is your Confirmation supposed to mean? And here, darling girls, I'm afraid I can't help you. I can't help you because the answer can only be expressed through *your actions,* not through my words.

If you think that you've learned a lot of *questions* the last two years, then you may be satisfied to frame your certificates prettily and call it a day. That will be one kind of an answer.

If you think that you've learned a lot of *answers* the last two years, then you will roll up your sleeves, open your white bibles and never close them — or the books about them — till the day you die. That will be another kind of an answer.

Old Rabbi Margolies can't help you there. You're on your own! But he can give you a little idea to chew on before class is dismissed: Shavuoth, your Confirmation day, is called "Zeman Mattan Toratenu", the time of the *giving* of the Torah, not the time of *receiving* of the Torah. The Torah, you see, can never be fully received — not at fifteen and not at one hundred and twenty.

> Adieu (or is it) Au Revoir,
>
> Your Aged Rabbi.

HANUKAH ● חנוכה

I

BRINGING HANUKAH HOME

Hanukah is here again and — are we with it? It is *such* a beautiful holiday, so rich in color, in symbols, in legend, in history, in meaning, in interest, in content, in pageantry, in timeliness, in timelessness. It is brimful of the stuff that Judaism is made of. It can be one of the most effective vehicles for the Jewish motivation, education and inspiration of the child. It is infinitely richer in pungent, muscular material than is the Christian Christmas.

How tragic, how wasteful then, to neglect the golden opportunity of exploiting Hanukah for all it is worth. Yet that is precisely what happens in countless Jewish homes year after year. Entering into such homes, one would hardly realize that the Hanukah season has arrived. Nothing is in visual, oral or olfactory evidence of the presence of the holiday. No tangible exhibits, no palpable spirit is to be met at all. The house is barren of Hanukah and its air is empty of the Maccabbean spirit. And the child must draw the subsistance of his awe and wonder and magic from the external atmosphere which is surfeited with Santa Claus, Jingle Bells and Yuletide.

This is a situation which we must combat vigorously with all of the resources at our disposal. We must bring Hanukah home — *literally.*

II

THE TRIUMPH OF THE LIGHT-SEEKERS

The period in which Hanukah was born may well have been the turning point of Jewish History. It is entirely conceivable that had the proverbial "draidel" taken a different turn Jewish history would have been terminated there and then.

*

The era of Hanukah was certainly a "showdown" era — but not in the way it is comprehended by most people. It was not a showdown between Jews and Macedonian Greeks. It was a showdown between Jews who wanted "in" and Jews who wanted "out".

*

These latter were not bad people. On the contrary. They were probably idealistic about their desire to assimilate and to be assimilated. Why not? Was not the civilization of Greece the most advanced, the most progressive and the most powerful on earth? Was it not ludicrous for microscopic Judea to pit its wretched way of life against such dazzling opulence and irresistible might?

*

If you can't beat them, join them, was the motto of these Jews who genuinely believed that both the physical and spiritual salvation of the Jews resided in Hellas. We are sick unto death of being a minority, was their battlecry. We want to be normal folk, with normal problems demanding normal solutions.

The other side was not to be persuaded by such "reasonable" argumentation. Had the criteria for the success of our people been "normalcy" and "comfort", they need never have left Egypt, said they. Egypt offered that in 1300 B.C.E. The Israelites chose first slavery and then the hazards of the wilderness because they refused the offer.

*

Babylonia, too, had attractive inducements for comfort-seeking Jews who were tired of war and exile and minority-status. Such Jews were, however, themselves a minority. The Voice of Ezekiel was much more sonorous than the Voice of Nebbuchadnezzar.

*

And even the benevolent Cyrus and Darius and the religion of Zoroaster could not induce the majority of the Jews to be comfort-seekers. The great god Ahura-Mazda was no source of light for them. Their light, they insisted, was the light of the Lord of the Universe, the Lord of Israel and the nations who created light and shadow and the sunshine and the twilight.

*

In 167 B.C.E. came the showdown between the "comfort" seekers and the light seekers. The light seekers triumphed.

*

Happy Hanukah!

III

HANUKAH VS. PURIM

The Rabbis say (Ta'anit 2, Jerusalem Talmud): "even if all the holidays should be abolished, Hanukah and Purim would remain."

This is undoubtedly because, more than any other holidays, Hanukah and Purim reflect the story of Israel, the people.

It is a story of perennial struggle with a perennial foe, a struggle of Life and Death.

In Purim is mirrored the image of a fiendish Haman who wants to destroy Jewry physically.

In Hanukah is mirrored the image of a devilish Antiochus
who wants to demolish Jewry spiritually.

*

The tactics are different; the effect is the same.

Purim Jews abound in every generation. They are targets by
the order of Haman. They are Jews whether they like it or not.
Haman makes victims of them.

Hanukah Jews, unfortunately, do not abound in every generation. Hanukah Jews are self made targets. They are Jews
because they like to be Jews and would be no other. Antiochus
makes martyrs of them.

The Purim motif is antisemitism. The Hanukah motif is pro-
Judaism. The symbol of Purim is the noisy Grager. The symbol
of Hanukah is the quiet Menorah.

*

Purim is negative. Hanukah is positive. Purim Jews
are negative Jews fighting with their backs to the
wall. Hanukah Jews are positive Jews fighting with their
eyes towards heaven. Purim Jews fight to escape darkness.
Hanukah Jews fight to remain in the light. Purim Jews owe
their primary loyalty to anti-defamation leagues. Hanukah Jews
pledge cardinal allegiance to the Synagogue. Purim Jews are
Hellenizers and assimilationists. Hanukah Jews are Hassideans
and loyalists. Purim Jews eat Hamentashen and Gefilte Fish.
Hanukah Jews light the Menorah and make kiddush. Purim
Jews breathe the air of Shushan. Hanukah Jews inhale the
atmosphere of Jerusalem.

Purimism is nothing for us to be proud of. It is the shameful
symbol of the weakness, the servility, and the materialism in
our ranks. Hanukah-ism is Judaism, a holy way of life and
a dedicated mode of living. It is *indeed* a feast of lights, a
festival of glory.

Down with the spirit of Purim ! Eight cheers for the spirit
of Hanukah!

IV

NOT BY MIGHT

Mattathias raised the banner of Judaic spirit aloft but his sons kept it waving. And that is Mattathias' strongest claim to glory.

*

Never in Jewish history had brothers formed so solid a front as did the original Maccabbeans. And that was the chief reason for the ultimate triumph.

*

Judah fell and Jonathan took over, Jonathan fell and Simon took over. Thus the Marathonian tradition of their Greek enemies was turned against them by the Judeans.

*

The most sensational achievement of the era were the well-nigh unbelievable victories of tiny Judea over the mighty armies of Syria. The least remarkable event was the purification of the desecrated Temple. Yet Hanukah celebrates the latter event and takes note of the former only in passing. Jewry has through the ages been forced to distinguish itself on the battlefield but its hold on immortality derives from the Book rather than the sword.

*

A Talmudic legend informs us that the first Hanukah Menorah was a makeshift affair fashioned by the Maccabbeans from eight of their own spears. In the Middle Ages the Popes reversed the procedure. They employed the fire of religious doctrine to inflame masses of people into the butchery which were the Crusades.

*

The word Maccabee is of doubtful meaning. Some say it means "The Hammer" while others find in it the Hebrew acrostic for the Mosaic Question: "Who is like unto Thee, O Lord, among the mighty?" Probably neither interpretation is correct but the second is much truer to the spirit of the Maccabees.

*

Jews have reached for the sword to defend sacred ideals but Jews have never elevated the sword itself to the level of an ideal. The moment they will have done that, they will have ceased to be Jews. Menahem Beigin please take note.

*

And if this be the kind of world in which the survival of Jewish nationhood can be guaranteed only by the laws of force and violence, then I say that the prize is not worth the price. The early Hasmoneans fought for the sake of a clean Menorah in the Temple. They triumphed. The later Hasmoneans fought for the sake of more territory and greater power and riches. They were defeated.

*

"And it came to pass, when Moses held up his hand, that Israel prevailed; and when he let down his hand, Amalek prevailed." (Exodus 17:11). Asks the Talmud: "Can the hands of Moses really cause victory, if they are raised; or defeat, if they are lowered? Scripture teaches that when the Israelites looked up to God. . . they were victorious; when they did not they were defeated."

*

That is the whole point of Hanukah.

V

"BROAD-MINDED" PARENTS

Some of us American Jewish parents seem to support a double standard in the business of educating our children. When something about which we really care is involved, we are very positive and emphatic in imparting it to our children *as we see it*. But when we are unconcerned with regard to some issue or principle we suddenly extend the vistas of democracy to include the exercise of the franchise by our little ones and we say: well, after all, he ought to see both sides of the question and then make up his own mind.

I was once again brought to mind of this double standard as a result of a question put to me the other day by a very fine Jewish mother and grandmother. Amongst the advance holiday gifts her grandchild recently received was a little book containing the story of Christmas and some of the better known carols. The grandmother was distressed to note that the child was being read to and sung to from this book. To her protests was accorded the parental rejoinder that after all the child must learn about these things too. Well, now, are they right, was the grandmother's question.

No, grandma, they are as wrong as Rocky Mountain Time is in Brooklyn. The child will learn about these things soon enough, whether she likes to or not. She will be literally swamped by them. At the same time her opportunities for learning something of her own holidays and of her own faith will diminish steadily as she grows older. (Such is the unfortunate fact of Jewish education in America). *Now,* therefore, is the time for the parents *if they really care* to extend themselves to the utmost as active and effective propogandists for the Jewish moment in the life of their very young daughter. This above all is hardly the time to administer to the child an academic dosage of "facts" on both sides of the

fence. Such dosage will impart to the boy or girl an acute case
of intellectual indigestion and spiritual confusion. If the child
is not given the full, unmitigated chance to assimilate Hanukah
before proceeding to Christmas, his holiday will be neither
"happy" nor "merry."

Of course in most situations parents who invoke the spirit of
"academic freedom" in such cases as I've described above are
really employing it as a camouflage of their own indifference or
even hostility to matters Jewish. If such is the case, very little
can be done to alter it. This essay is being written, however,
in the thought that there might be parents who despite their
undoubted concern with things Jewish may still entertain the
thought that their little child ought to learn all about Christmas
if for no other motivation than the "broadening" of the child's
perspective.

I say such "broadening" in the case of young Jewish children
is an illusion. There is no broadening here. There is only
disruption.

VI

ZEUS VS. THE MENORAH

From Modin, a tiny town, did the Maccabean Epic begin.
Size or volume are not material to the achievement of greatness.

An ideal must have a "father" but it will not endure unless
the "father" has sons who care for it. Abraham's ideal lasted
because of Isaac and the ideal of Mattathias endured through
his five sons.

Talent and seniority may often be confused in the United
States Senate but they were not confused in the family synod
at Modin. Simon and Jochanan were older but Judah, the third
brother, was more capable. Judah, then, succeeded Mattathias:
How true were the words of our sages: "He is senior who
hath acquired wisdom."

The King's Man arrived in Modin and said: Bow before the image of my sire and all shall be well with you". What a simple excercise is this! 'Twill not even strain an invalid. But it *will* make a straight spine crooked.

All in Modin stood up tall — all except one who chanced to be looking downwards and saw some silver on the ground. Ay, maties, silver *will* make a straight spine crooked.

No one else saw the silver for all other eyes were turned upwards to heaven and not by chance but by design.

For Old Man Mattathias, a priest of Modin, was leading the little congregation in prayer.

They prayed for the peace of Jerusalem but even at that moment Zeus was honing his bolt of lightning to be cast into the Temple of the Lord, God of Israel.

Who should have thought that there was a match for the fiery streak of Jupiter's bolt?

But there was. And it was more than a match. It overwhelmed the Titan from Olympus and changed the face of destiny.

Fire of one sort was fought with fire of quite another. Jupiter's bolt crashed headlong into a Menorah — and the rest is history.

Happy, happy, happy Hanukah.

PURIM • פורים

I

HAMAN'S ROPE

At the beginning of the Purim narrative we find King Ahaseurus in the middle of a 180 day long party. Apparently the king was in the habit of excusing himself from the affairs of state at the drop of a hat. And, of course, it is inevitable that while the king is busy "relaxing" the door is left wide open for Haman and his unpersian activities committee...

*

And talking of the drop of a hat, our collective hats must be off to Vashti, that unsung regal heroine, who defied the demogogic sensation mongers and refused to appear on public exhibition. She deserves a place in history as the first Susan B. Anthony of them all...

*

Let's not forget that the first Queen Esther beautty contest ever held was won by Esther herself. And this she accomplished without an iota of press-agentry to assist her. She didn't even send in a box top to qualify.

*

Mordecai would not bow and would not cringe. Though obviously an official at Shushan who "was sitting within the king's gate", he was not going to barter his Jewish pride away for a promotion to the post of some undersecretary's undersecretary.

*

Haman tried to equate Mordecai's defiance of himself with disloyalty to the state. "Who hates me," Haman must have "reasoned", is a subversive un-Persian". Yet while it must have been obvious even to the most accomplished fool in Shushan that Haman was both power-drunk and power-hungry (except to that biggest fool of them all — Ahaseurus), it was Mordecai who saved the king's life.

*

It was unfortunate that Esther's revelation of her Jewishness had to be engendered by a crisis. That crisis might never have come if she had the courage of her predecessor.

*

Haman was hanged with the noose he fashioned for others. But it didn't happen in accordance with the old and stupid adage about giving the criminal enough rope. That noose *had to be put there by others*. Given enough rope Haman would have hanged everybody else. Three cheers and a hip-hip hurray for Harbonah who knew enough *not* to keep his mouth shut.

*

And a happy Purim to you all, fellow Shushanites.

II

A KING IN HIS CUPS

Intoxication seems to run through the Purim story. Ahaseurus is forever tipping the goblet. Drinking parties are seemingly the order of the day (any day) in Shushan. Even Esther uses wine as a means for executing her counterattack upon Haman.

Let Alcoholics Anonymous worry about that sort of intoxication. All of us, however, should be mindful of the danger to society of the sort of intoxication with demagogy which allows a Haman to rise to power.

*

Legendary tradition relates that many of the Jewish elite in Shushan sat on the dais as the Ahaseurean banquet progressed through its tortuous six months. That the Persian King engaged kosher caterers for the affair is extremely doubtful, and such, too, must have been the piety of the Shushanite *landsleit*.

*

When Haman, with his characteristic and colossal egotism, was blandly assuming that the King desires nothing more than to render him homage, he asked for all the royal trappings except the combined TV and Radio facilities of S.B.S. (Shushan Broadcasting System). He couldn't very well ask for those since he had not yet been insulted coast to coast.

*

The un-Persian Activities Committee of which Haman was the chairman and only member, adduced not one iota of evidence against the Shushanite "subversives" save that they did their own thinking and did not fall all over themselves in their alacrity to pay tribute to Hamanism.

*

There was a woman behind Haman, too, giving him all kinds of advice, most of it wrong. Her encouragement of Haman to enter the construction business really boomeranged.

*

Ahaseurus, whatever else may be said of him, had a conscience. Insomnia plagued him until he paid off a long standing debt to Mordecai.

*

That sot of a king wasn't a really bad egg. He was just stupid. He acted in haste out of sheer laziness and then repented at leisure. His chief trouble was that he affixed his signature to all kinds of documents without reading the fine print. In general he wasn't very fond of reading. . . .

*

You know, friends, reading is a very good habit. Maybe that's why we read the Megillah.

III

MORDECAI'S MISTAKE

There are five scrolls or Megilloth in our Bible and Esther
is only one of them. Still when one says *the* Megillah one has
reference only to the Scroll of Esther. Of the other four scrolls
two (Canticles and Lamentations) are Poetry, one (Ecclesiastes)
is Philosophy, one (Ruth) is Idyll. Esther is cold, cruel fact.
Esther is the story of our life as a people in *Galut*. Esther is,
indeed, *the* Megillah.

*

Shushan, Granada or Berlin; Haman, Torquemada or Hitler
— the basic story is the same; the ingredients are identical.
There is the Jew in a strange land by sufferance of the autho-
rities. There is the vitriolic demagogue who would make political
capital out of them. There is the edict of extermination. There
is the "friend at court" procedure of fighting the edict. There
is or there is not a measure of success in postponing (that's all
it is — postponing) the "due-date" of the edict.

*

Maybe most Jews think the Megillah ends on a happy note.
After all, Esther is Queen, Mordecai prime-minister, Jews victory
— flushed, the King putty in the hands of our hero and heroine
— what more can you ask for? But even as a youngster I was
left with an empty, worried feeling at the end of the tale.
The victory seemed all too hollow to me. What, I asked myself,
is our assurance that another Haman will not appear at court?
Who is to guarantee the continued high status of Mordecai and
Esther? What if Ahaseurus should die? No, I never have been
satisfied with the outcome of the Megillah. It has always left
me strangely disquieted.

*

Mordecai's slant on the Jewish problem is all wrong. Mordecai is persuaded that the "right people" in the "right place" at the "right time" is all the Jews need for security in Shushan. The bald fact is however: *For the Jew there is no security in Shushan.* The Hamans of Shushan will always look upon Mordecai as an alien regardless of how many generations of his family have called Shushan home. Mordecai is a wishful thinker and a superficial one at that. What a humiliating thing it is to suspend the very life of a people upon the Golden Wand of an Ahaseurus! The shame of the very thought of it is far more profound than payment of conventional amenities to Haman. Yet Mordecai was horrified by the latter prospect while blandly accepting the former!

*

Mordecai, Mordecai, Mordecai—*there is no security in Shushan.* Nor will there ever be until the elusive millenium is achieved or the Messiah of all mankind is come. In the meantime, Mordecai, if you are indeed a man of pride painfully concerned with maintaining an upright backbone for your people, harness your undoubted talents to the cart that carries cargo to Jerusalem. Then you will be hitching your wagon to a stable star, not to a momentary meteor.

*

"There was a Jew in Shushan whose name was Mordecai... who had been exiled from Jerusalem..."

IV

DOES THE MEGILLAH HAVE A HAPPY ENDING?

Said our sages: "A Jew should drink on Purim to the point at which he cannot distinguish between 'Cursed be Haman' and 'Blessed be Mordecai'.

For a people in whom drunkenness is virtually unknown this is a mighty odd statement, indeed. Odd, that is, until one sees the reasoning behind it.

Our Rabbis did not share in the general enthusiasm engendered in Jews by the Purim story. Their cheers over Haman's defeat were not echoed from the rafters. Nor was there any particular zest to their huzzahs over the meteoric rise of Mordecai.

They were thinking people, were our Rabbis. And while the mob cheered and stamped its feet in wild ecstasy, they pondered the whole Shushan Affair most soberly and as they pondered they must have seen the following very salient aspects:

1 — The Jews of Shushan were "integrated" and "emancipated". They even had representatives at the "king's gate".

2 — The Jews of Shushan carried a very light religious burden, if they carried any at all. In the whole Megillah the name of God does not appear once.

3 — The Jews of Shushan tried to de-emphasize whatever Jewishness attached to them in every conceivable way. Neither Esther not Mordecai bore Hebraic names; indeed both cognomens denote pagan deities. And Esther carefully concealed her Jewish identity as she was taken to the court of the king.

4 — Haman's hatred united the Jews and forced upon them a Jewish consciousness which they had thereunto done their level best to submerge.

5 — The salvation of the Jews of Shushan derived from the petticoats of an attractive woman whom a lecherous husband wished to please. Nowhere in the Megillah is the argument for Jewish survival posited upon the inherent merit of the Jewish faith. The denouement of the enemy is encompassed by the diplomacy of feminine glamour and the success of Mordecai is the perennially banal story of political nepotism.

6 — There is a vaguely ominous aura emanating from the very end of the story. How about the citizens of Shushan and points North, east, south and west: do they now love the Jew "like a brother?" Has an effective job of plastic surgery been performed upon their erstwhile Jew-hating brains and have spite-

ful hearts been exchanged for hearts overflowing with understanding? And how about the Jews of Persian realm themselves:
What price Judaism for them? Has the Mordecai-Esther regime
effectuated a spiritual rennaisance or is all now *status quo ante?*

*

These are some of the questions our sages must have asked
themselves following their analysis of the Purim Story. Frankly
they were not sure of the permanency of either the Hamanite
suppression or of the Mordecaic accession. And this was the message they wished to convey in their Purim pronouncement.

"A Jew should drink on Purim to the point at which he
cannot distinguish between 'Cursed be Haman' and 'Blessed be
Mordecai'."

Fellow Shushanites, drink up!

V

SAME OLD MEGILLAH

Why did Haman hate the Jews?

He had his "reasons" and it is worthwhile analyzing them
if only for the proof they offer that with respect to antisemitism times have hardly changed since Susa, circa 400 b.c.e.

A — Haman was offended by Mordecai's presence in the
"King's Gate". He was irked by the Jew's social success, by his
rise to a high level of governmental responsibility, by his con-
fident, straight-backed promenading in the best circles and by
his adamant refusal to play the role of sycophantic boot-licker.
Mordecai and his people, mused Haman, must be put in their
place. Kneeling and cringing by Mordecais (whom Haman
deeply respected despite himself) would do more for Haman's
ego than like prostration on the part of anybody else. Mordecai's
obstinacy in walking about like a free man was a bug in
Haman's ointment, a constant exacerbation of Haman's deep-
rooted feeling of inferiority. Our Talmudic Rabbis sensed this

relationship intuitively in recounting the legend that Haman had begun his career as a stable boy and that Mordecai had "known him when".

B — Haman saw in the Jews a people scattered, unorganized and impotent. That they should be so vulnerable and simultaneously so successful was excruciatingly "unreasonable" to him. The powerful brute is always maddened by the sight of the successful runt. His boot just itches to kick out viciously to topple that miserable little creature who gives himself airs. Petty little minds in powerful, big bodies hate none more than the puny executive in the front office. *"And Haman said unto King Ahaseurus: "there is a certain people scattered abroad and dispersed among the people in all the provinces of the Kingdom".* Why does Hillary climb Everest? Because it's there to be climbed. Why does Haman kill Jews? Because they are there to be killed.

C — The Jews are different. They do not assimilate. They have loyalties extraneous to Susa. They exhibit peculiar mannerisms. They are not to be trusted. They are a subversive, international element. They are a menace to the throne. They stick out like a sore thumb. *"Their laws are diverse from those of every people; neither keep they the King's laws. Therefore it profiteth not the King to suffer them".*

All the elements of age-old Judaeo-Phobia are there, except the additional one obligingly supplied by Pontius Pilate in the year 33. The Jew is sharp, shrewd and dishonest. The Jew is too big for his britches. The Jew pushes himself too much. The Jew isolates himself too much. The Jews are a mammoth, international conspiratorial ring. Kill the Jews and solve the country's problems. Single out the Jews as the number one item on your campaign platform and you will surely rise to the top. (Said our Rabbis: "The demagogues who harass the Jews usually rise to power.")

Same old Haman. Same old Mordecai. Same old Megilla. Same old Swastika. Same old world.

And a very, very happy Purim to you, too.

לפרקים

•

OCCASIONAL

JEWISH BOOK MONTH

I

AM HASEFER OR AM HA'ARETZ?

Jewish Book Month is officially designated this year from November to December. — Religio-Cultural Jewish organizations throughout the country will take due note of these dates and will dutifully go through conventional motions of official openings, celebrations, exhibits and what have you.

*

But the really important question is whether Jewish Books will be read this month or any other month of the year by a number substantially larger than that which reads Jewish books because its professional occupation as well as its natural pre-ocupation is with Jewish matters — Rabbis, teachers, organizational directors, lecturers, article-penners and the like.

*

The above mentioned clan is already Jewishly literate to a lesser or greater extent — and the *main* problem of Jewish enlightenement is not posed by them. Rather is the core of the difficulty to be found in the vast masses of American Jews who know nothing or next to nothing of that civilization which since Abram of the Chaldees *Circa* 1800 B.C.E. and down to the present day has been a bottomless fountain of fecund thought, profound morality, and inspirational instruction.

*

Nothing has been more characteristic of the Jewish Nature for centuries than its passion for study, for learning, for enlightenmet! The Moslem faith recognized this fact 1300 years ago when it

labeled Israel "the people of the book". That was when the
Tannaitic dictum "The Study of Torah towers over aught else"
was a law of life for every Jew.

*

But American Jewish civilization has been laboring industri-
ously to eradicate Mohamed's judgment of his Mosaic cousins.
Where once the expression *am-ha'aretz*, a Jew ignorant of his
lore, was the most insulting epithet that could be used with
reference to a particular Jew, it is now a common occurrence
to hear an American Jew profess his Jewish illiteracy with no
sense of shame or guilt at all.

*

*Therein lies the tragedy and the danger. So long as we do not
return to our original concept that BITTUL TORAH, abstinence
from Jewish study, is the gravest of sins, so long will our hope
for the spiritual renaissance of American Jewry remain a wild
phantasy.*

Jewish Book Month must become the *Yamim Noraim*, the Days
of Awe and stock-taking in the realm of our Jewish intellectual ejuipment. We must pronounce the AL-Het over our neglect of that which has been labeled "our life and length of days".

*

Let us restore the biting sting to the expression *"AM Ha'a-
retz"*.

II

TO YOUR BOOKS, O ISRAEL !

Say our sages: "The book and the sword descended upon the
world together." This is tantamount to saying that the choice
between good and evil, malice and love, war and peace has —
from time immemorial — been placed within the hands of man.

Reach for the sword and you have made one choice. Reach for the book and you have made another. The two are incompatible.

*

For the book is knowdelge and knowledge is freedom and freedom is peace. And the sword is ignorance and ignorance is bondage and bondage is war. "See I have set before thee this day life and good and death and evil...therefore choose life, that thou mayest live, thou and thy seed." This, in the parting words of the Great Giver of the Book to the receivers thereof.

*

The Book he gave was the symbol and the secret of life. It was called *Torat Emet,* the Guidance of Truth — and has thereafter become for us the standard by which all worthy books must be measured — the standard of truth. The story of the Jewish people is largely the saga of devotion to the Great-Torah-Prototype in particular and to the seeking out of truth and the dissemination of learning in general. We were born by the book, we have lived by the book, we have died for the book and — paradoxically — have achieved deathlessness through the book.

*

We are a function of the book. As the book goes, so shall we. If the book is sustained and nourished and cultivated by us — it shall live and we shall live. If the book is spurned and starved and neglected by us — it shall become a dead letter and we shall be dead. For Israel and the Book are one — one and inseparable, as body and soul, as candle and flame, as lung and breath.

*

Ye people of Israel, thus saith the Lord: "And thou shalt study the Book by day and by night, for it is your life and length of days." Israel, Israel, Israel — return ye to the *Beth Hamidrash,* to the house of learning; return ye to the fountain of your youth and the sustenance of your age; return ye to the Heder and its twenty two Letters of Glory, emblazoned by the Flame of the Lord, the Eternal Light. Return ye, O Israel, return ye...

THE HEART OF ALBERT EINSTEIN

With the death of Albert Einstein, the world experienced a spiritual solar eclipse, for he was one of the great illuminating lights of the ages. His fantastic mind pierced through vast shadows of the unknown and cast rays of congnition upon some of the manifold mysteries of the universe. His theories were weapons which revolutionized centuries-old concepts of the physical world and which lifted the curtain upon the Atomic age — an age which may either be the last page in the history of total war or the first page in the history of total peace.

Einstein's life may be called the apotheosis of the quest for unity. He dedicated his colossal genius to an attempt at the formulation of an all-embracing theory of cosmic phenomena under which would be subsumed all the multifarious and seemingly unrelated manifestations of the universe. He firmly believed that there was plan and purpose in all of nature from its smallest to its largest detail. He could not accept the notion held by most contemporary scientists that probability rather than inevitability and chance rather than design played the major roles in the boundless arena of the universe. "I cannot believe", he said, that God plays dice with the cosmos."

In this belief Albert Einstein was Jewish to the core, for Judaism has ever seen the hand of a planning, purposeful, omnipresent God in every manifestation of the physical world. That, after all, is the inner meaning of our morning prayer: "(God) Who with mercy enlighteneth the whole earth... and in whose goodness every day reneweth the work of the creation. How great are Thy works, O Lord! In wisdom hast Thou made them all." It is interesting to observe and it is, moreover, no accident that these words form part of the introductory blessing to the very heart of Judaism — the Great Declaration of Unity: "Hear, O Israel, the Lord our God is One!"

Albert Einstein believed in the existence of God. With each successive unravelling of the mysteries of nature he sensed a closer proximity to the presence of the Master Builder, the Exalted and Absolutely Perfect Architect. "To know that what is impenetrable to us really exists, manifesting itself as the highest wisdom and the most radiant beauty which our dull faculties can comprehend only in their primitive forms — this knowledge, this feeling, is at the center of true religiousness. In this sense...I belong in the ranks of devoutly religious men..." Thus spake Einstein. And he added: "My religion consists of a humble admiration of the illimitable superior Spirit who reveals Himself in the slight details we were able to perceive with our frail and feeble minds."

The heart of Albert Einstein was comparable in magnitude to his mind. He loved his fellow man and he loathed injustice. He spoke out time and again for decency and freedom and peace and against malice and slavery and war. Although his incomparable mind was ever in the stratosphere of infinity and cosmic totality his heart was always here on earth and with mankind. His death is an enormous loss both to the science of life and to the science of living.

JEWISH EDUCATION

AN OPEN LETTER TO 120 YOUNG PEOPLE

Very dear boys and girls,

We are honored to have you meet within our synagogue at your Kinus under the auspices of the United Synagogue Youth Program.

We are honored because the greatest glory of a synagogue derives from the people who gather in it for the purpose of serving its ideals.

A synagogue in and of itself is not sacred; it is the human element within it that can impart sanctity to it.

The traditional reference to a Jewish community has always been in terms of a "holy congregation", not in terms of a "holy synagogue".

"And they shall build for me a sanctuary and I shall dwell within them" says the passage in Exodus, 25:8.

Upon which our Rabbis ask the logical question: "Should not the conclusion of the verse have read "and I shall dwell within *it?"*

And they answer: this demonstrates that the divine presence dwells within the heart of each individual in the synagogue.

In this great American Jewish community there is no dearth of synagogues and no shortage of worshipping space.

Rather is there a dearth of praying people and a shortage of studying people within the sanctuary.

If this should continue to be the case American Judaism will have left behind it towering monuments of stone, marble and ritual silverware.

The Jewry of Hellenistic Alexandria built one of the most beautiful and spacious synagogue structures in Jewish history.

But that was all they built and what meaning does ancient Alexandrine Jewry have now?

Now you, very dear young people, will inherit tomorrow the American Judaism of today.

I'm afraid that the legacy will be on the sorry side — — — unless you do something about it, *today not tomorrow.*

What? Why, everything!

I mean your all, I mean your love, your vitality, your enthusiasm, your dedication, your blood and marrow, the breath of your nostrils and the sinew of your soma.

It will take nothing short of all these to put skin and flesh upon the dry bones of American Judaism.

Your elders — for the most part — seem to "have had it"; even dynamite has no visible effect upon their immovability.

You are a different story. You are young enough to believe that obstacles are conquerable and naive enough to think that the conquest of obstacles is important.

The young of heart and the naive in spirit have been the mountain movers in human history.

Your challenge? To move mountains, specifically to move the mountain of lethargy off the center of the American Jewish Arena.

Having made the room for it, you must move a Mountain called Sinai into the center of that arena.

O ye potential movers of mountains — *birkat Ha'shem aleichem!*

MOTHER'S DAY

This coming Sunday is Mother's Day. Now I don't suppose that there is any theme more pregnant with sentimentality, more suffused with pathos than the theme "Mother". It is the kind of subject that helped Al Jolson bring down the house as he himself sank to one knee singing "Mammie". It is the sort of motif that brought Whistler a niche in the edifice of artistic immortality. It is the salvation of the tough-guy pugilist who after beating his opponent to a pulp redeems his humanity by barking into a microphone the immortal words: "Hi, mom, you can put the steak on."

Nothing is more destructive of an appreciation of true worth than the mawkish sentimentality showered upon it. "Mother" treated a la vogue emerges as a caricature, not as the truly beautiful concept that it is. The result frequently is the substitution of lip-service respect for the respect due to the flesh and blood mother who is the woman drawn from life, not from the Hallmark card.

Judaism has eschewed the practice of glamourizing motherhood out of its true proportions. Rather has it spoken plain and vital words on the subject which are calculated to impart reality to the image. At the very outset of the Bible the most crucial fact about motherhood is made abundantly clear. Says Eve in naming Cain the first man-child: "I have fashioned a man in cooperation with God" (Genesis 4:1). This is the Mother's claim to sublimity: doing the work of God by bringing life into the world. There is nothing more sacred and more important than that. Giving reverence to Mother is really giving reverence to life itself, respecting mother is respecting humanity. The killer and the hurter who "loves his mother" is a fraud. He loves his mother *not* for what she is and represents. He loves her out of a misguided emotionalism the source of which is his self-love.

Says the book of Leviticus: "Ye shall fear each man his mother and his father" (19:3). Now what is this "fear"? Is it physical awe? Assuredly it is not, for it applies to adults as well as to children. Obviously this "fear" connotes the deep sense of reverence associated with the Creator Himself. That, you see, is precisely the point. The parent is the agent of God, doing His work. Corrolary? This work which is human life is sacred and anything destructive or hurtful of human life is monstrous sin.

When Rabbi Joseph of the 3rd century heard his mother's approaching footsteps, he declared to his pupils:

"Let me rise before the Divine Presence which is about to enter." He intended no gushing sentiment here. He spoke the heart of the Mother as Judaism sees it.

Mother, God bless you!